TITAN
SHATTERED

TITAN SHATTERED

WRESTLING WITH CONFIDENCE AND PARANOIA

James Dixon

with Lee Maughan, Justin Henry
& Benjamin Richardson

www.historyofwrestling.co.uk

Published by History of Wrestling

This book is set in Garamond and Courier New.

10 9 8 7 6 5 4 3 2 1

This book was printed and bound in the United Kingdom.

ISBN 978-1-326-35581-4

We look at everything as an entertainment vehicle.
Nothing is sacred.

- Vince McMahon

FOREWORD
by Justin Henry

Oh, to be a twelve-year-old with blinders again. Not privy to the backstage dealings of the WWF in my pre-teen years, I was about the biggest Shawn Michaels fan that you could ever find. While the later discoveries of his insecurity-bred meltdowns and his rock-star junkie lifestyle did not exactly make me appreciate Michaels' body of work any less, there really is something about being in that un-jaded, almost incubated state of wrestling fandom.

I have been writing about professional wrestling since 2009, but I have been a fan for two decades longer. I was that happy-go-lucky kindergartner whose senses were met by an older brother's taped episode of WWF *Wrestling Challenge*, indelibly hooked for life by squash matches featuring the likes of Mr. Perfect and Tito Santana. I am still hooked twenty-six years later, though my views on wrestling have changed with age and knowledge - the customary evolution of thought that comes with the passage of time. I understand full well that it's a business with skilful actors that cushion their pratfalls as ably as possible.

I think I share the same sentiments as many fans who have been watching for this length of time when I say that I miss my wrestling naïveté - the sugar-bred energy that comes from too many marshmallow cereals and a Saturday morning filled with taped bouts airing in syndication after the cartoons. I miss hauling my cotton-filled "Wrestling Buddies" over to my friend's house on a warm afternoon, using his trampoline as our surrogate ring for a day of barely-controlled chaos - giggling as we deliver the Doomsday Device on poor inanimate Ted DiBiase, with one of us precariously playing Hawk, leaping off of the back porch handrail to deliver the clothesline. What a rush, indeed.

James Dixon's *The Art of Raw* is confirmation of the betrayal of my ignorant bliss. The year 1996 was the first time my home was wired with America Online, the home of two wrestling-specific entities: the WWF-produced website, and Grandstand Wrestling, the latter of which specifically targeted the more discriminating audience. My fandom - already corrupted by ECW's open hostility toward the "Big Two", and Eric Bischoff giving away *Raw* results on *Nitro* - was irreparably morphed by copy-and-paste dirt sheets, spoiler postings that listed all four or five hours of interminable *Raw* tapings, and free-flowing message board debates held between all walks of fan.

Bischoff, Vince McMahon, Steve Austin, The Outsiders, Brian Pillman, Joey Styles, and Mick Foley were pulling back curtain after curtain until everything laid bare. Once I was sucked into the internet wrestling community for the first time that year, it was a landscape void of partition. The Information Age had trampled my wide-eyed wonderment, and a twelve-year-old fan began to grow much hipper to what had previously been his combination cartoon/theatre.

Thus in reading through the manuscript to this book, I was familiar with some of the content, but having it bookended by soft cover recaptures my general feeling of the year. There was so much going on: Michaels' angst, Bret Hart's agonizing decision, Razor Ramon and Diesel's controversial exit, Ultimate Warrior's penchant for providing headaches, and Steve Austin's breakthrough. Much of that was obvious to most home viewers, a time where McMahon himself, the carniest of the carnies, pulled back his own curtains to pensively embrace a new era of wrestling - a necessity in changing times. Sprinkled within are the little stories that fill out the 1996 calendar, with Dixon providing as impressive a concrete anthology of the year as you could ever find.

The feeling it recaptures for me is an unblinking awe. 1996 redefined wrestling as I knew it, killing my personal sense of kayfabe before I reached seminal teenage years. The ramped-up, camped-out supercharge of *Saturday Night's Main Event* crumbled in the wake of the acid-tongued bombast of Scott Hall and Kevin Nash jumping the guardrail on *Nitro*, brandishing baseball bats. Razor Ramon and Diesel had grown up, and I took that as my cue.

On March 31, 1996, my happiest moment as a fan came watching Michaels - my favourite wrestler since he was a mulleted Rocker in neon spandex - superkick Bret Hart to become WWF Champion for the first time. I find it quite amusing in hindsight that the mark in me would be severely whiplashed by the sharp learning curve I was about to receive. The Information Age takes no prisoners, such was the theme of 1996 in professional wrestling.

Justin Henry
New Jersey.
May 2015

ONE

D ESPERATE TIMES CALL FOR DESPERATE measures, or so the old adage goes. As 1995 rolled into 1996, WWF premier Vince McMahon seemingly embarked upon a one-man quest to prove that to be true. In the eighties and early nineties McMahon had been the undisputed king of mainstream wrestling in North America. By 1996 he had lost his Midas touch as the pressures of having real competition for the first time in a decade began to take their toll. That competition came in the form of World Championship Wrestling, the Turner Broadcasting-owned Atlanta group, funded by the billions of media mogul Ted Turner, and driven by the non-traditional vision of progressive-thinking WCW Vice President Eric Bischoff. WCW's emergence since acquiring former WWF household names Terry 'Hulk Hogan' Bollea and Randy 'Macho Man' Savage' Poffo in 1994, and their cronyistic arrival on prime time television with *Monday Nitro* in September 1995[1], meant that McMahon's WWF no longer held the TV monopoly in the wrestling industry.

Loath to accept that anyone could threaten his vice-like grip on professional wrestling, McMahon had initially dismissed the fledgling Turner broadcast as a minimal threat to the WWF and its flagship *Monday Night Raw* television show. The weekly Nielsen television ratings painted the opposite picture; not only were WCW ably competing with the once untouchable WWF, they were frequently beating them. Bischoff was not afraid to play dirty in ensuring that remained the case. He employed guerrilla tactics, routinely giving away the results of pre-taped WWF broadcasts and snatching Federation talent from under Vince's nose with the lure of guaranteed money. He even had one former Titan performer, Debra 'Madusa' Miceli, disrespectfully throw her WWF Women's title into a garbage can live on *Nitro*, after Vince had carelessly neglected to retrieve the belt when he terminated her contract.

Though the Miceli incident was a relatively minor one - more insulting than harmful - the impudence of the act sparked something inside McMahon. As he would later say, "It was a tawdry thing to do. It was a shot across the bow, and pretty much a kick in the groin, I think, as it was meant to be." WWF official Michael Hayes concurred, "That was what got everybody's ire up. That is just something you don't do. You don't drop the

---

[1] Ted Turner owned the TNT network that *Nitro* was broadcast on.

flag on the ground, and you respect a title, a championship belt. It was the beginning of many traditions being broken."

Vince had initially been blindsided by the assault from Atlanta. Bischoff had beguiled him by not adhering to commonly accepted industry codes and practices. Namely, his belief that you did not even acknowledge the competition, let alone actively try to hurt it[2]. Nonetheless, when Vince McMahon was in a fight, he was not someone who stood in a corner and let his opponent throw blow after blow at him with no reply. Vince intended to fight back, and during an online chat on December 18, 1995, he finally let loose.

Vince ripped into Eric Bischoff, implying that he was merely a puppet for Ted Turner, willingly doing the mogul's bidding in his quest to put the WWF out of business. He slammed WCW for showing no regard for wrestling fans by scheduling *Nitro* directly opposite *Raw*, criticised their lax drug-testing policy, and claimed that the company treated its audience with contempt. Many who witnessed the comments cried foul, with Dave Meltzer at *The Wrestling Observer* arguing:

> While there is validity to some of what McMahon said, in many cases, such as treatment of fans, steroids, and knocking Turner because of his bank account, he comes off as someone with incredible gall for knocking exactly what put him on top and now knocking those very things when his grip on the top is weakening. Let's face it, how much regard for the wrestling fans of America did McMahon show when he was putting everyone out of business, and when he was making up his own storylines and trying to push his own washed up or untalented headliners because their name could still draw money?

WHEN THE first episode of *Monday Night Raw* of 1996 aired on New Year's Day, Vince lined up a retaliatory shot against WCW's months of attacks, which he felt would swing the momentum back in the WWF's favour. For the first time since he had been at the helm of the WWF, he decided to respond directly to another wrestling company on his television show. Before that, the Federation had always led fans into believing that professional wrestling barely existed outside of the WWF bubble. Now

---

[2] There was an irony to this, given some of McMahon's own tactics in dealing with promotional rivals in the past. Among other things, McMahon scheduled the 1987 *Survivor Series* to go head to head with the NWA's *Starrcade* in a purposeful attempt at sabotage. He even told the pay-per-view companies that if they didn't opt for *Survivor Series* ahead of *Starrcade*, then they would miss out on pay-per-view cash cow *WrestleMania*.

Vince was not only going to acknowledge another promotion's existence, he was going to viciously, and unrelentingly rip them to shreds.

His method of achieving that was typically brash; commissioning a series of satirically cutting parody skits titled *Billionaire Ted's Wrasslin' Warroom*. The idea was first broached in a creative team meeting as a way to amuse McMahon. When he laughed, the rest of the room jumped on it and started throwing out further suggestions until Vince decided to do it. He handled the scripts for the segments himself, making sure they expressed the exact message he wanted to convey. They were forums for his own personal brand of vengeance, and he was determined to use every malicious weapon in his arsenal in the effort to sully the names of WCW and Turner.

Though *Raw* would expand to two and eventually three hours as the years elapsed, it was still only airing for a single hour per week in 1996. Regardless, Vince was determined to devote precious WWF television time to his personal vendetta against Turner, despite the pretext of the sketches being lost on the majority of his primarily adolescent fan base. The first in the series was fairly humorous, seeing 'Billionaire Ted' (Turner) asking 'The Huckster' (Hogan) and 'The Nacho Man' (Savage) to deliver more action in their performances, while footage of current WWF wrestlers performing flashy manoeuvres aired in the background. Both men recoiled at the prospect, then posed and danced upon Ted asking what exactly they *could* do. The voice over stated, "You can't teach an old dog new tricks," in a jokey tone, before signing off with the witty tagline: "The WWF New Generation; on top of the hill, not over it."

Though portraying WCW's former WWF stars Hulk Hogan and Randy Savage as decrepit reeked of irony (both had been WWF Champion within the past three years, and current title holder Bret Hart was only a few years their junior), the content was generally inoffensive and served the purpose of promoting the current WWF product as superior. If Vince had stopped there the segments probably would not have attracted much attention - but he was merely getting warmed up.

If this was war, then the first instalment of the *Warroom* was merely a warning shot compared to the second - the wrestling equivalent of a nuclear blast. The subject was taboo for Vince and Titan to be dabbling with in light of their own murky past: steroid abuse. In a sketch aired on the following week's show, Vince shot a skit strongly implying that Hogan and Savage were once again on the juice since defecting to WCW.

It started out innocently enough, with Billionaire Ted searching for a fresh motto for his "wrasslin" company. After dismissing one idea for having been stolen before (the "uncooked, uncensored, uncut" slogan for

WCW's *Uncensored* pay-per-view, which aped the marketing for early editions of *Monday Night Raw*), and another for being too truthful (the suggestion that Hogan and Savage were old), The Nacho Man came up with, "This is where the big boys play." It was hardly a coincidence that it genuinely was WCW's marketing phrase of choice at the time. Vince proceeded to give its meaning an entirely different and far more slanderous edge, having Nacho Man ask, "But what if our stars have to take a legitimate drug test for steroids?" The Huckster inflammatorily replied, "Don't worry about that brother; we're not in the WWF anymore."

Vince was cute about the whole thing. Realising the comments aired in the parody left Titan open to a lawsuit, immediately after the broadcast he released a statement that claimed the WWF had used satire to demonstrate a point regarding the two company's respective drug testing policies. By using the term "satire", Vince believed he had a watertight get-out clause that would grant him legal immunity from slander or libel lawsuits.

He had also faxed a letter to Ted Turner prior to the airing of the segment in which he challenged him to compare WCW's drug testing policy with the WWF's under the jurisdiction of an independent drug policy advisor. Crack Titan lawyer Jerry McDevitt forwarded the same memo to WCW attorney Nick Lambrose. Eric Bischoff could not resist the chance to spar publicly with Vince, and decided to interject himself into the situation. His response was to draft a personal letter to McMahon that read:

Dr. Mr. McMahon:

Your letter dated Jan. 3, 1996 to Mr. Ted Turner and your subsequent letter of January 10 have been directed to my attention. Although initially mildly amusing, the WWF programming that you refer to as a "satirical vignette" has become defamatory and disparaging to WCW and its wrestlers. Accordingly, we have referred this issue to our legal counsel for review. In addition, Mr. McDevitt's letter of Jan. 11, 1996 on your behalf to Mr. Lambrose of this office has similarly been referred to legal counsel for review. By copy of this letter, we are informing Mr. McDevitt of this referral and advising him that we found his previous letters wholly without merit and undeserving of a response. In light of WCW and WWF programming ratings, we understand your concern about the content of our programs. Your encouragement is duly noted; however, WCW programming decisions are the responsibility of WCW and Turner Broadcasting. Finally, as you are aware, WCW has a comprehensive Substance Abuse Policy, which includes drug testing.

While we can appreciate your intent in combining the efforts of the WWF with certain facets of our program, we are not so inclined.

Signed, Eric Bischoff,
Senior Vice President, WCW

Looking for a modicum of retribution for what he perceived to be Bischoff's past sins against his organisation, Vince took great delight in showing freeze-frames of the communiqué on his television shows. He hoped to embarrass WCW's senior VP, but much to his chagrin Bischoff remained nonplussed. Rather, he found the whole exercise to be somewhat hypocritical. "Accusing *us* of not having a drug testing policy defined the old expression, 'the pot calling the kettle black'," he protested. Despite the executive's front of bravado and his declaration that McMahon had no say in WCW policy, there was a minor ripple effect. The company's tagline for *Nitro* of "where the big boys play," was quietly dropped for a few weeks because of McMahon's insinuations. Turner execs didn't want "big boys" to equate to steroids in the minds of the viewers, as had been subliminally planted by McMahon. Once the memory of Vince's stunt had diminished, the strap-line duly returned.

The flagrant hypocrisy of McMahon's finger-pointing and sudden holier-than-thou attitude regarding steroids was not lost on industry commentators. Dave Meltzer dubbed it, "the biggest irony of all," adding that McMahon's interest in protecting his performers only came about when his hand was forced by a federal investigation. Most could see the truth of Vince's frustration; he was restricted in his practices while Turner was not. Now that WCW was a legitimate rival and a threat to the WWF, he was increasingly unhappy about it.

THE WEEKLY airing of *Billionaire Ted's Wrasslin Warroom* continued into March, with the joke quickly wearing thin once the tone of the pieces became progressively petty and spiteful. McMahon soon abandoned any lingering pretence that he was presenting light-hearted satirical commentaries. Once the facade slipped, he proceeded to take great delight in directing savage, personal attacks at Turner and his former Federation employees.

Projecting the demeanour of a jilted ex-lover, McMahon called out Hogan and Savage as disloyal has-beens, allowing his true inner feelings of resentment to spill out increasingly with each passing week. Another of McMahon's former staffers, "Mean" Gene Okerlund, was the next target for his vitriol. Vince presented an onscreen facsimile of the announcer - whom he dubbed 'Scheme Gene' - promoting an extortionately priced premium rate phone number as a direct attack on Okerlund's own controversial WCW hotline.

The timing was deliberate, coming a few weeks after WCW fought off a lawsuit from their former performer Richard 'Ricky Steamboat' Blood for using his name as a hook to get people to call Okerlund's 1-900 line. Okerlund had promised callers they would find out the truth regarding Steamboat's upcoming appearance at a special ceremony on *Nitro*; though in actuality no discussions between Blood and WCW had ever taken place.

Blood was already locked in a legal wrangle with WCW over the way he had been fired while injured on the job in 1994, outraged that WCW had failed to honour the remainder of his contract. He was piqued that his name was used without consent to make premium rate money, especially as the story was a total fabrication. Blood's lawyer forced Okerlund to issue a retraction of sorts on his hotline, with the announcer admitting that Ricky Steamboat was not associated with WCW in any way.

The following weeks saw Vince try to goad Turner Broadcasting stockholders. He had Billionaire Ted crow about wasting investors' money rather than his own with "play thing" WCW, and then looked to sabotage an imminent Time-Warner/TBS merger.[3]. He was purposely trying to sew kernels of doubt in the minds of the deal-brokers by alluding to the company honcho's apparent carefree attitude and inherent avarice.

Nevertheless, Wall Street movers and shakers were hardly *Raw*'s target demographic. McMahon remained unconvinced that the segments would be seen by those in charge at Time-Warner, thus negating their effect. He decided to squander further company resources to fuel his vendetta - the selfsame tactic he complained Turner was employing in his own apparent quest to kill the WWF - by attempting to take out the following advert in various financial magazines:

Attention Stockholders: Has Ted Turner lost $40 Million dollars of YOUR money in his personal vendetta against the World Wrestling Federation? Where are these losses reported in TBS financial statements? Time-Warner Beware!

Most magazines rejected the advert on the grounds that it was too defamatory, though the *New York Times* did allow an edited version to be

---

[3] At the time TBS was negotiating a merger deal with Time-Warner that successfully went through a few months later, but ultimately cost Ted Turner his power.

printed. Vince was undeterred, airing a lingering freeze-frame of the original ad during *Raw*, giving viewers enough time to read and digest the message. The executives who mattered in the Time-Warner merger deal paid little if any attention to the Titan propaganda. Most others merely saw it as a petty assault; a cry for attention from a sinking company fighting dirty to keep afloat.

Vince felt he was justified in his actions, because he considered WCW's existence to be born out of a personal rivalry Turner had with him. He cited Turner's "lack of business ethics" as the reason the pair fell out in the eighties, though the reality was actually the opposite. The tension started during McMahon's national expansion of the WWF, after Turner had unequivocally rejected McMahon's offer in 1984 to buy Georgia Championship Wrestling's plum television slot on Turner's WTBS station. In response, the WWF head decided to employ an anomalous approach to negotiations: he bought the whole promotion.

Now forced to work with the WWF, Turner demanded that Vince provide his station with first-run programming featuring competitive matches each week as GCW had, which was to also include a number of bouts taped at the TBS studios. McMahon agreed to the terms, then almost instantly reneged on the deal by unflinchingly broadcasting months-old WWF footage of one-sided squash bouts and previously aired arena cards.

On July 14, 1984 - a day that would later become known in wrestling folklore as *Black Saturday* - GCW host Freddie Miller introduced McMahon to the TBS audience for the first time. The WWF chairman confidently stated he was sure TBS fans who had watched GCW's *World Championship Wrestling* program would enjoy his show just as much. They did not. The station's viewers were outraged at the WWF force-feeding them their outlandish brand of sports entertainment. They felt it was a galling circus masquerading as professional wrestling, rather than the traditional athletic-based grappling they favoured.[4]

Ratings for the WWF show nosedived, with appalled GCW fans tuning out in droves. Turner balked and wanted out of the deal, and with Vince having broken his promise of original programming, the TBS boss decided to act. Determined to bring traditional southern-style wrestling back to TBS, he turned to Bill Watts and his *Mid-South Wrestling*, to whom he gave a Sunday afternoon slot on the channel. Furthermore, he added Ole Anderson's *Championship Wrestling from Georgia*, the spiritual successor to GCW, to the station's Saturday morning line-up. Both quickly outperformed the WWF in the ratings.

---

[4] Colloquially referred to - with both positive and negative connotations - as "wrasslin".

Turner was trying to drive the WWF off TBS and McMahon was livid about it. He believed purchasing GCW - and with it the TBS Saturday night timeslot - gave him exclusivity on the channel. With the venture losing money and proving to be embarrassing for the company, McMahon had few options. He soon sold GCW to rival Jimmy Crocket for $1 million, then left the station forever. The whole ordeal resulted in the ill feeling between Turner and McMahon, both believing they had acted within their respective rights. The reality was that McMahon had violated the pair's business agreement, not Turner.

Vince never forgave Turner for unceremoniously forcing him off WTBS. He hated to lose to anyone at anything and simply despised that someone had beaten him at his own game. Turner soon bought into the wrestling business himself, bailing out Crocket when he fell on hard times in 1988. Wrestling had been good to Turner during the early days of TBS, serving as the ever-reliable foundations for him to build his empire. With Crocket given the exclusivity on TBS that McMahon had desired, there was nothing else to replace Crocket's show with if he went under. Turner did not want to lose wrestling from the station, so he bought Crocket out. Still annoyed with how McMahon had acted while with TBS, Turner then called him and gloated that he was "in the wrasslin' business". The contention escalated from there.

WHILE THERE was obvious malice to what Vince was doing with his weekly digs at Turner, there was at least a modicum of truth to his claims regarding TBS bookkeeping. The corporation had recently released financial figures that claimed WCW had turned a profit in 1995 for the first time since Turner took over the business, serving as proof that the mogul had the nous to turn around the fortunes of ailing brands and forge them into successful entities. The ability to present an apparently profitable front was imperative in the ongoing negotiations of the Time-Warner merger, because it strengthened Turner Broadcasting's bargaining power in the deal. Like virtually everything else in wrestling, what was released to the public wasn't the full truth. Turner accountants had massaged the figures and fudged the results to reach a borderline fraudulent conclusion.

In the prior seven years, WCW had lost a cumulative $30 million, but in 1995 - despite significantly higher running costs due to the advent of the weekly live *Nitro*, and some major name acquisitions on substantial guaranteed contracts - WCW claimed to have made a profit. Due to the make-up of Turner's empire, some of the figures on the wrestling side were heaped onto the books of other already profitable sectors of the company.

Thus, Hulk Hogan's multi-million dollar salary was for the most part written off and included as part of media branch Turner Home Entertainment, with the justification that it was payment for his *Thunder in Paradise* television series and various roles in low-budget, straight-to-video B-movies.

WCW was also internally gifted $4 million from Turner Broadcasting for the production of its cable shows, something that had never been done previously. If the same donation had been given in years prior then WCW would have turned a profit in most of them. However, back then it didn't matter whether the wrestling company showed losses, because there was no corporate merger imminent in those days. To most industry observers it was obvious that the payment was a disingenuous token gesture concocted to balance the sheets and make WCW look like a money generating arm of the TBS package, one which Turner was insistent remained active should the amalgamation transpire.

The figures were also helped by the inclusion of two successful pay-per-view events from the end of 1994 (*Halloween Havoc* and *Starrcade*) on the 1995 books. The far less profitable 1995 editions of the same events were deferred to the 1996 report, by which time the Time Warner deal would be closed and it would no longer matter. In addition, WCW failed to disclose a number of other incurred expenditures from 1995, including but not limited to venue hire, live event costs, production overheads, and a host of minor sundry outgoings. These too were dumped onto the 1996 books to ensure that WCW appeared to be profitable in 1995, thus reducing the possibility that Time-Warner would want WCW out of the picture.

VINCE MCMAHON was an astute businessman with an almost unrivalled understanding of how the wrestling industry worked, so he was well aware of the tricks WCW had pulled. He was not shy about letting the world know about them either. On *Raw*, he increased the intensity of his Turner character assassination in the *Billionaire Ted* skits, where he also made sure to highlight his findings. In one of the skits the script called for 'Larry Fling' (a send-up of long-time Turner ally Larry King) to call out Billionaire Ted for writing off The Huckster's salary to a more profitable wing of the company. Shocked that he had been caught out, Billionaire Ted was suddenly at a loss for words.

What would turn out to be the final instalment of the series saw Ted investigated internally at a board meeting, where the demeanour of his character took a sharp turn from light comedy relief to something much more sinister. The episode accused Turner of coveting a wrestling monopoly and desiring sole ownership and control of the national media, each in a concerted effort to kill the WWF. The piece ended with a name and address for viewers to write to if they shared the WWF's concerns that the upcoming Time-Warner/TBS merger could lead to Ted Turner owning or influencing half of the cable networks in America.[5]

The skit was so spiteful that USA Network Chairwoman Kay Koplovitz became concerned. McMahon's methodology had always been radical, and more often than not, he was a law unto himself. Even though Koplovitz found Vince an occasional headache to deal with, she had always turned a blind eye to his more questionable behaviour because his shows remained successful. When the content of Raw started to threaten the future prosperity of her network, she had no choice but to intervene.

Turner controlled cable stations across America, which accounted for nearly fifteen percent of the homes that USA aired in. She could ill-afford to risk losing such a significant proportion of her network's audience over a childish rift between two rival wrestling organisations. Because she felt Vince could no longer demarcate himself, Koplovitz demanded that he cease production of the Billionaire Ted skits effective immediately. In addition, all future Monday Night Raw scripts were to be looked over by an intermediary acting on her behalf, and vetted for approval. The man chosen for the thankless task was USA's Vice President of Sports Programming, Wayne Becker. More at home in the genteel world of golf broadcasting, Becker was horrified to be given the role.

The feeling was mutual on the Federation side. Vince hated anybody telling him what to do, though he harboured a particular disdain for pushy executives whom he felt could not relate to the wrestling business. However, with his ratings at their lowest point since Raw had debuted three years earlier, McMahon realised he was hardly in a position to argue back. He signed off on the skits by degenerating to new levels of crass, having The Huckster and The Nacho Man both keel over and die in the ring from heart attacks during a "match" on the WrestleMania XII pre-show. He then had a representative from the Federal Trade Commission turn up at ringside, the sight of whom caused guest referee Billionaire Ted to collapse and die from a fear-induced heart attack. "Another Turner classic. So long, Ted," chortled McMahon heartlessly as the screen faded to black.[6]

---

[5] The ultimate hypocrisy was that Vince eventually became the very monster he claimed to despise. In 2000 he became a billionaire - on paper at least - when he floated the WWF on the stock market. A year later he bought WCW and ECW, merging both into the WWF and creating the wrestling monopoly that he had always coveted. In the years that followed he snapped up every piece of wrestling footage available for the eventual launch of his very own WWE Network in 2014, as things came full circle.

Ultimately, the only purpose the skits served was informing people who did not already know that there was an alternative to the WWF featuring names they adored from their childhoods. Vince had wasted considerable airtime and company resources in boosting the competition without making so much as a chink in the WCW armour. "It made fans turn on WCW to see if Hulk Hogan was really pushing a walker. It made people look to see if I was really that washed up," observed Hulk Hogan.[7]

Vince did not care about that. He simply wanted to paint Turner and any ex-employees he felt had jilted him in as negative a light as he could. Specifically, he wanted to needle at Ted personally by calling into question his virtuousness. His aim was that inquisitive executives within TBS and Time-Warner would see through the parody aspect of the skits and realise that many of the messages peddled were actually true. He hoped that would in turn make them start to question Turner's leadership, and indeed whether professional wrestling was something they wanted to be putting up with at all.

TURNER HAD been in the business world far too long to let a handful of vindictive parodies on a pugnacious business rival's wrestling show bother him. He was accustomed to having enemies - that was business. He merely let the jibes about his personal life and the ethics of his business decisions wash over him. As Eric Bischoff noted, "Ted laughed his ass off when he saw them. He thought they were funny as hell."

Turner backed up Bischoff's statement, "I was not that offended by 'em," he stated, "I said, 'Vince must be hurting to be resorting to this kind of stuff.'" Turner himself would never be directly drawn into the mudslinging. He felt he was above the pettiness, and was more than willing to let Bischoff be his public voice of combativeness. Bischoff did take the opportunity to respond, but his rebuttal was somewhat half-hearted. He simply aired a bumper on WCW's weekend TV broadcasts that showed

---

[6] Originally this was going to be on the main card, but a threatened lawsuit from WCW caused it to be moved. WCW were unhappy with the use of the Huckster, Nacho Man, and Billionaire Ted characters for profit, and sought a restraining order that would ban the match at *WrestleMania*. To avoid the issue, McMahon gave it away on free-to-air television, and was thus able to present what he was doing as a further parody rather than a money making exercise.

[7] Hogan was more offended by the digs at him than he ever publicly let on. He was particularly slighted with one segment that portrayed him as an egotist with an aversion to losing matches, so he decided to counter. In a transparent move, he had Bischoff approve his first pinfall defeat on WCW television, losing to Arn Anderson on an episode of *Nitro*. Being the master publicist that he was, Hogan waited until *Raw* was pre-empted before going through with it, thus ensuring as many eyeballs as possible were trained on him that night.

former WCW talent who now worked for Titan getting handily beaten, with the message conveyed that the much vaunted WWF New Generation were actually a bunch of WCW rejects. Bischoff had more pressing matters to concern himself with. One in particular was the issue of what to do with the overpriced Hogan, whom the Southern audience that WCW attracted were refusing to accept as one of their own. McMahon was merely an annoyance for Bischoff; he was no longer his primary concern.

Frustrated that the Billionaire Ted sketches provoked such little response from Turner brass, Vince decided to change tact. He utilised his battery of in-house lawyers and had them draft a letter to Turner Broadcasting that threatened a lawsuit for restraint of trade. The WWF claimed that airing *Nitro* in direct competition to *Raw* was an intentional move to sabotage the Federation show, given that Ted Turner owned the network and could have picked literally any timeslot to air it.

"The threats didn't scare me," claims Eric Bischoff, "They hoped to scare us off. They couldn't really figure out what we were doing, or maybe they couldn't really admit to themselves that we were smarter than they were, so they tried to scare us. They stirred the legal pot, hoping to rile the board of directors and shareholders." Vince's move failed. Turner and Bischoff had little tolerance for McMahon and what they perceived as an arrogant belief that he owned pro wrestling in the United States. They found the threats to be nothing more than a transparent attempt to create a scare within the corporation that would result in pressures to cancel *Nitro* and shelve WCW.

The two companies ultimately became entangled in a petty legal battle. Titan sued WCW for anything they could cook up, though the basis of their argument was essentially that WCW's mere existence was a threat to their well-being. Naturally, WCW disagreed. Feeling they were clear of any wrongdoing other than providing hearty competition, they counter-sued. The lawsuits were little more than posturing bluster and juvenile one-upmanship, a mess of he-said-she-said accusations that no judge worth his salt was ever likely to take seriously. After all, this was the wrestling business. To those outside of it, the WWF and WCW came across as two rivals squabbling like children, petulantly pouting whenever one lost ground on the other.

In one of the countless letters to the Turner Corporation drafted by Jerry McDevitt, he claimed the Billionaire Ted jibes were simply a response to WCW's own months of disparagement towards the WWF. Specifically he noted Eric Bischoff's belittling of their product and giving away results, as well as copyright infringements, trademark infringements, contract tampering and frequent derogatory comments about the WWF on Mark Madden's WCW Hotline. He later added during a live online interview that Turner had repeatedly attempted to purchase the WWF in the past decade, and that the consistent, unequivocal rebuttals had made him bitter towards the company. According to McDevitt, this served as inspiration for Turner's hell-bent drive to put Titan out of business.

"The WWF is a family-owned business and Vince is a third-generation promoter," noted McDevitt, "He doesn't want stock in TBS; he is a wrestling promoter. When it became obvious [to Turner] that the WWF was not for sale, we started hearing the statements that Turner was going to try and put the WWF out of business." The "family-owned business" approach to fighting the Monday Night War in the courtrooms was one that McMahon and McDevitt loved to employ. They felt it made Vince look like a sympathetic figure, an honourable family man trying to keep his wife and children fed and clothed, while an evil corporate tyrant was hell-bent on ruining him due to misplaced resentment. "It's personal and it's *damn* personal, it is my life. It is the life of my daughter, and my son," McMahon once insisted to a sceptical reporter, a story he would repeat to anyone prepared to listen.

Wrestling historians and journalists scoffed at the notion. In portraying himself as a poor, downtrodden proprietor of a quaint family business, one fighting for its survival against the mighty Turner-led WCW, Vince managed to conveniently forget his own history. The methods he had used to establish the WWF as the leading brand of professional wrestling for the masses were every bit as ignoble as those he claimed Turner was employing.

HEALTHY-FINANCED and with the strong New York market already well-entrenched thanks to three decades of foundations built by his father, Vince McMahon Jnr., waded into the promoting game in 1982 and swept away memories of his dad's esteemed reputation throughout the industry in a matter of years. He ambushed the ill-prepared regional promoters, calculatedly crossing long-held territorial lines and invading their provinces to seize local television slots by over-paying for syndication. Those he was unable to out-spend he assaulted from the inside, snaring away top talent and leaving the rival promotion combating a fatal dearth of star-power. In building his international wrestling empire, McMahon had wantonly violated years of tradition in a business built on handshakes, where a man's word was his bond. He left the rest of the industry a beaten, bloody mess, with everyone on the outside of the WWF feeding on scraps from the dying carcass of the once-thriving but now irreparably bludgeoned territorial system.

Vince would always vehemently oppose the suggestion that he was responsible for the demise of the status quo. "I didn't put the territories out of business, they put themselves out of business," he argues, "I had nothing except creative skills, a really strong work ethic, a lot of luck and a large set of grapefruits." It was McMahon's firm belief that the regional promoters were content with their lots and unadventurous in their business practices, unwilling to invest in the future of their respective companies. He felt the territories were already on the brink of extinction anyway. The advent of cable television had made America a much smaller place virtually overnight, opening the whole country up to would-be national entrepreneurs like him. He had merely been ahead of the curve and more technologically savvy than the rest. Seeing that cable television was a game-changer, he took more risks than his opponents, speeding up their demises rather than causing them.

The level of McMahon's accountability may have remained open to debate, but the tremors of his multi-faceted assault on wrestling's hidebound modus operandi were felt in all facets of the industry. Where there had once been dozen's of places throughout the length and breadth of America where a performer could earn a respectable living, suddenly there was only a handful. Significantly, the only place to become truly wealthy was Vince's WWF, though to do so one had to forgo family life and leisure time, trading it for a nomadic existence living on the road for three-hundred days a year. Anyone who ended up on the receiving end of Vince's ire now found themselves with few other options. McMahon had tried to - and virtually succeeded in - creating a wrestling monopoly, the specific thing he accused Ted Turner of trying to achieve in 1996.

Most in the real world purely saw Turner's actual motives as creating spirited competition. If anything, Turner was looking to break the WWF's own industry stranglehold by giving viewers and wrestlers a viable alternative to McMahon's ingrained brand of sports entertainment. The only difference between McMahon's war in the eighties against the regional promoters and his battle with Ted Turner was that Vince was on the other side of the fence; he was the one tasting the bitterness of defeat. McMahon had always thought himself to be unsinkable after overcoming every obstacle he had faced, be it the federal government, bankruptcy, an abusive stepfather or a general condescension from the outside world towards the wrestling business. Now he was the underdog, steering the ship of a once-flourishing but rapidly sinking organisation, while the lavishly assembled WCW ark sailed off into the distance.

His solution to the WCW problem was inspired in part by the response to the controversial *Billionaire Ted* skits. Even though they had not moved ratings, and if anything had harmed his own show, McMahon was buoyed by the talk they generated in the industry. He decided that bolder programming all-round was the answer. He would gradually stop presenting a wrestling show aimed towards children, instead reimagining the WWF with a daring product that catered to young adults.

TWO

VINCE'S NEWFOUND SELF-RIGHTEOUS PUBLIC stance opposing steroid use in wrestling was not without a degree of irony. Compounding that further, at the same time as he was taking Ted Turner to task for WCW's sketchy drug testing policy he was also deep in negotiations with a man who had no qualms admitting he used "the juice" to enhance his physique: Jim 'The Ultimate Warrior' Hellwig.

One of McMahon's biggest stars a few years prior, the face-paint-wearing, neon-emblazoned superhero incarnate had been away from the mainstream long enough for the business to change significantly since he had last featured. Ironically, in 1992, the last time Hellwig had worked for McMahon, he had admitted taking Human Growth Hormone to help chisel his massive bodybuilder frame. Vince could not risk having anyone on his roster that was so obviously using while the government was investigating his company for that explicit reason; Hellwig was promptly let go.

With media interest regarding steroid use in pro wrestling at its lowest in years by 1996, Vince had to make a moral decision regarding Hellwig. Undoubtedly, the Ultimate Warrior would be a significant boost to his ailing business, a ready-made remedy to help combat the ongoing threat of WCW.[8] On the other hand, he was an unabashed user of steroids, a remnant from the eighties when everyone on the roster was jacked up to the gills, their godly physiques injected straight from a bottle. It was the sort of ethical quandary that Vince would encounter multiple times over the year, and the outcome would prove to be no different from any of the others; morals were a virtue unashamedly left by the wayside. After all, there was a war to fight and dollars to make.

The discussions were tense. Hellwig and Titan had been locked in an ugly lawsuit over trademarks and rights to the Ultimate Warrior brand, so bad blood still simmered on both sides as a result. At his meeting with McMahon, Hellwig made a series of demands; primarily that he would still own and retain the rights to the character rather than Vince. Hellwig had a number of non-wrestling projects he was working on which involved the

---

[8] While McMahon was fascinated by Warrior and felt him the solution to the WWF's problems, most others in the promotion felt he was nothing more than a nostrum, a relic from the past whose dated persona no longer connected with the modern wrestling audience.

use of the Ultimate Warrior name and intellectual property, and he was not willing to give them up for a return to the ring.

Vince was unaccustomed to talent dictating contract terms, so he had mixed feelings about how to proceed. Worried that there would be a locker room revolt if the already unpopular Hellwig received anything approaching special treatment, Vince instead decided to fax him a generic Titan contract and hope for the best. Hellwig was incensed. He felt the offer was a disrespectful slap in the face, and he flat out refused to continue negotiations. A proposed return date at January's pay-per-view the *Royal Rumble* was nixed. The deal was dead.

ANOTHER NAME from the WWF's halcyon days of the eighties did agree to swallow his pride and return to work for Titan: Aurelian 'Jake the Snake Roberts' Smith, Jr. Once one of the most recognisable names on the roster in the Hogan era - partly down to his penchant for hauling a fifteen-foot Burmese python to the ring and placing it over beaten opponents after matches - Vince was willing to forgive Roberts for holding him up for a contract release moments before his scheduled bout with The Undertaker at *WrestleMania* in 1992. Lured by an inflated guaranteed deal from Kip Frye at WCW, Jake was so determined to leave that he refused to wrestle unless Vince acceded. As with Hellwig, McMahon was willing to forgive Roberts' past sins so that he could mine what little star power he had left and turn his fading name value into merchandise dollars.

Having spent the majority of his career battling crippling addictions to alcohol and crack cocaine, Roberts had recently become a born-again Christian. He had decided to get out of the wrestling business in 1994, and spent the ensuing two years trawling the country and preaching gospel, in addition to appearing on weekend evangelical shows extolling the virtues of Jesus Christ. Despite the $1500 per gig he was receiving for spreading the word of God, by 1996 he was no longer generating enough revenue to fund his drug habit. He was broke, so a call from Vince offering him a place in the *Royal Rumble* came at an opportune time. McMahon was instantly intrigued by Roberts' newfound religious demeanour. Feeling it would make a wholesome character trait for the Jake Roberts persona, Vince recast him as a Bible-thumping babyface. "It was bad for the character in the sense of what is marketable. I regret that," Roberts later rued.

Eyebrows were raised by the reacquisition of Roberts. On television, Vince was openly lambasting WCW for utilising aging former WWF talent whose peak of success came in the eighties, yet he was resorting to doing the exact same thing. Roberts was already forty years old when Vince came calling - only two years younger than the supposedly decrepit Hogan - and life away from the ring had taken its toll on his physique. Never a body guy even in his prime, Roberts returned overweight, balding, lacking visible muscle definition, and with a face that bore the wrinkles and creases of his decades of substance abuse and life on the road, all of which made him look far older than his years. "I'd let myself get out of shape, I hadn't taken care of myself," Roberts admits, "There's nothing worse than getting in that ring and not being able to give those people what they want. It hurt."

ANOTHER VETERAN booked for the *Royal Rumble* was even older. Dory Funk, Jr. was a former NWA World Champion who had last appeared for the WWF in the eighties, competing as 'Hoss Funk' alongside brother Terry. Dory was a major star in his seventies heyday and one of the finest workers of his generation, but the business had long since passed him by. The majority of Vince's youthful audience had no idea who the fifty-five-year-old was when he was trundled out at the pay-per-view.

That mattered little to McMahon; Funk's involvement in the match was purely political. He had seen the success Eric Bischoff was enjoying through importing performers from New Japan Pro Wrestling to his roster, and despite having mocked WCW for appropriating WWF practices, he intended to steal a page out of their book. Vince forged a deal with New Japan's fierce rivals All Japan Pro Wrestling, with Funk set to act as a liaison between the groups. His entry into the bout was a favour from McMahon to AJPW promoter Shohei 'Giant' Baba, and All Japan regular Takao Omori was brought along for the ride under the same circumstances.

The decision to strike up a working relationship with All Japan marked a significant shift in McMahon's ideals. He had never before so much as contemplated working with an outside group - though he had loaned talent to and maintained relations with small-time promotions the United States Wrestling Association (a relationship which granted unknown-outside-of-Memphis ten year veteran Doug Gilbert a berth in the Rumble match to fill out the numbers) and Smoky Mountain Wrestling because their respective promoters Jerry Lawler and Jim Cornette were members of his roster - but he recognised the need for change and a fresh approach to the way he conducted business. With Bischoff getting the jump on him in snapping up talented grapplers from around the world like Chris Benoit, Eddie Guerrero, and Rey Misterio, Jr., McMahon felt he needed to follow suit.

While the All Japan union proved short lived, the WWF versus WCW rivalry was quickly becoming an all-encompassing industry-wide war. Both sides were forging precarious allegiances with other promotions, be it enlisting them as feeder companies, or as a means to increase the visibility of their own performers. It was a call to arms; a readying of troops and a stocking of arsenals for what promised to be a protracted and draining battle.

MCMAHON REALISED that relics from the past alone would not be enough to combat WCW; to truly compete he needed a fresh influx of talent - a neoteric new breed. He asked around his closest and most trusted members of staff for potential names. Of those suggested to him, one in particular stood out: Mick 'Cactus Jack' Foley.

Thirty-year-old Foley had left WCW by his own volition in 1994 in favour of working in Japan, and he had been carving out a niche for himself in Philadelphia-based hardcore group Extreme Championship Wrestling for the past year. The WWF's interest in him represented another surprise move from McMahon. Possessing a doughy teddy bear physique, a violent unrefined ring style and an unsightly scar-covered appearance, Mick Foley was everything that Vince *did not* look for in a WWF "superstar". However, he also possessed a confidence, aura, and passion when delivering interviews that few could match, and his grasp of in-ring psychology was much greater than the bloody barbed wire matches he frequented seemed to suggest.

Jim Ross was the key driving force behind the decision to begin talks with Foley; spending months convincing McMahon that it would be in his best interests to hire him. As he explains, "I kept pitching and pitching and pitching Mick to Vince, because I knew in my mind that once Vince saw Mick, he'd like him. Secondly, once Vince got to know Mick on an individual basis, he would *love* the guy"

Foley was initially cautious when Ross contacted him in late 1995 with a potential job offer at Titan. "Vince has a new idea and some of us think you would be perfect for it, so he has agreed to set up a meeting," Ross told him. Growing up in New York, Foley had aspired to work for the World Wrestling Federation since the days he spent in his teens diving off garage roofs in an effort to emulate his hero Jimmy Snuka, but he was not a star-struck fan anymore. He knew that business in the Big Apple was struggling, having been regaled with horror stories from his close friend Troy 'Shane Douglas' Martin about what conditions in the company were like financially and politically. He was also reluctant to give up years of hard work perfecting the Cactus Jack character for Vince to repackage him as something unmarketable or career-shattering, as he felt the WWF head had a tendency to do.

Despite his concerns, Foley agreed to the meeting and anxiously drove to Stamford to meet with Vince and front office executive J.J. Dillon at Titan Tower. It was there that McMahon told Foley he wanted to put him under a mask and rebrand him as something resembling Hannibal Lector, then have him work a program with Mark 'The Undertaker' Calaway. Foley balked and expressed his disappointment, asking McMahon why he couldn't just be Cactus Jack, a character he had been honing and refining for over a decade. Vince's response was typical of his mindset when it came to talent, pointing out that the WWF had to differentiate itself from its competition to appease their licensees.

Even though Vince was willing to take steps that moved the WWF in a new adult-oriented direction, he was still reluctant to drop too many of the principles that had served him so well. The rebranding of talent was one of them. He was in favour of implementing edgier characters, but they had to be self-created and pre-approved, not shoehorned in from elsewhere. Dillon pressed a contract into Foley's hand as he left the building, which contained within it zero guarantees and merely the promise of an opportunity. It was Vince's standard offer. Guaranteed money was something he was still unwilling to contemplate, despite what had happened with Randy Savage in 1994 and Lex Luger in 1995, both of whom had been signed to lucrative guaranteed deals by WCW right under his nose.

Foley was dejected when he returned home. After giving minimal consideration to the deal, he called Dillon to tell him, "thanks but no thanks". Unlike his friend Shane Douglas, he did not intend to allow Vince to turn him into a two-bit cartoon act with a limited shelf life. A frank call from Ross outlining the possibilities for growth in the Federation eventually changed his mind. Finally convinced about the merits of a job with Titan - and of McMahon's commitment to the new character - Foley reached an agreement with the WWF.

Foley met with Vince again a few weeks later. Unlike most recently signed Titan acquisitions granted an audience with their employer, he was not afraid to let his true feelings be known about McMahon's proposed 'Mason the Mutilator' gimmick. He expressed dissatisfaction with the attire that had been provided for him, and made it clear that he didn't care for the handle 'Mason'. Foley instead proposed 'Mankind', outlining the various scenarios and possibilities that the name's double meaning offered.

When McMahon agreed to the changes, Mick Foley was officially the newest member of the WWF roster. Unfortunately for Vince, he was unable to start with the group until after *WrestleMania* due to commitments in Japan and with ECW that the professional Foley was determined to honour.

He was a no-go for the upcoming *Royal Rumble*, so for that, the WWF was forced to once again look elsewhere.

ONE ECW name that the WWF could not agree terms with was Terry 'Sabu' Brunk. The nephew of one of wrestling's great heels, Ed 'The Sheik' Farhat, Brunk was a hot commodity in 1996 due to his propensity for breaking ringside tables with his own body. Brunk called J.J. Dillon to express an interest in working for the WWF, and Vince believed him to be the sort of innovative performer he was looking for, so agreed to use him. A one-time deal was made that would see Sabu compete in the *Royal Rumble*, with Titan agreeing to let him perform his trademark table spot to eliminate himself from the match and thus protect his aura. The group went so far as to promote Sabu's appearance in the match on its hotline and television pre-tapes, but then ECW promoter Paul Heyman put a spanner in the works.

Heyman was uncomfortable with the WWF treating ECW as a feeder company, especially after many of his top stars had recently been snatched away by WCW. He managed to talk Brunk out of doing the show, and then openly discussed the situation with the audience at an ECW Arena event. He wanted to make sure that everyone knew Brunk's options, and presented it in such a way that if Sabu did appear at the Rumble, then ECW fans were pre-programmed to turn on him. Brunk was unhappy being used as the rope in an inter-promotional tug-of-war, so following the advice of close friends he decided to appear at the *Royal Rumble* anyway.

To appease Heyman, whom the WWF wanted onside as part of their drive to rally opposing forces to WCW, office executive Bruce Prichard offered him a deal that would see a number of WWF-contracted undercard stars appear for ECW. Heyman rejected the proposal, worried that if his audience saw an influx of WWF talent on the shows they would turn against what was promoted as an outlaw, anti-authoritarian product. To have WWF wrestlers work for him would be viewed as the WWF and ECW having endorsed one another. Heyman felt that would harm his business much more than it would help it; such was the mentality of his fan base and the overall ethos of ECW.[9]

Instead, Heyman continued to pressure Brunk not to do the WWF show, and as was usually the case, his silver tongue got him what he wanted.

---

[9] Heyman inevitably ended up doing exactly that just a few months later, agreeing to a secret working agreement with McMahon and the WWF that allowed them to exchange talent. Little over a year later, Heyman and Vince even reached a deal that saw ECW take over *Monday Night Raw* as a way to hype interest in the group's debut pay-per-view *Barely Legal*.

A master manipulator, Heyman convinced Brunk that he was the biggest star ECW had, so him appearing on a WWF pay-per-view would hurt their chances of presenting a paid event of their own in the future. He claimed the providers willing to take a chance with the group on pay-per-view wanted a contemporary, alternative brand to the WWF and WCW, and that it would be in jeopardy if Brunk did the show.

His logic was patchy. Having someone who would be on a potential ECW pay-per-view compete for a mainstream wrestling organisation as a one-off would bring only exposure; it would hardly mean Sabu was a WWF performer. Heyman was convincing enough that Brunk backed out, leaving the WWF red-faced and frustrated, with some in the company determined not to do business with Paul Heyman again.[10]

WITH THE Hellwig and Brunk deals having fallen through, Mick Foley tied up with commitments elsewhere, and half-hearted grandstand plays for UFC fighter Dan Severn and ex-boxer Peter McNeely coming to nothing, Vince felt he still needed a big name debutant in the *Royal Rumble*. He eventually found one in the form of recently released ex-WCW World Champion Leon 'Big Van Vader' White.

A bull of a man who hit harder in the ring than most men did in real fights, Vader had a fearsome reputation. So intimidating was he during his WCW peak that as Mick Foley recounted, "Some of the newer guys used to actually leave the arena if they saw their name on the board opposite Vader. Other guys would hide until that evening's card had been drawn up, and then come out of hiding if Vader wasn't their opponent."

White had been a top star in WCW for years, holding the WCW World Heavyweight Championship three times, more than anyone else at that point[11]. However, the arrival of Hogan had seen his status reduced, and he had last held the company's most prestigious title in December 1993. The advent of *Nitro* in 1995 was set to be his return to the fore, with Eric Bischoff looking for something shocking and unexpected to pique interest in his new broadcast. His idea was that Vader would dethrone Hulk Hogan on the second episode of the show, ending a record reign that spanned over a year. When Hogan learned of the plan, he instantly vetoed it. Unwilling to lose on television, he was able to refuse the request thanks to a clause that

---

[10] Sabu would eventually get his Royal Rumble spot and table elimination eleven years later at *Royal Rumble 2007*, when Kane eliminated him with a chokeslam from the top rope through the announce desk.

[11] Though that is strictly WCW World Title runs, and does not include the NWA World Title lineage that WCW often claimed as their own.

had been written into his contract giving him complete creative control over his character's storylines.

White was annoyed by the news but hardly surprised. He was tired of the Hulk Hogan circus dominating WCW, frustrated that his role had been downgraded from killer heel to Hogan fodder. He was also forced to severely limit his hard-hitting in ring style when working with Hogan, given strict instructions to go easy on WCW's top drawing card and forced to work at Hogan's pace. Despite the more deliberate tempo of the contests, White suffered injuries to his shoulder and chest during a bout with Hogan at 1995's *Bash at the Beach* pay-per-view. His temperament was not helped by management forcing him to work through the pain in matches that put further strain on his already damaged body, rather than letting him have time off to get the surgery he needed. He had to work, they told him, because the company needed him. White acquiesced, but refused to work non-televised live events. Soon he started to mix drinking heavily with downing handfuls of Percocets in an effort to numb the pain.

ON A seasonally warm late August afternoon at Centre Stage in the heart of midtown Atlanta, an incident with Paul Orndorff caused White's WCW career to come to an abrupt end. White was asleep in his hotel room the morning of a WCW television taping when he received a stern phone call from Eric Bischoff, who was frustrated that White had missed a number of scheduled photo shoots recently. The VP told him in no uncertain terms that he was to attend a rescheduled shoot that afternoon at the CNN Center, warning he would be fined a few thousand dollars if he failed to show up. White was not even aware he had missed any of the other shoots, but duly complied with Bischoff's demand and fulfilled the obligation. His ensuing three-mile journey back to the site of the evening's taping came during heavy rush hour traffic, meaning he did not arrive at the building until ninety minutes after he was scheduled to be there. The event was the catalyst that changed the course of his career.

White was not worried about his tardiness, because Bischoff had sent him on the assignment and knew why he was late. He had also promised to pass on the information to the agents and executives working at the tapings. Unbeknownst to White, informing others of his whereabouts had slipped Bischoff's mind due to myriad other issues coming up - as was always the case during a television shoot. When White finally arrived at the building he was greeted by his friend Tonga 'Meng' Fifita, who expressed surprised at his lateness because it was so out of character for him. "Where you been? You're never late! They've been looking for you..." Fifita warned him.

White wondered exactly who "they" were, but did not concern himself with it. Once again, he felt assured in the knowledge that he was following direct orders from his boss.

When road agent Terry Taylor wandered into the room and began questioning him about why he was late, White started to become irritated. "Terry, Eric told me I had to do some photos," he stated flatly. Taylor understood once the situation had been explained, but informed White that he needed to change quickly into his ring attire so he could head down the hall and film some promos. Already behind schedule, the team were about to wrap up. If WCW didn't get the final shots filmed straight away then they would have to pay double to have the crew stay on longer.

White agreed and was about to get changed, when another agent - former wrestler, Paul Orndorff - burst into the room. Orndorff had been on top of the business in the mid-eighties. One of the key players in the WWF's glory years, he had wrestled in the main event at the inaugural *WrestleMania* and headlined across North America with Hulk Hogan, where the pair had routinely drew monster sell-out houses. During the run with Hogan, Orndorff damaged his neck when he was kicked in the chin during a match in Canada. He had needed surgery, but put it off because he knew that the time it would take to heal would spell the end of his run as a main eventer. By the time the run was over it was too late to fix the problem, which left him with permanent damage on the right side of his body. He once justified his decision to work through the pain during a conversation with Kevin Nash, telling him, "I was on top with *the man*, I was printing money." However, by 1995 Orndorff was reduced to the role of occasional wrestler and backstage agent. What remained was a jacked-up bipolar veteran with an atrophied right arm, who was angry at the world as a result.

Orndorff had been sent to find White that fateful August afternoon by Bob Armstrong, a grizzled fifty-seven-year-old veteran who had been in the business for three decades and had trained all four of his sons to be wrestlers. His current employment with WCW was also as a road agent; he was the man in charge of getting the day's promos completed on time. Armstrong was annoyed the filming was behind schedule, so he was deeply irritated with White not showing up. To hurry things along, he sent Orndorff to tell him to get a move on.

"Where the hell you been? You're late!" Orndorff demanded tersely, and White sighed, fed up with having to explain himself yet again. He didn't get the chance; Orndorff had no time for excuses, he only wanted to make sure the promos were shot. White was less than impressed with Orndorff's curtness and told him he would have to wait until he was changed. The notoriously intense Orndorff saw red and started yelling at White, who already irritated, growled back that he was late because he was on a Bischoff-ordered photo session, and that Orndorff was not his boss so should change his tone.

Both men had always been cordial to each other prior to the blow-up, even teaming up a couple of times a few years earlier, though Orndorff felt White could be a bully in the ring. Any remaining semblance of friendship and professionalism disappeared at that point. "Goddamn you, you fat-ass fucking prima donna," yelled Orndorff, who by now had worked himself up into a frenzy. White refused to be talked down to in front of the boys and other agents, so shouted back, "Hey Paul, go fuck yourself. If you're gonna talk to me like that, then get the fuck out of the room."

Though he was still seething, Orndorff walked away. White on the other hand remained livid about the way he had been treated, growing angrier and angrier as he stewed over it. He decided to confront Orndorff again and demand an apology, feeling he had done nothing wrong to justify the torrent of foul-mouthed abuse. He left the locker room and immediately spotted Orndorff in the hallway, deliberately shouldering into him, igniting the powder keg. The pair quickly squared up, going nose-to-nose and barking expletives at one another. "Make your move fat-ass, go ahead, take your best fucking shot, 'cos I'm gonna kick your fat fucking ass," screamed Orndorff.

Given the circumstances and setting there was little chance of either man backing down. It hardly even mattered that both felt they were in the right; predominantly neither man dared risk losing face with the growing crowd of intrigued locker room members. White struck first, smacking Orndorff hard in the chest with his bear-sized palm and knocking him clean off his feet. Orndorff's head cracked off the floor with a thud, immediately causing White to worry that he might have gone too far and accidentally killed him.

"Paul, are you alright?" he asked tentatively, but was shoved away. For White the near miss diffused the situation somewhat. He backed off, but Orndorff was still enraged and wanted to continue the fight. When he made it back to his feet, he pounced with three quick punches to the face, as members of the locker room half-heartedly tried to pull the pair apart. Orndorff then caught White in the side of the head with a powerful left hook that would have floored a rhino, sending him tumbling to the ground. Orndorff, who was wearing flip-flops, proceeded to kick White repeatedly until the skirmish was finally broken up, and Orndorff was led away into the agent's room. Observer Brian Pillman would later note that if Orndorff had been wearing a real pair of shoes, then he might well have killed White before he was pulled away from him. As Bob Armstrong remembers it, "Paul just beat his big fat… I mean he beat him 'til he was bleeding. It was a mess."

As a company official, Orndorff should have known better than to engage in a fistfight with a member of the talent roster. However, he was not a corporate suit - he was a wrestler foremost - and wrestlers handled business in different ways than real world executives. He recounted the tale to the gaggle of impressed announcers, linkmen and other agents who had quickly surrounded him. Orndorff justified his actions, explaining that he was merely defending himself because White had sucker punched him first.

Meanwhile, White was on the floor for several minutes recovering from the impact of the blows and trying to regain his bearings. Orndorff's assault had left him bruised, bloodied, and embarrassed. He wanted to save face. At any rate, he had a tough guy reputation to protect, one that would be irreparably damaged if word leaked out that he had been humbled by an older man half his size who had the use of only one arm.

He stormed into the agent's office and called out Orndorff for another round, telling him that he had not wanted to fight before, but had since changed his mind. He goaded him, yelling how he was yet to throw a single punch, whereas Orndorff had to hit him four times in the face before he went down. Gene Okerlund stepped in and cautioned White that he could not fight in the executive's room, so the two spilled outside and brawled again, this time in a more even ruckus. When Orndorff looked to be getting the upper hand again, Tonga Fifita intervened and pulled him off before he could do any more damage. The result was a black eye for Orndorff, with White suffering further damage to his eyes and lip. Orndorff would later state that if not for his inability to use the right side of his body, then he might well have ended up in jail for having killed White.

When Eric Bischoff finally learned what had transpired, he immediately sent White home. He understood his position and sympathised that the situation had become so out of hand because of his own failure to communicate White's whereabouts to his staff, but matters had escalated far beyond that being an acceptable reason. The way Bischoff saw it, White had thrown the first punch and then reignited the situation when he came looking for Orndorff. He had no choice but to suspend him. Orndorff on the other hand wrestled on that evening's tapings, with his fresh black eye clearly visible as he defeated enhancement performer Barry Houston in a routine squash bout.

The altercation meant Bischoff had to act and punish White, because he could not be seen as tolerant of such miscreant behaviour, no matter what the original justification behind it was. He told White to go home and cool off, then offered him a six month unpaid suspension with the caveat that he could work as many dates in Japan as he wanted during that period. To White that was the equivalent of a $250,000 fine, which he felt was excessively harsh considering the circumstances. On the advice of his lawyer, White rejected the offer. He later admitted he had felt pressured to do so, and confessed that it was a mistake. Bischoff even tried to caution him as such, warning, "Leon, we've got a whole floor filled with attorneys. Do you really want to do this?" White did not, but his attorneys did and he listened to them. "It was bad advice," he later conceded.

As White sat at home brooding, the sharks were circling in Atlanta. Hulk Hogan and Ric Flair were both in Bischoff's ear, self-servingly advising him that WCW didn't need Vader, and that he should be released from his contract for his actions. It was a political play from both. With Vader out of the way, it would free up space in the crowded main event scene. Bischoff was au fait with Hogan and Flair's respective camps pulling him from both sides, though rarely did they share the same opinion. He relented to the pressure - in part so he could free funds to make a statement of intent by signing the WWF's Lex Luger - and released White from his four-year contract. Due to the manner of his dismissal, cited on the grounds of disorderly conduct, WCW were not required to pay him a penny in severance money.

WHEN WHITE wound up sat in Vince McMahon's office in early January 1996, he made sure to be on his best behaviour. The WWF was the only alternative to WCW if he wanted to remain in North America. He had no interest in embarrassing himself by working for low budget independent operations or going somewhere small-time like ECW. Even though he had options in Japan where he was already a star and would be given a much lighter schedule, White wanted the WWF job. He needed shoulder surgery, and a contract with Titan meant the costs of the operation would be covered. In addition, like Mick Foley, he was a closet 'mark' for the WWF name at heart, feeling that for his career to be judged as a success he needed to "make it" in New York.

From the start White was upfront with McMahon, informing him that he was injured and would need surgery. He outlined two realistic options regarding a deal; he could come in and work through the injury for as long as possible then get surgery, or he could appear at the *Royal Rumble*, then take time off immediately and return months later. McMahon contemplated the two options and suggested a third; that White worked the Rumble show and the following evening's *Raw* tapings, on which they would run an angle that caused him to be suspended, allowing him to get the surgery.

White agreed to the compromise and the deal was struck, then Vince moved on to another issue: his ring name. McMahon had always looked to repackage performers who came in to the WWF with reputations built elsewhere. He felt that his marketing machine could not fully get behind something dated and pre-existing; they were better equipped to push and promote something original and vibrant. As he had with Mick Foley, Vince suggested an alternative alias.

"Vince wanted to change his name to 'The Mastodon'!" remembers an incredulous Jim Cornette, "I said, 'It's fucking Vader! He's a former WCW Champion; everyone in the world knows who he is!'" White did not want to change either and argued his case. Vince eventually relented and agreed that White could remain as Vader, a decision that the performer ultimately regretted. "Vince wanted to create a whole new character, and you know what? I should have done it," he rued. "The WWF would have owned it, but Vince would have marketed [the character properly] if it was his. That was a mistake, and that was stupid on my part. I should have said yes."

After twenty minutes of the *Royal Rumble* match had elapsed, Vader arrived as the bout's thirteenth entrant. Flanked by motor-mouthed manager Cornette, he was immediately allowed to shine and display the same dominance that had made him into a star during his WCW peak. He wasted little time in making his presence felt, dumping four contestants out of the ring and surviving for ten minutes before falling victim to Shawn Michaels.

Following his elimination, Vader proceeded to lay a beating on Michaels and anyone else in his way, then the following night on *Raw* he was made to look like a monster as he demolished Savio Vega. So vicious was Vader's destruction of the Puerto Rican that figurehead company president Gorilla Monsoon intervened. Then in a shocking angle, Vader crushed Monsoon with his impressive Vader Bomb finishing move, which led to the storyline suspension McMahon had suggested. It was captivating television, roundly praised by critics as one of the best angles to appear on Titan programming in some time.

White was extremely satisfied with how he had been booked and presented on his WWF debut. Little over a week later, he underwent his scheduled shoulder surgery and his spirits were high. Despite the discomfort he was in, he was confident that his future with the company looked promising once he returned. White convalesced at home, taking his recovery steadily with the knowledge that he had ten months to heal, cautious about putting too much strain on the repaired limb too soon. White's relative positivity quickly dissipated upon receiving a call from his agent two weeks after the operation telling him that he was scheduled for a return to action in six weeks. Vince wanted him to be back in time for *WrestleMania* and a match with the gargantuan Yokozuna.

"What? No! That's not the deal. I can't do it! I can't come back from this surgery that soon," White exasperatedly told him, demanding that he fix the situation immediately. It was too late. The deal had already been struck and Vince expected White to honour it. "Two and a half months ain't shit on a shoulder," pointed out Steve Austin. "From my own experience when I had shoulder surgery, it took me eight or ten months minimum to get that thing back. There's absolutely no way you can come back from a severe shoulder injury in a two-and-a-half-month time period. Any injury is bad, but with something like a shoulder? There goes most of your offence. You're at a severe disadvantage."

Despite suffering a significant lack of movement on one side, White had no choice but to return to work or else he would be in breach of his contract. It was the same situation he had found himself in at WCW, forced to work in constant agony for the benefit of the company. Unlike Eric Bischoff, McMahon did at least have some sympathy for White's plight, but ultimately he was a businessman and he wanted every weapon he had at his disposal in his fight against Turner. Nevertheless, he agreed to a compromise, canning the scheduled singles bout with Yokozuna and changing it to a six-man tag to take some of the onus off White.

Demoralised by the situation, White was satiated as best he could be, but he realised the restructured contest was an obvious demotion for him. A throwaway multi-man bout at the biggest show of the year might have been necessary for him to be able to compete on the card, but it meant his WWF career was stalling before it had even properly started. He already knew he had a task on his hands to win Vince over because of his rejecting the 'Mastodon' name change. This situation hardly helped. It would be the story of his WWF tenure.

ROUNDING OFF the unprecedented number of unfamiliar faces in the *Royal Rumble* were The Headhunters, Manuel and Victor Santiago. They were a pair of 5'11, 350-pound identical twins from New York, who had made names for themselves in Japan's off-the-wall extreme violence promotions Frontier Martial-Arts Wrestling and IWA Japan. Agile and swift for men of their size, what they lacked in wrestling acumen they made up for with a willingness to bleed buckets and inflict brutality. Their only North American exposure of any real note had come in the formative years of ECW, so they were complete unknowns to nearly everyone in the WWF audience.

Though only brought in for a guest spot to make up the numbers, Vince couldn't resist putting his own stamp on the duo and rechristened them 'The Squat Team'. The irony of naming the stumpy, vertically challenged tandem as such was lost on McMahon. For the brothers, the Rumble appearance was an easy $5000 apiece - the going rate for an outsider's appearance on the show - as in the match they only lasted for a collective ninety-five seconds.

As had been the case in striking a deal with Mick Foley, bringing in a duo best known for their work in ultra-violent promotions was a significant diversion from Vince's usual hiring policies. Those in the know realised that he was up to something; he had never before considered performers of that nature an acceptable fit for his sanitised, family-friendly wrestling promotion, even for one night. If he was suddenly willing to change his ethos, there had to be a reason behind it.

There was of course; Vince still intended to take the WWF in a new creative direction as a response to WCW, a decision he had so far kept largely to himself. Some had noticed that McMahon was allowing elements to slip through on his broadcasts in late 1995 that he had formerly outlawed, such as turning a blind eye to the use of blood and profanity from some of his performers. It was a deliberate play of ignorance on his part; he wanted the WWF to become more edgy and move away from the overplayed, stale and childish programming that he was currently presenting.

McMahon realised that reinvention was the key to keeping ahead of the curve. Incorporating blood, violence and smutty sexual content into his programming was a concept that WCW could not replicate thanks to the restrictions of working under the TBS umbrella. It was something he had wanted to do sooner, but he had been hamstrung by the steroid trial and forced to adopt a clean image until the spotlight was shining elsewhere. WCW's rise to prominence had forced his hand. With each passing week of the war he felt the time to forge ahead with his mooted cutting-edge direction was imminent.

THE REST of the *Royal Rumble* match consisted of Vince's regular troupe of burned out performers, a typically diverse cast that in itself was representative of the hotchpotch of mismatched ideals prevalent throughout the company. Veterans mixed it up with rookies, hackneyed stereotypes competed against dual career specialists (as with the example of Isaac Yankem, a zany wrestler-cum-dentist), and above all there was a definite dearth of realistic contenders to win the match. Among the participants were:

Veteran part-timers Bob Backlund and Jerry Lawler, who were generally used sparingly as in-ring performers due to their advancing ages. They were wheeled out because of the incredibly shallow roster depth that Vince was working with following a string of cost-cutting releases in 1995. He used both as light-hearted comic relief, with Backlund gurning and stomping around the ring like an overblown caricature, and Lawler chosen as the man to be draped with Jake Roberts' giant python Revelations, before spending the majority of the match hiding under the ring.

Also making an appearance was Robert 'Bob Holly' Howard, who had been used primarily to put over the likes of Goldust and the Body Donnas in the weeks leading up to the show. It was a rare television outing for the California native, whose bookings had dried up significantly following Titan's canning of lesser 'B' house shows in 1995. Howard was one of a number of performers in the match constrained by a cartoonish gimmick that called for him to have an outside vocation (in his case a racing car driver) as well as wrestling. The Bob Holly character was practically the epitome of the WWF's creative problems, failing as it did to resonate with any demographic watching.

Plenty of characters were similar to Holly. Another was doe-eyed garbage man Mike "Duke" Droese, who was given the number thirty berth in the match following a victory over Hunter Hearst Helmsley in a bout aired for free before the pay-per-view broadcast. Droese had been with the WWF since 1994, though this was only his second appearance on pay-per-view, with the first having come a year earlier in the 1995 edition of the Rumble. Like Howard, Droese had not connected with the audience and had little chance of doing so. Once he realised that his career was going nowhere he asked for and was duly granted his release in July, taking up a somewhat less physically draining job at a local elementary school in Tennessee.

Elsewhere, Kensuke 'Hakushi' Shinzaki and Chris 'Tatanka' Chavis were both portraying outdated cultural stereotypes and were reaching the end of their tenures with Titan. Shinzaki was supremely gifted inside the ring, but he was limited by his ethnicity in a world where being foreign was considered a negative trait. Unable to deliver interviews in English, he was treated as an afterthought and placed in opening matches where he would routinely lose to inferior workers. Realising that his upside was limited in the WWF and that by staying there and losing each week he was damaging his credibility elsewhere, he left the company never to return in February, heading home to Japan.

Chavis' appearance was his first for the company since August 1995. At that time, he was removed from the active roster for his alleged part in a seedy situation involving David 'Jimmy Del Ray' Ferrier and a female fan from Anaheim, which had resulted in a lawsuit. There was little evidence to suggest that Chavis had done a great deal wrong other than find himself in the wrong place at the wrong time, but Vince felt he could not have the stigma of suspicion hanging over one of his performers and suspended him. By the time the *Royal Rumble* came around, the legal suit had been dropped.

It was a case of excellent timing for McMahon, who was struggling to fill the battle royal. However, Chavis - who had been working in pay-per-view main events in 1995 - had lost steam having been off television for five months. He left the company in March having barely won a match since he was reinstated. Like Shinzaki and Droese, he asked for his release and was granted it, citing family issues as the reason behind his departure. Eric Bischoff immediately offered him a deal with WCW upon learning of his free agent status, but Chavis declined, preferring to work on the independent circuit due to the free time it gave him to spend at home. He would not return to work for Vince for nearly a decade.

Nelson 'King Mabel' Frazer had worked in a pay-per-view main event as recently as *SummerSlam* in August, where he squared off with Kevin 'Diesel' Nash in a poorly received WWF Championship match. Frazer's notorious clumsiness in the ring had caused him to accidentally injure Nash in the contest, and then he did the same to the Undertaker six weeks later. At first, Vince had been fascinated by the five-hundred pounder's immense girth, but he soon became irritated with him injuring his top stars. He could not risk losing any more by putting them in the ring with Frazer, so Mabel was phased out. Defeat against the Undertaker in a casket match at December's *In Your House* event appeared to spell the end of the road for the character.

However, the thinness of the roster meant that Frazer was given one final chance and he was brought back for the Rumble match. Unfortunately, for both McMahon and the wrestler, it was the same old story. Frazer injured Mark 'Henry Godwinn' Canterbury during the bout, and the pig farmer had to be eliminated from the match earlier than planned. There would be no more chances for Frazer in 1996. The *Royal Rumble* appearance was his last match for the company until he was brought back as a one-off on *Monday Night Raw* in 1998, then rehired permanently in early 1999. When it came to big guys and Vince McMahon, there was always one more opportunity in the offing.

At over 800lbs, Rodney 'Yokozuna' Anoa'i was even bigger than Frazer, though he had rather the opposite reputation. Anoa'i was known for being safe in the ring and protecting his opponents at all times. He realised that at his size something going wrong was not just an injury, but potential death. McMahon was initially so impressed with Anoa'i's ability to move quickly around the ring despite his five-hundred pounds frame, that he had made him his top heel and WWF Champion in 1993, all within a year of signing him. As the years elapsed, Anoa'i increasingly piled on the weight until he was a barely mobile seven-hundred pounds mass of lardy flesh. He had headlined two consecutive *WrestleMania* cards in 1993 and 1994, not to mention unceremoniously ending Hulkamania at *King of the Ring* in 1993, but by early 1996 he was washed-up far sooner than he should have been.

A heel throughout his run, saddled with the typically trite "evil foreigner" gimmick that Vince loved to give his top villains, the character had grown stale and was in dire need of a revamp. Thus, the *Royal Rumble* would prove to be the start of a surprise babyface run for Anoa'i, thanks to a smartly booked altercation during the match with the debuting Vader. It was a false dawn. With the babyface side of the roster already overcrowded, the turn proved to be merely a relegation down the ladder for Anoa'i. Come April, Yokozuna was written off the show with an injury angle and sent to a fat farm to drop weight.

Anoa'i's close friend Charles Wright (both members of backstage clique the Bone Street Krew) was also about to embark on a hiatus. Despite being booked to reach the final four of the match, his Kama persona bowed out at the Rumble. He had not been seen on television for months, but like Mabel and Tatanka he was brought back to flesh out the contest. A series of defeats to The Undertaker over the summer had damaged the character, and Wright was taken off television after the pay-per-view until mid-1997.

A number of other competitors in the bout were reaching the end of their usefulness too, having no place in Vince's vision for a new-look WWF. Jobber-turned-superstar Barry Horowitz was among them, unable to retain the momentum he had generated in mid-1995 following a first ever WWF television victory over Chris 'Skip' Candido. The Rumble appearance would be his final on pay-per-view before he was shunted back down to the prelims, with Vince having quickly grown bored of his feel-good Jewish underdog story.

Anoa'i's cousin, Solofa Fatu, Jr. who simply worked as Fatu, was portraying a smiling, reformed street-thug babyface at the time of the Rumble, advising youths to stay off drugs and pledging to "make a difference". He did not. Fatu was the exact type of generic, intelligence-insulting persona that Federation fans were fed up with. He too had no place in Vince's grand design and was eventually repackaged in August, albeit with an equally dismal gimmick: The Sultan. It was another of Vince's infamous racial pigeonholes, and like Fatu, it failed to get over.

AMIDST THE sea of deadweight and clichéd personalities in the match were a handful of wrestlers Vince was relying on to carry the WWF's in-ring action throughout the year. Brothers-in-law Owen Hart and Davey Boy Smith were two of them. Both were talented bone-benders who commanded a great deal of respect amongst their peers for their in-ring abilities, but as far as Vince was concerned, as main event stars they were yesterday's news. They had both already been given their chance as headline acts, but having failed to move business to McMahon's liking they dropped down the card into a no-man's land underneath the top stars. Because they were of average size compared to McMahon's circus of giants and freaks, they were not afforded a second bite of the main event cherry. They remained fairly well placed thanks to their family ties to WWF Champion Bret Hart, but in Vince's eyes their days on top had been and gone.

Backstage political powerhouses The Kliq (Shawn Michaels, Diesel, Razor Ramon, Hunter Hearst Helmsley and 1-2-3 Kid) were expectedly given prime spots in the match and allowed to look impressive, making sure to manipulate the booking of the contest so they would only be eliminated by each other. Even in a battle royal environment with thirty competitors, the Kliq were still unwilling to let anyone on the roster get one up on them.

Paul 'Hunter Hearst Helmsley' Levesque's entry at the number one spot ensured there would be a Kliq presence in the match from start to finish. It was a chance for Levesque to prove himself worthy of competing at a higher level than he was typically being booked, and he was given nearly fifty minutes - far longer than anyone else - in which to do so. He gave an accomplished performance, showing impressive levels of stamina and cardiovascular conditioning, confirming that he was receiving a push based on merit rather than because of who his friends were. Sean '1-2-3 Kid' Waltman was also allowed to shine with a respectable fifteen minute spell in the bout before he was ousted by his buddy Shawn Michaels. Earlier in the night he had set up a future program with another Kliq member, Scott Hall, by interfering in his match against Dustin Runnels' homoerotic Goldust persona and costing him the Intercontinental title.

Recently the quintet had decreed they would only do programs with each other, or guys they knew and trusted. It was a decision made following a series of unsavoury incidents working with Kliq adversaries Carl 'Pierre Lafitte' Ouellet, Troy 'Dean Douglas' Martin, and Nelson 'Mabel' Frazer. Hall in particular was upset with his program opposite Runnels. He was worried that having a flamboyant bi-gender kook making plays for him and caressing him in the ring was not the message he wanted to be sending home to children, especially his own. Booking Hall in a program with best friend Waltman was a way for Vince to appease him.

Waltman had already been sent packing from the Rumble by the time Kevin 'Diesel' Nash joined the fray towards the end of the contest. Nash was allowed to eliminate a number of performers en route to reaching the final two before he ultimately fell short of victory. Like last year, the match belonged to his best friend and Kliq ringleader Shawn Michaels.

Michaels was McMahon's shining light. He was a unique type of babyface; rudimentarily white meat, but with a brash braggadocio that set him apart from the rest. In the ring he had few if any equals in the WWF, but for every inch of praise heaped on his wrestling ability from all quarters, there was a simmering cauldron of negativity bubbling underneath. Behind the curtain he had a poisonous reputation as a headache to deal with. He had been kept off television for the two months prior to the *Royal Rumble*, selling the effects of an elaborate concussion angle that aired on *Raw* back in November. During his time away the WWF had been running a series of promotional videos tracking his recovery, building anticipation for his return. Even the most susceptible fan knew that Michaels was the obvious winner of the bout, and unlike in later years, Vince did not change his storyline to avoid predictability.[12]

Michaels had long been deigned as the WWF's chosen one, and in 1996 Vince was ready and willing to pull the trigger on his ascension to the pinnacle of the company. Michaels was on a journey to the WWF Title, and a *WrestleMania* win over Bret Hart was set in stone. Despite his numerous shortcomings outside of the ring and the ill feeling towards him in the locker room, McMahon knew that Michaels better than anyone fit the mould of what he wanted the future of the Federation to be. He was

---

[12] Vince changed the finish to the following year's *Royal Rumble*, diverting from the plan of putting Bret Hart over in the match because Vince 'Vic Venom' Russo predicted Hart would win it on *Livewire*. McMahon's knee-jerk response was to change the booking and put Steve Austin over instead.

youthful, athletic, flamboyant, and possessed a sex appeal that his female audience adored. Not to mention he possessed a sizeable dose of attitude that may have irritated agents and his peers, but translated into entertaining television when the cameras were rolling.

AS MICHAELS superkicked his friend Nash out of the ring to win the bout for the second consecutive year - a feat only ever managed by Hulk Hogan - Bret Hart was stood backstage running through the spots he had planned for his WWF Championship defence against The Undertaker one last time. He glanced over at the monitor and was disturbed by the image of Michaels celebrating his victory by dancing a striptease, nearly exposing himself to the hordes of families with young children in the crowd. He was at a loss to explain McMahon's apparent fascination with the flamboyant showman. While he could not deny Shawn's undoubted in-ring ability, he did not stand for any of the strong values and rich traditions that Hart himself embodied. In his eyes Shawn was in no way a wholesome role-model for children watching the show, like he had been for the past four years. If this was the man that Vince wanted to carry his company, he pondered, then they were going to hell in a hand basket.

Hart was known for consistently bringing a high standard to his performances - he prided himself on it - but his plodding match with the Undertaker was a disappointment. Ironically, he found himself in the same position as former champion Kevin Nash had been in the year prior when Hart himself had been his challenger: a babyface champion booked to work with a fellow fan favourite in the *Royal Rumble* title bout. Hart could see through Vince's half-hearted justification for booking the match; he knew he was positioned in such a way only so that when the match with Shawn at *WrestleMania* rolled around there would be little doubt about who the crowd were supposed to support.

The way the contest was scripted to play out did little to fill Hart with any confidence that McMahon was behind him. Instead of beating Undertaker and looking strong going into the annual supercard, Hart was made to look inferior to his foe, only saved from certain defeat by a timely Diesel intervention. By the time the match concluded, Hart felt he was merely a pawn in the Diesel versus Undertaker storyline that Vince was promoting as *WrestleMania's* second main event. "The pay-per-view ended with me bent over in the ring having injured my knee for real, lucky to still have the belt. It did little to build me for *WrestleMania*," he complained.

McMahon didn't concern himself too much with the stuffy Hart's grumblings about his portrayal. He mused that he had pushed 'the Hitman' as a main event talent for years and he did not need the WWF machine behind him anymore. Shawn Michaels was the man groomed for the top spot - it was he who Vince wanted to concentrate his attentions on.

Once the *Royal Rumble* concluded, for the first time in months McMahon was optimistic about the future. He was even happier when the buy-rate for the show came in. In keeping with the recent price increase of his *In Your House* series, McMahon had also raised the cost of his "big five"[13] pay-per-view shows by $5 to $29.95, with *Royal Rumble* the first.

Consequently, McMahon's expectations were that the show would draw fewer viewers as a result, but that the increase in price would offset the lost buys and the card overall would still generate more revenue. However, off the back of the group's worst pay-per-view buy-rate in their history with December's *In Your House*, many in the office suspected that the *Royal Rumble* number would be another embarrassing one for the company. When the figures came in, they shocked the industry. Even with the higher price the WWF had pulled a phenomenal 1.1 buy-rate - more than three times what *In Your House* had drawn - which translated to around 265,000 buys and a company gross of over $3.5 million. While looking for an explanation, Dave Meltzer wrote:

> The figures defy explanation given the trends in the industry of late. It is clear that the cat-fighting on television, along with the more violent style in the ring, and going back to juice is increasing overall interest in both [WCW and WWF] products. Both companies are also going balls out to bring back big names from the past and prominently feature them, and that's getting a lot of people who have lost interest in wrestling over the past few years back to the table. The reports we have from the WWF are that the show shocked everyone both in the WWF and the PPV industry, coming off the string of nose-diving buy rates. Nobody was at all expecting this, even within the WWF.

Some prematurely declared that the number was a sign the corner had been turned and the WWF was finally ahead in the nascent Monday Night Wars. Momentarily at least, they were. Vince's bold vision, his decision to rehire past names, freshening up his roster with new faces, and pushing Shawn Michaels as the group's biggest star, were now starting to pay off. The WWF had survived the initial onslaught from WCW over the past four months and they looked to be regaining lost ground. Then little over three

---

[13] The *Royal Rumble, WrestleMania, King of the Ring, SummerSlam* and *Survivor Series*

weeks later everything fell apart when two of the company's biggest stars handed in their notice and declared they were defecting to Atlanta.

THREE

THE ROYAL RUMBLE MAY HAVE been an unexpected success for Titan, but the last year had been amongst the worst for business in company history. Many of the low-profile opening match specialists in the locker room were struggling to make ends meet as a result. Twelve-year veteran Scott Hall was amongst the upper echelon performers in the company and was hardly living hand-to-mouth, but he too was frustrated that his payoffs had been stagnant for over a year and that there appeared to be no chance of upwards momentum for his Razor Ramon character. Hall wanted to be on the same pay scale as Kliq allies Kevin Nash and Shawn Michaels, not to mention Bret Hart and Mark Calaway. At thirty-seven years old and with four years of solid WWF service under his belt, Hall felt he was due a raise that would bring him parity with the industry's top earners.

Hall had first expressed that opinion to Vince McMahon in early 1995 during a private backstage conversation at a television taping, querying him about what he had to do to be considered a top guy. "Vince, does my ring work need to improve?" he asked the chairman. "Oh, absolutely not. I'm more than happy with your ring work, you're one of the best," McMahon replied. "My microphone skills then? What about those?" Hall pressed. "No, you're one of the top talkers we've got," McMahon told him. Hall then reached the purpose of his questioning, asking, "I'm just curious because, y'know, my pay has kinda plateaued over the last few years and I'm wondering what I can do to make big money like the guys you perceive to be [big stars]. I'm asking you what I need to do to be successful. I'm asking for your help here. I wanna be here, I want to be part of your team."

Caught somewhat unawares, McMahon remained silent, but from his hesitant expression Hall could tell that he was heading down a futile avenue. Hall understood his boss's position; any extra money he made would be coming directly out of Vince's own pocket, so he jumped in before McMahon could feed him any excuses about why he could not afford to pay him more money. "Look Vince, I know how it works; there's only so much revenue from house shows and pay-per-views. But what about merchandise? How about moving that decimal point in the royalties just one place?" Without even considering it, Vince told him no.

Hall was undeterred, "Okay, how about Japan? I still wanna work for you, but can I have fifteen weeks a year to go work for them? Make their money instead of yours? I won't miss [WWF] TV, but I don't need to be on the smaller house shows in front of a few hundred people. Let the young guys do those instead." Hall knew what he was pitching was a long shot at best. McMahon had seldom afforded anyone a deal with that level of freedom before. Vince knew that he would be opening up a can of worms if he agreed to those terms. He liked the wrestlers under WWF contract on his watch and his alone, because it was the only way of guaranteeing they were protected as entities. He did not want to risk someone he had under contract getting injured elsewhere, or someone from another organisation trying to make a name for himself by taking a shot at a WWF guy. He realised that if he made that allowance for Hall, then everyone would want the same deal. Thus he countered the proposal with another non-negotiable rejection.

Hall was beaten and admitted defeat. He realised there was little choice but to ride out the remainder of his contract and reassess the situation in twelve months time. At which point he would take the option not to renew his deal, either forcing Vince's hand at the prospect of him leaving or allowing him to pursue options elsewhere.[14] When the time for his contract renewal came in early 1996, Hall was conflicted. He wanted to stay with Vince and help turn the WWF around, but contrariwise he was tired of the infamously gruelling Titan schedule, the rampant politics, and getting paid far less than what he felt he deserved. He mused that he had two children at home whom he was growing estranged from because he was rarely there, and was instead spending all of his time entertaining other people's kids. He joked to his Kliq buddies that he shared a more intimate relationship with the four of them than his wife Dana, but behind the jovial banter was a real sense of simmering resentment. "What good is the money when I can never spend it?" pondered Hall, "I'm never home."

The way McMahon's contracts worked - and had always worked - gave each performer the promise of ten dates per year[15] at a paltry $150 per shot, which covered the block taping television schedule that the WWF employed at the time. They were known amongst the boys as "opportunity" contracts due to McMahon's infamous opening line in any contract negotiations: "All I can guarantee you is an opportunity." It was as close as Vince came at that

[14] Despite the conversation with McMahon, Hall actually ended up making even less in 1995 than he had in 1994, pulling in around $250,000 (before accounting for road expenses and tax) compared to $400,000 the year prior.

[15] This was simply a token number to guarantee a performer a minimum set revenue and tie them down to a long-term deal. An active member of the roster could expect to work anything up to three hundred dates per year for the company.

point to offering a guarantee of any sort, but it was a tried and tested method that had worked for over a decade.[16] Invariably most of his wrestlers would make a lot more thanks to pay-per-view payoffs, house show payoffs, merchandise royalties and bonuses, but at $1,500 per year before tax, the contract was offering some $21,500 less than the country's national average wage. As Steve Austin later mused, "It was a starving artist, rock and roll contract. You put your name on that motherfucker and you weren't guaranteed shit, but it was your opportunity to [be part of] *the show.*"

While individual contracts varied in length, each of them locked in the performer for a number of years with no get-out clause. The only way for a wrestler to leave was by giving notice prior to the final ninety days of the agreement's duration, stating they did not want their deal to roll over. Then, after the ninety-day period (which Vince would use to 'bury' the character by having him lose repeatedly on his way out if he didn't negotiate a new deal) they would become a free agent.[17]

ON FEBRUARY 21, 1996 that's precisely what Scott Hall did when he faxed a letter to McMahon stating that he did not want his contract to continue. Far from doing it on a prayer and a whim, hoping that McMahon would suddenly change his policy and offer him a generous contract, Hall already had another offer: from Eric Bischoff at WCW.

As much as Bischoff had dismissed the content of Vince's *Billionaire Ted* skits as the petty grumblings of a bitter competitor, he also realised that there was at least a kernel of truth to their message. One thing that struck him as accurate was that he did have an aged roster headlining his cards. While his opening matches were increasingly filled with exciting young talent, he also knew he needed someone younger at the top of the card with name value to further increase WCW's visibility. He had been made aware of Hall's contract status thanks to his neighbour and friend Page 'Diamond Dallas Page' Falkenburg, who was close with Hall from their days in WCW together earlier in the decade.

---

[16] As always Hulk Hogan was the exception to the rule, as in the eighties McMahon had given him a contract that contained within it various guarantees. Though, it wasn't the same as WCW's guaranteed contracts that promised a set salary regardless of box office performance.

[17] There was also the option of giving "late" notice, or asking to break the contract prior to the final three months. That may still have resulted in a release, but would likely be a "conditional" as opposed to "unconditional" release. What it meant was that the WWF would let the wrestler in question leave, but would impose restrictions on where they could work. During the Monday Night Wars, that meant WCW. Usually the ban would remain in effect for the duration of what the contract should have been, leaving the departed with few options. Thus, this was rarely actioned.

With his contract coming up for renewal, Hall had sent feeders out to WCW via Page to gauge whether there was any interest in him. Page called Bischoff, "Look, here's the deal: I've been talking to Scott Hall and he wants to make the move here," said Page matter-of-factly. Bischoff was initially apprehensive, "Things were going so well with WCW that I just didn't want any trouble, I didn't want to deal with the pressure of an unhappy camper of that magnitude. I had heard about the stuff that was going on in the WWF with [the Kliq], and I said, 'Why do we want to bring that in?'"

Much like Steve 'Sting' Borden had managed to pressure Bischoff into changing his mind and bring in Lex Luger six months earlier, Page eventually convinced the WCW chief that hiring the problematic Hall was a choice idea. Bischoff did not need too much convincing; he had recently privately devised an audacious angle that he wanted to run with, and he realised Hall was perfect to feature in it. In addition, signing Hall would solve WCW's aging main event problem in one fell swoop. As Bischoff tells it, "I thought, 'What the hell? We need more talent.' *Nitro* at the time was beginning to get some traction, the numbers were growing, the revenue was growing, the company was growing, and we were doing more house shows. We needed some fresh faces."

Even though he was well aware of the reputation Hall had as a trouble-causer, a manipulator, and a drug abuser, Bischoff also saw the potential that having him in WCW could bring. Not only would Hall strengthen his own product, but his departure from Titan would weaken the WWF. It also sent a message to fans that WWF stars would rather be working for WCW than in wrestling's supposed Shangri-La. With that in mind he offered Hall - via agent Barry Bloom - a gigantic $750,000 per annum, three year guaranteed contract. The deal was made even sweeter with a date cap of one-hundred-and-fifty shows per year, and a "favoured nations" clause that promised to match any contracts that WCW may offer other performers in the future.

WCW had guaranteed contracts before, but they were primarily in the $104,000 to $156,000 range. Other than Hogan and Sting, Hall was the first to command such a high figure. "We had to pay that if we wanted to compete with the WWF," Bischoff argues, "Guys made a lot of money with licensing royalties there, but WCW didn't have that. You either matched it and gave a guarantee, or you didn't compete. What we offered Scott probably wasn't as much as he would have made if he had worked three hundred days [in the WWF] and everything clicked, but it worked. The maths worked. To guys back then, one-hundred-and-fifty days a year was like a vacation, it meant more than money, because it meant they could have a life. It was a competitive advantage and we used it."

"I was all about money then," Hall admits, "At that point guys were making that sort of money - maybe - for Vince, but they were working three hundred days for it." Earning more money, guaranteed, for the equivalent of six months less work meant that for Hall there was only one logical choice: he accepted the deal.

As soon as Vince received Hall's fax, he sank down in his seat and let out an irritated sigh. 1995 had been a tough year, but 1996 had started well and the WWF seemed to be on an upswing. Hall's resignation was more than a blow, it was a proverbial kick in the groin. What annoyed Vince the most was that Hall had spent the last two days with him at television tapings in Ohio and West Virginia, yet had not breathed a word of his intentions. Titan had already shot angles to promote Hall's match with Goldust at *WrestleMania*, one of which had aired two nights earlier on *Raw*, but Vince wasn't going to waste a payoff from the group's biggest card on someone deserting him. He immediately axed the Razor-Goldust program, before penning a memo to his producers telling them to remove all hype for the match at 'Mania from the television shows they had in the can.

As coincidence would have it, the day Hall handed in his resignation was also the time McMahon found out that the wrestler had failed a drug test after testing positive for marijuana use. McMahon felt the failed test was perfect justification for him to remove Hall from the single biggest WWF payday of the year. He defended his actions to the *Pro Wrestling Torch*, noting that no matter what people thought, Hall had genuinely failed a test and it was simply coincidence that it occurred on the same day as his resignation. He added that he was aware others would draw their own conclusions but it was not his problem, and that the wrestlers would have nothing to worry about if they stayed clean.

While some suspected Vince might have brushed the indiscretion under the carpet had Hall not quit, McMahon's explanation was backed up by Jim Cornette. "I think the suspension was a case of coincidental timing. I don't think that would have been covered up if Hall hadn't quit," he offers, "The news about Scott's test failure just happened to come to light at the same time as he faxed his notice. Vince's reaction went from wondering what the hell we were going to do about it to, 'Well, fuck it.' Scott leaving meant we didn't have to work around it anymore."

ONCE SCOTT Hall had given his notice, Vince realised he needed to act quickly to replace him on the roster. A few days later he was putting the final touches on an exhumed deal to bring back Jim 'Ultimate Warrior' Hellwig. Many felt that McMahon's failure to land Hellwig for the *Royal Rumble* had permanently signalled the end of negotiations between the two parties, especially as they were so far apart on the terms offered. Nonetheless, McMahon was so concerned with the lack of star power on his roster that he firmly believed the Ultimate Warrior was his answer.

Hellwig remained annoyed with how McMahon had dismissed him during their earlier negotiations. To help smooth the issues over, Vince's wife Linda was called in to act as a go-between because Hellwig liked and respected her. Linda met with Hellwig at his Phoenix home and talked terms on a deal, with Hellwig determined that the only way he would get on board was if the WWF granted him some hitherto unheard of concessions. Namely he wanted the group to plug his various individual projects - including a new comic book that featured him as the superhero lead, and a wrestling school called Warrior University - but without having any direct involvement. Hellwig wanted Titan's support and promotional backing, and nothing further; he simply did not want them interfering beyond that.

The other remaining bugbear was with regards to naming and licensing. Hellwig and McMahon had already battled in court over the issue, with Hellwig stating that he created the Ultimate Warrior persona, symbolism and ideology, countered by McMahon making his own claims to the character's intellectual property rights. He felt they belonged to him because he had given Hellwig the platform on which to perform and become a star in the first place. Eventually a compromise was reached that gave the WWF the trademark "Feel the Power" in relation to the Ultimate Warrior as a WWF Superstar. Hellwig's recently coined "Always Believe" slogan and iconic logo were his and his alone, for use with his comic book and outside projects, and under no circumstances could they be used by Titan.

No deal like it had ever been struck by McMahon, who had always insisted on having a despotic grip on the movements, performance rights and actions of his stars. Jim Hellwig was an atypical talent; he realised that the WWF needed him a lot more than he needed them. With Scott Hall lured to Atlanta by gigantic money, Vince understood that he was in a war more than ever, and eventually, semi-reluctantly, he signed off on the deal.

McMahon felt the return of Warrior would give an adrenaline shot to his floundering company by boosting live attendance and pay-per-view buys, not to mention merchandise revenue, though few could believe that he was willing to bend over backwards for the notoriously difficult-to-handle Hellwig. It was clear that he was desperate. "He just wanted some stars back," says Jim Cornette, "Vince was the one guy in the world who believed that Warrior was as good as Warrior thought he was. And Warrior thought he was the biggest star in the world."

IF SCOTT Hall leaving was viewed by Vince McMahon as a shot below the belt, then Kevin Nash's decision to follow suit almost immediately was considered a hammer blow. Vince had invested the last three years in the six-foot-nine Nash, getting his Diesel character over as one of the top stars in the company and giving him a year-long run with the WWF Championship along the way. He had stuck with him on top despite his failure to draw on pay-per-view or at live events, and regardless of that he intended to jump too. McMahon was livid.

Like Hall, Nash had not given him any prior indication that he planned to leave, though it was hardly a secret in the locker room. Hall had first told Nash of his own deal a few weeks before handing in his notice, to which Nash flatly responded that he was staying with Vince. When Hall shared the lavish terms of the offer he soon decided to reconsider. As Nash recalls, "Scott was approached first, he said, 'I got an offer to work for Turner,' and I said, 'How much?' and he told me that it was "Sting money"[18]. I said, 'For how many days?' It was one hundred and fifty days, and I said, '*What?*"

As far back as early February, during a Federation tour of India, Nash had confessed to Bret Hart that he had been offered a guaranteed deal in Atlanta. When Nash told him how much the offer was worth, Hart made a mental note that Nash was going to be getting paid more than he was currently receiving as WWF Champion. With his own contract up in six months time, WCW was a possible avenue he might decide to explore. He was in the same boat in regards to his advancing age and running out of time to become rich from the business he had dedicated his life to, rather than simply well-off.

When Nash had mentioned the deal on the table to Hart he was still unsure whether he was going to accept it. He did not want to leave the WWF; he simply wanted the terms of his current contract with the group to improve. Nash hoped that Vince would match the WCW offer, deciding that if he proposed the same guaranteed money as Bischoff then he would stay, even if it meant working more dates. Despite the intentions behind his resignation, Nash refrained from sending the fax for a few weeks after making his decision. He realised he was potentially burning a bridge and losing a friend if he did, so wanted more time to mull everything over before he committed himself to anything.

[18] In reference to Steve 'Sting' Borden, who in the industry had a well-known large guaranteed contract that was only surpassed by Hulk Hogan.

IRONICALLY, IT was an incident involving confidante Bret Hart that led to Nash finally making the decision to walk out on the WWF and accept the offer from Eric Bischoff. During the WWF's sixth incarnation of *In Your House* from Louisville, Kentucky on February 18, three days before Scott Hall gave his official notice, Nash was working in the pay-per-view main event; a cage match with Hart. Prior to the bout, the proposed booking called for Hart to appear beaten following Diesel's powerbomb finisher, only to have The Undertaker burst through the ring and pull Diesel through it, allowing Hart to clamber out of the cage unopposed to win the match. The idea was designed to give symmetry to the Diesel-Undertaker program, with Diesel having already cost Undertaker his title match with Hart at the *Royal Rumble* thanks to similar machinations.

There was a problem: Hart refused to go along with it. He argued that it would not do anything for his character to appear beaten again only to be saved at the last minute, and that it was not a strong way to build him up for his *WrestleMania* showdown with Shawn Michaels. Nash implored Hart that it would not hurt him because he was still the one winning the match, but 'the Hitman' had made up his mind. Frustrated with Hart's snub, the normally reserved Calaway leapt out of his seat and exasperatedly yelled, "Motherfucker! It's not always about *you*! This helps *our* match mean more at 'Mania." The plea fell on deaf ears and Hart remained resolute in his refusal. Come show day he had talked to McMahon, who made the decision that Diesel did not need to do his powerbomb at the finish after all.

That was the final straw for Kevin Nash. He realised that his time at the top of the mountain was over and he would likely be employed to put others over from that point forward. He felt that McMahon had lost faith in him. After his match with Hart, Nash jumped in the showers beside Scott Hall, who was trying to wash baby powder out of his hair.[19] He leaned over to his friend and whispered quietly, "Tell Bischoff I'm in." Hall was so thrilled that he was not heading to Atlanta alone that he nearly hugged Nash, but thought better of it when he realised they were both buck naked.

Nash then told officials that he had separated his shoulder in the match with Hart and took two weeks off from in-ring action to heal. In reality, he was using the time to iron out the finer points of his proposed contract with Bischoff via lawyers and intermediaries. His shoulder *was* injured, though not to the point that he could not compete. He just did not want to risk getting hurt on the road and have his life-changing deal taken off the

---

[19] Hall had been involved in a humiliating "cry-baby" match with Sean Waltman early in the card, with the winner dressing the defeated man in complete baby garb, from diaper to pacifier.

table. Then on March 5, the final day before his Titan contract rolled over, Nash finally, heavy-heartedly, faxed his notice to McMahon.

"The way that Hall and Nash did their deal was bullshit," crows Jim Cornette, "First Scott came up to Vince and told him, 'I'm with ya Vince. I would have been nothing if it wasn't for you,' and then two days later he resigned. Kevin Nash did the same thing. He even told Vince that he would call a meeting with all the boys to tell them he was staying. I was actually at Vince's house when the news about Kevin came through on his private fax. He wasn't really mad, his reaction was more, 'Can you *believe* these guys?' Mine was pretty similar, I was like, 'Fuck! These fucking guys!' I don't care if you stay or go, but don't say one thing to the guy's face and then do the opposite. Here you have these big tough guys who, for all the balls they were supposed to have, didn't want to tell Vince to his face that they were leaving. They just told him what he wanted to hear and took the easy way out. Maybe they did have to give their resignations in writing officially, but that doesn't mean they couldn't have told him first.

"I guess Vince can be pretty persuasive and they didn't want to be pressured into something they didn't want to do. He had even managed to do that to me a couple of times; talking me out of things that I was absolutely convinced I was doing, and making me see the "error" of my ways. I don't blame them for leaving - most guys would have left for that kind of money because no one was making that then. I blame them for not having the decency to tell the guy that made them that they were going."

WHEN NASH encountered Vince at a subsequent television taping, McMahon asked him curtly what deal Bischoff had offered. When he revealed the unprecedented figure, he could have sworn that he saw the chairman gulp like a cartoon character. Other than this fleeting involuntary response, McMahon barely reacted. He simply turned around and walked away, before turning his head back and growling, "I thought we were *family.*"

Nash knew that Vince was hurt by his decision and tried to explain himself as best he could. "We are family, man, but I've got a wife at home who is seven months pregnant, and it is hard to run a family based on whether you are booked at *WrestleMania*, and don't know if you are going to have a good year or not."[20] The WCW deal was especially enticing to both Nash and Hall because it was the first time they knew what they were going

---

[20] For the WWF roster, *WrestleMania* was the be all and end all as far as payoffs were concerned. A good spot on the card meant a large payoff that would sustain most for the year, with everything else being a bonus. Not being booked meant a year of hardship and a struggle to make ends meet.

to earn in advance of actually making it. They could potentially come close to the same figure in the WWF, but that relied on business being hot, *WrestleMania* and other pay-per-views being successful, and the booking placing them in key spots throughout the year. With Nash having figured that his time as champion and top guy had been and gone, he concluded that the future looked uncertain for him if he stayed with Titan.

Nash wanted what was best for his family, but he also wanted to be loyal to the man who had put him in a position to be able to command such a substantial contract in the first place. He told Vince he wanted to remain with the WWF, telling him to simply match the offer of guaranteed money and he would stay. McMahon point-blank refused. "I can't do it," he stated bluntly, "If I do it for you then I would have to do the same for Bret, Mark, Shawn... I can't afford to do that." Nash sympathised with his boss's predicament, but realised he had to take care of himself firstly. "Look, I hope we stay friends but I gotta do what I gotta do," he told the disappointed chairman.

"Nobody except Hogan had ever gotten money like that before," clarifies Jim Cornette. "Lex Luger was famously given $350,000 by Jim Crocket in 1986, the Road Warriors in the late eighties got $500,000 apiece, but Vince couldn't start guaranteeing that sort of money because it would have upset the whole applecart. Doing it for Hall and Nash would have raised everyone's money, not just at the top of the card but the underneath guys too. They would have figured that while they might not warrant the same money, they were worth at least half."

Nash's impending departure put McMahon in a predicament. He had already spent valuable television time and company resources promoting a first-time-ever Diesel versus Undertaker confrontation at *WrestleMania* as the show's second main event. It was too late to change booking plans, so he turned to Nash and asked him to do him three favours, or jobs, on his way out. Those were losing to The Undertaker at *WrestleMania*, Shawn Michaels the following month at *In Your House: Good Friends... Better Enemies*, and then the soon-to-be-returning Jim 'Ultimate Warrior' Hellwig on *Raw*. Vince wanted to use Nash's final ninety days to have him put over as many of his roster as possible. It was a time-honoured tradition in the business, a way to devalue Nash in the eyes of fans before he turned up in WCW.

Nash briefly contemplated the request, then told McMahon that he would be honoured to put over Calaway and that he would do anything for Shawn. Hellwig was another matter. "Hey, if he can take one on me, it's all his," Nash told McMahon, implying that Hellwig would have to beat him for real in a *shoot*. "I guess we won't have that *Raw* match then," Vince replied. "Probably not," warned Nash. Once the ink was dry on his lucrative WCW deal, Nash lived up to his word. He returned to the road for the WWF, laying down night after night for Hart, Michaels, and Undertaker without complaint as he worked out his notice period.

News of Kevin Nash and Scott Hall's departures from Titan spread throughout the industry like wildfire, and inevitably so did the numbers involved in their deals. "Everything changed when it came out that Nash and Hall had signed with the opposition," remembers Bob Holly. "WCW had been gaining ground and were trying to sign a lot of our guys, but everyone was shocked when they quit. After everything Vince had done for them, they showed him absolutely no loyalty. Before they got to the WWF they were nobodies. Vince took care of them, paid them well, made them who they were, and they shit on him. Loyalty didn't mean a damn thing to those guys. All of the other boys worked hard, put Hall and Nash over, and then they just upped and left. They were making tons of money while none of us were making any. They deserved to have their asses kicked."

Immediately there was a backlash in Atlanta. Multi-decade veterans Randy Savage and Ric Flair - who had both done far more in the business than Nash and Hall, over a much longer period of time - were particularly riled that the new acquisitions would be earning roughly double what they were. Not to mention the top of the card in WCW was about to become a lot more jammed, which would hamper their earnings potential further.

The massive contracts were symptomatic of the weekly ratings war that WCW were competing in. Overpaying for talent was something prevalent throughout the sports industry, especially when similar competitive situations arose. As Dave Meltzer explained in his *Wrestling Observer Newsletter*:

> If you look at pro sports in competitive as opposed to monopolistic economic situations in the past, in every situation it ends up with guys whose owners are trying to make team or league moves being paid way above what had been the scale for people of their level.

Hulk Hogan was typically vocal against about the pair's arrival too, expressing to Eric Bischoff that he would rather see the money spent bringing in proven draws, names like Yokozuna and the Ultimate Warrior. It was a classic Hogan political machination. The imminent arrival of WWF power players Nash and Hall unnerved him because he was worried about how his own position on the card would be affected, especially with the WCW audience having never fully connected with him to begin with. There was also a more egomaniacal motivation: Yokozuna and Warrior were the only two wrestlers he had ever lost to cleanly in the WWF without exacting his revenge, and he was desperate to rectify that. Hogan wanted Bischoff to hire the pair simply so he could beat them, thus rebalancing the extraneous win/loss books back in his favour.[21]

A FEW days after receiving Nash's resignation, McMahon released a statement via the WWF's *America Online* website that lambasted Turner for using his chequebook to buy already established WWF performers.[22] The statement began:

> Kevin Nash and I are friends. I think from my perspective, he didn't make a good business decision. Diesel could have become an icon here in the World Wrestling Federation, an icon which he would be able to derive great benefit from financially and aesthetically for the next twenty years, perhaps far outlasting his time as a wrestler in the ring. But, yes it hurts, and the people in Ted Turner's organization know that it hurts. Athletes must have a love for the business they are in, a strong work ethic and a sense of loyalty to remain here in the WWF. Many performers here make very large sums of money, and those athletes that have confidence in themselves and in the company compete very, very well with Turner's guaranteed contracts. Turner's organization has no idea how to make a star, all they can do is buy them. The idea to acquire the services of Kevin Nash is so Diesel ceases to exist, thus hurting the World Wrestling Federation.

In actuality Turner had little to do with hiring Nash and Hall other than agreeing to sign off on the deal that Eric Bischoff had made. Using the mogul as a scapegoat was simply McMahon's standard narrative practice at the time. Years later, he was more reflective about the situation, remembering, "They really didn't want to leave, but I wouldn't guarantee a contract in those days. From a business standpoint they really had no alternative but to go. If I had been them, I think I would have taken the

---

[21] Hogan got his wish with Warrior in 1998, convincing Bischoff to hire him to a big money deal purely so he could restore parity in the record books. Hogan pinned Warrior at the *Halloween Havoc* pay-per-view in a bout that was roundly criticised as one of the worst in the history of mainstream wrestling, and Warrior disappeared soon thereafter.

[22] This was yet another hypocritical stance for McMahon to take, as he had done much the same thing during his talent drive in the eighties, snapping up established talent from across the length and breadth of the country as he expanded the WWF nationally.

money." As disappointed as Vince McMahon was to see Hall and Nash depart, few were as dejected by the news as Shawn Michaels. He had spent the better part of three years on the road with them and they were as close to him as family. They were also two of his few allies in the locker room, and both had his back if he found himself in a sticky situation - and with a tendency to run his mouth without thinking, he had found himself in plenty of those down the years.

Nevertheless, Michaels did not try to talk the pair out of the move because he knew what a favourable deal they were getting in Atlanta. As he remembers, "I wasn't married. I was single at the time, whereas they had responsibilities. How do you look at your buddies and not say, 'You gotta go for the dollars?' They had those things to worry about like kids and family that I didn't."

Others within the WWF were not afraid to let their feelings on the matter be known, with Bret Hart appearing on a Chicago-area talk show and stating, "It's a personal thing. Everyone has a right to take care of themselves the best they can. I think some of them made the decision because maybe they were forced into it, like Randy Savage, but at the same time, there are other guys who have left that I think, even in the case of Diesel, I think he did it maybe for the money. If that's the reason, I don't think his career is going to go forward anymore. He'll miss where he was. I think Hall and Nash will be miserable about two years from now because they'll realize they went to a second-rate organization that is never going to take them to the heights they were at before."

VINCE MCMAHON had started to realise that he was short of top names on his roster even prior to losing Scott Hall and Kevin Nash. Once again he had been forced to turn to the past, rehiring Roderick 'Roddy Piper' Toombs on a short-term contract. Piper had been one of Vince's frontline soldiers in the WWF's national expansion of the eighties, acting as the antagonist heel for the ultimate babyface superhero Hulk Hogan on MTV joint venture *The War to Settle the Score*, as well as at the inaugural *WrestleMania*. By 1996 he had not worked a full schedule for years, preferring to return to the company intermittently before going on hiatus to keep himself fresh.

Piper's disappearing act had been going on since 1987 when he had bowed out in style following a victory over rotund effeminate heel Adrian Adonis at *WrestleMania III*, but the time spans between his eventual re-emergences were steadily growing. The last time he wrestled for McMahon was in 1994 at the *King of the Ring*, where he had headlined a poorly received, archaic-style match opposite fellow forty-something part-timer Jerry Lawler. It was Piper's only match for the group since a blood-soaked classic with Bret Hart in 1992, with Vince deciding against offering him any further dates due to how disappointing the *King of the Ring* return had been.

However, desperate times called for desperate measures, and with few stars of any real note from the eighties available thanks to so many of them having wound up in WCW, McMahon made the call. He wanted Piper to return as a regular television character and step into Gorilla Monsoon's role as on-screen company president. Piper agreed, and on an episode of *Raw* aired January 29, he was introduced by McMahon to a rousing reception from the Stockton, CA crowd. At first he served merely as a spokesperson for the onscreen booking, but in late February Piper received another call from McMahon, this time requesting an even bigger favour: he wanted him to return to the ring.

Having suspended Scott Hall, and with Kevin Nash on the shelf supposedly injured, Vince needed someone to step in at the live events the missing pair were absent for so he would not be out of pocket thousands of dollars due to refunds. Piper was the only person on the roster not already booked who had the name value to make a difference. He agreed to the deal to help out McMahon, and on February 24 took to the road for the first time in nearly half a decade.

With Hall also set to miss *WrestleMania*, McMahon turned to Piper again, asking him to step in and work Hall's scheduled match at the supercard in his place. Piper duly agreed and signed on for a part-recorded, part-live contest with the controversial androgyne Goldust in a bout dubbed the "Hollywood Backlot Brawl". Once again, the irony of McMahon criticising the age of WCW's headliners while simultaneously promoting a forty-two-year-old in a match on his biggest show of the year was not lost on anyone.

THE UNPRECEDENTED level of talent movement in the industry continued the week following Kevin Nash's resignation, when on March 11, 1996, Marc 'Johnny B. Badd' Merowitz quit WCW.

A former bodybuilder and *New York Golden Gloves* tournament winner in amateur boxing, the bronzed Buffalo native broke into the wrestling business in early 1991 after training under the respected Malenko family. He was hired by WCW a few months later. Booker Dusty Rhodes was so taken by Merowitz's resemblance to Little Richard that he repackaged him as a flamboyant look-a-like of the rock and roll icon, then rechristened him 'Johnny B. Badd', a less than subtle nod to Chuck Berry's classic song 'Johnny B. Goode'.

The gimmick had started out as a colourful and overtly effeminate version of Richard, but Merowitz toned down the campiness of the character significantly over the years due to his strong belief that someone in his position should be a positive role model. His argument was that he told kids to believe in themselves, and could not do that with any sincerity while playing a glitter-gun shooting, make-up wearing fruit.

By March, Merowitz had been working without a contract since his deal expired on February 28. He wanted to commit to WCW, but he was reluctant to sign the deal that Bischoff had offered him due to how heavily it was weighted in WCW's favour. Specifically, he did not care for a ninety day rolling clause that allowed WCW to fire him for any reason, nor a four month non-compete clause that prevented him working elsewhere after it expired.

On March 4, five days after his contract ended, Merowitz received a call from WCW's head of public relations Alan Sharp asking him to attend a race meeting as a WCW representative on March 9. Merowitz was one of Sharp's go-to guys because he was amenable, and always willing to take part in extra-curricular appearances. It so happened that on this occasion he had a scheduling conflict: March 9 was his adopted daughter Mariah's fifth birthday. He had already rented out a play gym and arranged a party, so he asked Sharp if, just once, he could find someone else to do it.

Sharp told Merowitz it was no problem, but four days later the wrestler received a phone call from an irate Eric Bischoff. "Johnny, what's the problem?" he demanded, to which a confused Merowitz asked, "Problem about what?" "Why aren't you going to the races?" Bischoff wanted to know. Merowitz told him the same thing that he had told Sharp; that it was his daughter's birthday. As far as Bischoff was concerned that was no excuse. "Lots of people have missed their kids' birthdays to help build this company," he yelled, "When someone calls you and tells you to be somewhere, you be there!"

Merowitz was surprised with how hard Bischoff was coming down on him, especially given he was not even technically under WCW contract. However, wanting to keep the peace - and his recently tabled $300,000 per year deal - he told Bischoff, "Look, no problem Eric, I'll miss my daughter's birthday and I'll be there." It was too late. The damage had been done and Bischoff was fed up with Merowitz. He told him flat out not to bother attending the race. Merowitz assumed his boss was merely annoyed with him for the initial snub so called up Sharp to ask him where to be on the Saturday, but was told in no uncertain terms that Bischoff wanted him nowhere near the track.

A further issue of contention for Merowitz concerned a storyline he was involved in with Diamond Dallas Page. He felt the program had long since ran its course after five months of bland, repetitive matches, but sensed that WCW did not have anything worthwhile left for him to do. His dissatisfaction with the company's creative direction turned to outrage when he was forced into an onscreen union with Page's real-life wife Kimberly. The angle deeply troubled the fiercely religious Merowitz, who felt it was a violation of his Christian faith to be parading around with another man's wife. Bischoff dismissed his concerns, arguing that Merowitz was simply playing the character of Johnny B. Badd in a wrestling angle, and in doing so was not committing an actual sin. "I don't want to have to run every storyline by Jesus Christ for approval," Bischoff carped.

Merowitz felt he had been treated unfairly, especially after five years of local service to the company. Mindful of his free agent status, he decided to give Vince McMahon a call out of the blue on the off-chance that he was interested in negotiating with him. As it happened, McMahon had once caught glimpse of Johnny B. Badd on a tape of WCW programming. He had immediately become a fan of the provocative garishness of the character, a trait that appealed to his penchant for the showbiz side of wrestling. As Jim Cornette remembers it, "Vince had discovered Johnny B. Badd and loved the gimmick. I guess he saw a tape of him or something. He thought he was going to be the biggest star on television."

When Merowitz called McMahon at his Stamford home on March 8, he was somewhat startled when the notoriously in-demand WWF honcho answered the phone. He was even more surprised at how excited McMahon was upon finding out he was available. "Give me chance to think this over and to think about a gimmick, and I'll call you back tomorrow," Vince told him. True to his word, McMahon called back the following day and offered Merowitz a first of its kind long-term deal with the Federation. It would mean him working five or six days a week compared to only two or three at WCW, but it was also for more money than Bischoff was offering once royalties were factored in.

"Royalties were a big deal," explains Cornette, "Usually they were bigger than the contracts. When I first started in the WWF managing Yokozuna I would always be hot when we were in the dark match at a taping and it was ten to midnight, but Yoko would be telling me, 'Oh brother, royalties!' because it was filmed for Coliseum Video. I didn't even know what they were, but then my first monthly royalty cheque came in and it was for like $6,000!"

Unbeknownst to Bischoff, Merowitz had already verbally agreed to the WWF deal by the time the two met in an airport on the morning of March 11, prior to a live *Nitro* in Winston-Salem that evening. Merowitz confronted Bischoff, telling him that because he was working without a contract he wanted some protection. He would board a plane to *Nitro* only if he was given a written guarantee stating that the WCW contract offer currently on the table could not be retracted if he was injured in the ring that night. Merowitz had observed what had happened to Ricky Steamboat and Steve Austin, who were both let go after getting injured on the job. He wanted reassurance that it would not happen to him.

Bischoff promised that would be case, reminding Merowitz that his new contract was already drawn up and waiting to be signed. Merowitz countered that he was still unhappy with a great deal of it, before finally admitting that he had been given a better offer from the WWF. An embittered grimace immediately etched itself onto Bischoff's face. "Well, I guess we had better go and sit down then," hissed the nettled VP. The two found a secluded spot where they could talk privately, and Bischoff asked, "What can I do with the contract to change it?" By that point, Merowitz was unwilling to compromise. Bischoff's attitude towards him over the past few weeks and his failure to give written protection for that evening's event had firmly made up his mind to sign for Titan. "Look, it's not about changing the contract anymore," the wrestler admitted, "I'm not happy with how everything has been handled this past week. I want to give you my two weeks' notice, even though my contract has already expired, because it is the respectable thing to do after being here for so long."

Bischoff was annoyed. He told Merowitz he could work *Nitro* that evening and put over Lex Luger, then as far as he was concerned, that would be Johnny B. Badd finished with WCW. Merowitz still refused to back down on his earlier stance, reiterating that he would not go ahead with any match that evening unless he had written assurances covering him if something went wrong. Similarly stubborn, Bischoff refused to provide any documentation to that effect, and the two become locked in a standoff. Merowitz tried to break the deadlock, not to mention the rapidly increasing tension, offering, "Eric, I don't want to leave on bad terms." He attempted to shake Bischoff's hand, but by now it was too late for pleasantries. "You aren't leaving on good terms," Bischoff barked angrily as he pulled his hand away, "You will never work for this company again."[23]

---

[23] As is usually the case in wrestling, "never" was finite. In this instance it translated to "four years", with Merowitz briefly returning to the WCW fold in 2000.

Three days later, Vince McMahon flew Merowitz and his wife Rena out to Stamford to finalise their verbally agreed WWF deal. McMahon was instantly besotted with Rena, a former *L'Oreal* model with perfectly styled blonde hair, a silicone-enhanced bosom and a *Baywatch* body. "What a lady!" he commented to his aides admiringly. Immediately Vince told booking assistant Bruce Prichard that he wanted Rena as part of the package to act as Marc's valet, so she too was offered a lucrative guaranteed deal. It was far more than the couple had bargained for. Not only would they be earning more money than they ever dreamed of, but they would also be able to travel the road together, thus negating the one negative aspect of the WWF contract compared to WCW's: the extra dates.

Not everyone working in the Titan office was in favour of the decision to hire Rena alongside her husband, with booker Jim Cornette particularly baffled. "I warned them that they were gonna get heat all over this guy to start out, because they [the fans] would all be looking at this fucking girl and it would bury him. I also pointed out to Bruce Prichard that everyone thought Merowitz was black - even though he isn't - and that it was going to get him a lot of heat in the south being with this white girl. Bruce didn't believe that anyone even thought that about him, so I showed him on the internet and *everyone* thought it."

Prichard and McMahon ignored Cornette's concerns, booking Marc and Rena to debut at *WrestleMania* little over two weeks later. Rena was given the moniker Sable, but Marc's persona posed more of a problem. Because the name and traits of Johnny B. Badd were WCW trademarks, the WWF could not present anything that resembled the character. His role had to be something entirely different to the one he was familiar with performing in WCW. Upon his request, Merowitz was allowed to compete using a slightly trimmed version of his real name, becoming simply Marc Mero. It was a rare concession from McMahon, who usually insisted on putting his own explicit branding on a performer, or at the least changing their name enough to trademark it so they could not profit from their WWF-built reputation elsewhere once their time with the company had expired. In Merowitz's case, Vince simply added 'The Wildman' in front of his truncated name, and gave him the vaguest vestige of a gimmick.

As Jim Cornette explains it, "Despite what everybody told him, Vince didn't realise that with Marc he wasn't getting Johnny B. Badd, because Johnny B. Badd was a WCW-owned character. The problem was, Merowitz had been trained by WCW and had been trained only to play the character *of* Johnny B. Badd, with the promos, seven-minute matches and characteristics of that persona. Then the WWF stuck his wife with him.

With the big fake breasts, she overshadowed him, and for Marc it didn't work out."

McMahon may not have been able to use Johnny B. Badd like he had hoped, but with Sable, he was getting *exactly* what he wanted. Playing the role of sultry sex-kitten, she was the definition of what Vince was looking for to make the WWF more adult than - and thus different to - WCW. She became another essential piece of his new grand design. Within two years Sable would become one of the most recognisable faces in the world, posing nude for *Playboy,* pulling in over a million dollars in personal revenue in a single year and earning far more than even her financially astute husband.

Marc Merowitz remained unique in that he was the recipient of the first guaranteed contract Vince McMahon had ever offered. The situation with Hall and Nash had forced him to change his stance and accept the reality of the talent arms race he was involved in. While he was still not in a position to match the monster main event contracts that Nash and Hall were getting from Turner's organisation because of the certain backlash he would receive from other top names in the locker room, he could certainly tie up newcomers on his roster in such a manner. He did it under the guise that it was a necessary tactical move he was forced into making to compete with WCW. He argued that if he did not give guaranteed contracts to new signings then WCW would greedily vacuum up all available talent instead.

Eventually, McMahon had no choice but to start offering his entire roster something more than an opportunity. He started strong-arming his stars into signing heavily weighted contracts that favoured the WWF, securing them long-term to protect Titan from any more departures to Atlanta. Vince called them *downsides,* which promised a token amount of money to a performer each year should the business bottom out, but assured them they would make more per annum in royalties and licenses than their contract stated. For those towards the top of the card, that meant around $300,000-$400,000 per annum, and the biggest stars such as Shawn Michaels and Mark Calaway eventually pulled in almost $700,000 - similar money to what Nash and Hall would be making in WCW. For everyone else it was between $75,000-$125,000 guaranteed yearly. When taking into account tax, accommodation, travel, expenses and living costs on the road, it meant that most were still on the breadline.

The downsides did not make much difference in stopping grumblings about pay within the locker room. Mick Foley and Steve Austin in particular were vexed when they learned that Marc Mero was receiving a considerable guaranteed contract, as they had both recently signed for Titan on the starving artist "opportunity" deals that Vince was otherwise famous for. "Mero's deal pissed off a bunch of guys," says Cornette, "He had never sold fifteen cents in Chinese money and yet they [Vince and the office] were fawning over the guy and gave him this massive contract." Later in the year when Mick Foley was under pressure to pen his own downside deal, he cited Mero's inflated contract as a source of contention, claiming it was one of the main reasons he had yet to sign his own much smaller downside. "Vince, I just can't on principle sign a contract that has me earning less money than Marc Mero," he told the chairman in disgust.

WITH THE players now firmly in place, Vince was ready to concentrate on *WrestleMania,* and plan for the future of the WWF without Razor Ramon and Diesel with a fresh influx of talent both new and old. For the first time in recent memory there was a more positive vibe in the air, with many in the locker room pleased to see the back of Hall and Nash due to the disruption they and their Kliq allies were known to cause, but also because it created two glaring gaps at the top of the card. "We were happy to pick up the pieces," says Mick Foley, "Losing so much talent may have actually helped the WWF. Not only did it make for better morale in the dressing room, but it also ignited the wrestling war that spring-boarded the sport's resurgence."

Morale in the WWF was boosted further two weeks prior to the supercard by the group drawing its first sell out house at Madison Square Garden in seven years. One year earlier the WWF had struggled to get 7,000 people into the building, so a crowd of 17,000 (with people turned away) was rightly considered a roaring success for Titan and a sure-fire sign that business was finally beginning to pick up.

Some pointed to the onscreen journey of Shawn Michaels as the reason for the uptick in business, the man slated to headline *WrestleMania* as he vowed to achieve his "boyhood dream" of becoming WWF Champion. He was making a difference to the bottom line, with his return at *Royal Rumble* having helped the show pull a strong buyrate after an all-time low *In Your House* number in December. That in turn gave him even more political stroke behind the scenes and confirmed to McMahon that he was justified putting his eggs into the 'Heartbreak Kid' basket, regardless of the reservations of the boys, the agents and other members of his staff..

Others were less quick to praise Michaels, instead crediting Bret Hart's return to the WWF summit as the reason for the improvements across the board. On many of the promotion's recent strong houses, it was Hart who had headlined rather than Michaels, and *In Your House* in February with Hart wrestling Diesel in the main event had also drew a healthy buy rate. A further theory attributed the strong business to the increased popularity of wrestling in general thanks to the Monday Night Wars, which had seen *Raw* and *Nitro* set records for combined viewership in the preceding weeks. Being challenged on a weekly basis had caused Vince's creative juices to flow. The still slight but noticeable shift towards a more adult-themed product was seemingly paying dividends.

FOUR

VINCE MCMAHON SHOWED ONCE AGAIN how his business mentality and wrestling preferences could shift on a whim year to year with his presentation of *WrestleMania XII*. For over a decade the name *WrestleMania* had become synonymous with the biggest wrestling show of the year in the eyes of the casual audience. Celebrities from the non-wrestling mainstream were routinely brought into the fold, boosting perception of the event to non-fans by giving the WWF a star-power "rub". While Mr. T, Liberace, Muhammad Ali, Cyndi Lauper and a host of other icons of their era had been involved in the original showcase piece, few other 'Mania cards had featured so much direct celebrity involvement as the prior year's *WrestleMania XI*.

The main event saw NFL Hall of Fame star Lawrence Taylor competing in his only professional wrestling bout, working opposite the gargantuan tattoo-headed Bam Bam Bigelow, and winning. While Mr. T had been in the headline attraction at the inaugural *WrestleMania*, he was simply the mainstream cherry on top of an already well iced Hulk Hogan and Roddy Piper cake. To have an entire show built around a singles bout featuring a football player was a wholly different direction altogether for McMahon to venture, and it bombed horribly.

WrestleMania XI had been both a commercial and creative disaster. As well as flopping on pay-per-view, it also failed to inspire critics, and McMahon was determined not the make the same mistake again. He made one of his characteristic immutable decrees: there would be no celebrity involvement at *WrestleMania XII* whatsoever. Then WWF Director of Promotions Basil V. DeVito Jr., justified the decision, "As the product changed and the performers at the top of the roster became increasingly athletic, the notion of involving celebrities at *WrestleMania* lost a bit of its appeal," he states. "If they served no other purpose than window dressing, it almost detracted from the event - at least during this period."

The truth was a far more sobering denunciation of the mainstream malaise towards Titan. Such was the nadir to which the WWF's reputation had fallen that few in Hollywood wanted to associate themselves with an ailing company no longer in vogue. Any celebrities with credibility and name value were well aware of the national lampooning that Lawrence Taylor had received from his own sports press after agreeing to don the tights, and few were willing to risk their careers to jump into bed with Titan.

As a marketing executive from one major toy franchise had told Federation marketing officials earlier in the year, "You guys are a dead brand." It was a stark contrast to the first *WrestleMania* in 1985, which had seen celebrities throw themselves at the WWF because of the group's popularity with the bourgeoisie hipster fad crowd, the key demographic directing America's tastes and spending at the time.

Instead, Vince was forced to rely on the old-fashioned art of professional wrestling to attract the masses, offering them a potential mat clinic between his two finest workers in a sixty minute "Iron Man" main event, and a host of blasts from the past embodied by the appearances of enduring eighties' icons Roddy Piper, Jake Roberts, and The Ultimate Warrior.

For the live gate, the strategy worked and the arena sold out with nearly 15,500 people (a figure inflated to 18,500 by the WWF) in the building, with 12,500 paying to the tune of $750,000 in revenue. While the number was low on the attendance list compared to other *WrestleMania* shows, it was actually more impressive than it appeared on the surface. The WWF had made the decision initially to offer tickets only via mail order - a crafty ploy to generate a mailing list made up of their most loyal fans for future marketing purposes. Furthermore, an increase in ticket prices meant it was the highest grossing card in North America since the prior year's *WrestleMania*. Further positive news came with the merchandise revenue, with the company generating a further $175,000 at the stalls, a substantially larger dollar figure per head than at other *WrestleMania* events.

But the show was not entirely positive. Titan may have claimed a sell out, but giving away tickets as local concessions which were then not used meant hundreds of seats in the building were visibly empty on camera. The WWF had suspected this was going to be the case and opened the venue's box office right up until show time. They even resorted to giving away free tickets in the parking lot prior to the card's first match, though it was too late to make a difference.

THE OPENING match of the pay-per-view broadcast saw Vader making his *WrestleMania* debut, teaming with veteran big show performers and fellow Camp Cornette members Owen Hart and Davey Boy Smith, lining up opposite returned veteran Jake Roberts, the increasingly obese Yokozuna and another *WrestleMania* debutant in Ahmed Johnson.

The portrayer of Vader's, Leon White, was in a permanent bad mood having been forced back into the ring early from his shoulder surgery, and he already knew he faced an uphill battle to keep his WWF career on track.

Thus the last thing he wanted or expected was to be told what to do and when to do it in his matches. However, this was the micro-managed WWF, a vastly different organisation to what White was familiar with. When it came to the story told in the matches, everything had to adhere to Vince McMahon's strict guidelines, especially at *WrestleMania*.

Jim Cornette, who juggled his time between acting as an on-screen manager with a job on the creative team, was assigned the task of helping to lay out the contest. White was perplexed that Cornette was the man tasked with laying out the structure of the match. As Cornette began explaining a sequence that McMahon wanted the sextet to enact, White immediately looked at Yokozuna and Smith with an expression of befuddlement. Unhappy with what was suggested, he stood up and asserted, "Jim, that's not the way we were going to do it." According to White, Cornette countered that it was what McMahon wanted and thus the way it had to be done. "It was bullshit," foamed White, "He was calling the match and it was horrible. We [the wrestlers] all knew it. He didn't have a clue what he was talking about. We knew what to do, how to do it and when to do it. We didn't need any help."

Cornette tells a starkly different story. "I have no memory of this happening. As an agent for the WWF, I never recall once laying out a match step-by-step for the top talent. TV matches with job guys? Yes. Angles? Sure. Finishes? Absolutely. But not matches. No agent laid out the entire match for top talent back then, and only the finish and/or "theme" of the match was ever laid out in booking meetings. I often suggested spots, but never *insisted* on anything except what I was instructed to, or when I knew without having to ask that something might violate some WWF policy or sensibility. Leon knows this as well as anyone.

"I certainly knew this match would be a lacklustre affair going in, mainly because of the babyface team. I barely remember it, but I know I never once told talent that Vince McMahon wanted something a certain way unless Vince McMahon wanted something a certain way. More often than not, I would accompany this statement with, "I don't like it either, but he's the boss." Unless, I thought he was right of course.

"So what happened? I don't know. Maybe Leon didn't like the finish I gave and now remembers it as the whole match, maybe the guys were trying to do one or more of the "pet peeves" that Vince got from time to time and I said no, or maybe Vince wanted someone protected and to look stronger.

"To accuse me of playing "the Vince card" to strong-arm personally laying out a match I barely gave two shits about is ridiculous. To accuse me of not knowing how to lay a match out is even *more* ridiculous. Hey, there were a lot more great Midnight Express matches than there were great Vader matches. Leon's WWF run was hampered by bad booking, Vince not "getting" the Vader gimmick, and Shawn Michaels and his butt buddies not wanting to work with him because he was too stiff. To be perfectly honest, Leon's incessant whining and griping to Vince about items both major and minor caused Vince to roll his eyes every time he spoke Vader's name. Leon should have been a major star there and he wasn't, but on the list of reasons why, Jim Cornette and his *WrestleMania XII* match don't crack the top one-hundred."

FOLLOWING THE six-man tag came Dustin 'Goldust' Runnels' encounter with the veteran 'Rowdy' Roddy Piper in a match dubbed the 'Hollywood Backlot Brawl'. Few watching realised that what they were seeing was not live, but had in fact been filmed over two weeks earlier on a lot at Universal Studios. To even call it a pro wrestling match was something of a stretch. The action between the two was more akin to a fight scene in a blockbuster movie, which happened to be exactly what Vince was hoping to achieve.

McMahon, with Bruce Prichard in tow, headed to Los Angeles with Runnels and Piper to direct the contest. He had already gone to the trouble of having a Cadillac spray painted gold, and had a brand new white Ford Bronco stationed at the scene of the shoot, because McMahon had grand plans for the presentation; he intended to recreate the infamous O.J. Simpson car chase that had dominated the news headlines two years earlier. It stemmed from an idea first pitched by Bruce Prichard - prior to Vince's no celebrities decree - for Simpson to compete in a grandstand match with Piper at *WrestleMania*, a move the WWF felt would generate even more publicity than Lawrence Taylor had a year earlier. "We wanted controversy," admits Prichard sheepishly.

When the Simpson talks failed to materialise beyond general enquiries, and with Goldust's originally scheduled opponent Scott Hall having been suspended, the company put the two remaining participants together, determining they actually made apposite foil for one another. "Goldust represented everything that Piper wasn't. It was a tremendous clash of personalities," notes Jim Ross.

After a brief dress rehearsal on the backlot that allowed the performers to get a feel for the cars they would be driving at the onset and conclusion of the piece, they fought hell-for-leather in a one-take shoot. Barely in shot were a horde of paid screaming extras, who encouraged the faux Scotsman to smash the rapacious homosexual in the head with a baseball bat. Because of how much his audience despised Goldust, Vince had instructed Runnels not to mount any offence, instead commanding that Piper be in control for the duration of the skirmish. It made for uncomfortable viewing. As Shaun Assael wrote in his critically acclaimed book *Sex, Lies and Headlocks*:

> It scarcely mattered to the McMahons that Goldust was giving millions of teenagers their first images of what gay men acted and sounded like. He was a heel, and in the moral nexus of Vince's world, there was only one way to deal with someone like that. You had to beat the shit out of him. In any other context, it would have been called a hate crime. But the rules were different when you called it wrestling.

The spliced-together footage ran for around five-minutes. Piper dominated the entire time, getting his jollies from violently beating Runnels with a bat and punching him so hard in the head that he broke his hand. "I hit him hard with the bat; it sounded like a watermelon," he recalls with little hint of remorse, "Tough kid." Following the ostensible attempt to recondition Goldust with physical abasement, Piper hosed him down like an amorous dog - a non-too-subtle metaphor even by WWF standards. On the show's live commentary, McMahon laid bare his prevailing mind-set from behind the announce desk, noting that Goldust was, "being taught a lesson".

Goldust's only offence came when fleeing the scene. Jumping in his Cadillac, he backed into Piper's Bronco - though failed to properly execute a planned spot that had called for him to knock the door off its hinges, then lurched the vehicle forwards towards Piper. "I was driving pretty slowly because I realised we had one take and I could kill him if I wasn't careful," remembers Runnels. "I was getting closer and closer, and I saw that he wasn't moving. All of a sudden his eyes grew bigger and bigger, and we were looking right at one another. It was like everything was happening in slow motion."

As Runnels rammed the car towards Piper, the veteran wrestler jumped at exactly the right moment and landed on the bonnet, making it look as if the vehicle had ploughed straight into his knees. Runnels drove gingerly for twenty feet with Piper clinging to the car, then carefully hit a dumpster to allow him to roll off in a controlled fall. Disaster nearly struck for the WWF when the dumpster was sent careening towards a studio executive's parked $300,000 sports car. Had it hit, Titan would have been left footing the bill. The cost of repairs would have wiped out a percentage of the company's

WrestleMania gate. Fortunately a well-placed cameraman was able to intercept the rogue receptacle before any damage was done.

Following the hit and run, Goldust sped out of the lot and was quickly pursued by Piper in his Bronco. It was the O.J. Simpson homage that McMahon had coveted. Two weeks later during the live *WrestleMania* broadcast, Titan's production team spliced in police footage from the actual Simpson chase, which the WWF claimed was Piper pursuing Goldust. It wasn't a stretch to infer a dark message in what the WWF was presenting: Goldust, and all other gay men, were to be treated in the same was as those wanted for murder.

Clad in the same unwashed blood-soaked attire as they had worn two weeks earlier, Runnels and Piper waited patiently for their cue. They were finally given the go-ahead to drive down the ramp into the Anaheim Pond for the conclusion of their scuffle, and a battered Goldust stumbled into the arena. The first person he saw was Pat Patterson - one of the most notable openly gay men in the industry - in what was a far from coincidental cameo. Piper stalked his victim to the ring, where the bout soon took a turn for the avant-garde when the 'Rowdy Scot' grabbed Goldust's crotch, planted a lingering kiss on his lips and then stripped him down to his underwear. As per his own creative incentive, Runnels' underwear was racy black women's lingerie that he had picked out with his wife Terri earlier in the day. It was a final zany exclamation point on the most outrageous match that McMahon had presented to date.

THE MATCH that the majority of the Anaheim crowd had come to see ended up not much of a match at all. It was the long-awaited comeback after a near four year exile of the flamboyant Ultimate Warrior, returning to the event that had seen him reach the pinnacle of his career. Six years earlier at *WrestleMania VI* in Toronto, Warrior had been allowed to pin the hitherto unbeatable Hulk Hogan in the middle of the ring before over 60,000 people at the Toronto SkyDome. Beating Hogan meant Warrior became WWF Champion, a shift in power that was supposed to position him as the star of the WWF for the nineties.

It did not work out. A combination of unfavourable booking and resentment from irked Hogan fans resulted in declining interest in the product while Warrior was on top. Hogan riding off into the sunset to make movies, at least for a few months, seemingly gave Warrior a clear stage on which to excel. Instead, he found himself suffering as the result of the ex-champion's pre-sabbatical megalomania, coming up against perennial Hogan victim Curt 'Mr. Perfect' Hennig around the loop in flat matches that rarely drew. Fans across the country had already seen Hennig try and fail to dethrone Hogan. In an era of kayfabe, they had little reason to suspect that the one man who had beaten Hogan would ever lose to Hennig.

There was also resentment from the boom-period generation of fans. While willing to overlook Hogan's inferior ring work because he launched the WWF into the stratosphere, they were less readily prepared to tolerate the haymaker-swinging, neon-bedecked Warrior as a credible champion. Though they tolerated him as an upper midcard act, parading around with the Intercontinental Title and squashing hapless foes without breaking a sweat, to many the WWF Champion needed to offer more than a colourful gimmick and rippling muscles.

Coming off the career plateau of his title win Warrior's popularity began to slide as 1990 progressed. He repeatedly found himself main eventing as part of six-man tag matches alongside the recently debuted Road Warriors (known as the Legion of Doom in the WWF) opposite the Demolition triumvirate (Bill 'Ax' Eadie, Barry 'Smash' Darsow, and Brian 'Crush' Adams), where the extra bodies could hide his shortcomings. McMahon had tired of the Warrior experiment by early 1991. He had him drop the title to perceived midcarder Sgt. Slaughter, a veteran who had been a star babyface for McMahon at his peak in the pre-*WrestleMania* era. Slaughter had since turned heel and been recast as an Iraqi-sympathiser right in the middle of the real Gulf War. All mooted plans for a Warrior and Hogan sequel were off, leaving Jim Hellwig rudderless. He was trapped in a wrestling purgatory between the midcard and the main event, and he was peeved with the demotion.

By July 1991, Hellwig was fed up of the WWF, and decided to confront McMahon about recent payoffs he deemed substandard. He felt that as he was billed on the same level as Hulk Hogan at *SummerSlam* - teaming with him in a much-hyped main event opposite Sgt. Slaughter and his dastardly foreign lackeys - he should be getting equally remunerated. He demanded McMahon put it in writing that he would receive equal terms to Hogan, which included equal pay at pay-per-views they both appeared on, or else he would pull out of *SummerSlam*. Not wanting to jeopardise his main event, on which thousands of dollars had been spent on promotion and marketing material, McMahon agreed to Hellwig's demands.

Immediately after *SummerSlam*, McMahon suspended Hellwig and removed him from all Titan programming. Despite having given the tetchy performer written confirmation that he would pay him the same as Hogan, he reneged on the promise. Instead he sent Hellwig a vitriolic letter telling him in no uncertain terms that he was nowhere near the level of star that Hogan was, before hitting Hellwig with a jab that would stick in his craw until near the end of his life: "You have become a legend in your own mind." As a further act of contempt towards Hellwig, McMahon paid Hogan a $15,000 bonus for *SummerSlam*, ensuring he ended up receiving more than him for the show.

As he would be again in 1996, McMahon was desperate when he called Hellwig in early 1992 and asked him to return to the fold at *WrestleMania VIII*. The WWF was having its name dragged through the mud thanks to ill-advised comments made by Hulk Hogan on the *Arsenio Hall Show* denying ever having used steroids to enhance his physique. The resultant fallout was a steroid scandal that quickly engulfed the company. Many notable stars from the era were allowed to fade out of the spotlight, with Hogan, Roddy Piper, and Jake Roberts each set to depart after *WrestleMania*.

McMahon needed stars so turned to Hellwig, and the two enjoyed a relationship that lasted nearly eight months before again capitulating. It was a situation that eventually mimicked itself in 1996, though this time no one was sure how the audience would react to a relic of a long-gone era. The landscape had changed beyond recognition in the WWF since 1992, with an almost entirely different troupe of performers now filling the locker room. Of the faces still around from the last time Warrior worked a pay-per-view for the company, only Bret Hart, Davey Boy Smith, Shawn Michaels, and The Undertaker remained as active in-ring performers.

That was a fact not lost on Hellwig, who noted, "I didn't know half of the guys. All I knew was that the guys now on top were B-team players when I was there before, and I had come back to make an impression." The man tasked with helping him do that was his return night opponent Paul 'Hunter Hearst Helmsley' Levesque, a member of the Kliq. McMahon knew Hellwig's strengths and weaknesses as a performer well. He had no intention of the much ballyhooed Ultimate Warrior return match stinking out the joint, so he relayed an edict to his agents that the bout must be kept short and Warrior should be made to look strong. All the booking stated was that Warrior must have his hand raised in short order, the meat of the match was left up to the participants.

Hellwig had never met Levesque prior to the show, and would later claim his opponent offered no suggestions for the match when they first discussed it. Instead he outlined his own plan that would see Helmsley hit his Pedigree finishing move straight away, only for him to kick out, respond in kind, and win the bout quickly. He was looking to recreate one of the most rapturous responses he had received in his career, aping a contest from *SummerSlam* in 1988 at Madison Square Garden. On that evening he was booked to beat then Intercontinental Champion the Honky Tonk Man in twenty-seven-seconds, ending his record fifteen-month reign with the belt. It was a moment that had launched The Ultimate Warrior character into the upper echelon of the WWF, and he was eager to replicate that same level of fan adulation that he had once commanded.

Levesque had turned up at the building excited about making his *WrestleMania* debut opposite one of the WWF's biggest ever stars. He was expecting to be slotted into the Rick Rude, Ted DiBiase, and Randy Savage roles of years prior - as the man expected to carry Hellwig to a respectable match. As he listened to the radically different vision Hellwig was proposing for their bout, Levesque simply nodded in agreement. He expressed no hint of having a problem with the brief one-sidedness of the contest, so Hellwig left the conversation there and headed off to get changed. "It wasn't a malicious plan to hurt Hunter," he would later state, "It didn't matter if he was squashed anyway. You can easily fix things like that in wrestling."

"It was never supposed to be so one-sided, but what they did in the match was up to those guys, we only gave them the time that it was allotted," notes Jim Cornette. "But y'know, don't just shit in the guy's mouth. Have a decent match for what time you've got." Despite having remained a silent witness as his proposed career assassination was laid out in front of his eyes, Levesque evidently did have a problem with how Hellwig wanted everything to play out. Troubled by the plan, he sought out respected veteran road agent Jerry Brisco for advice.

As a decorated former amateur wrestler and a professional wrestling traditionalist, Brisco had little time for a character like the Ultimate Warrior. He advised Levesque not to kill his finish in the manner that had been suggested and shared his belief that the contest should be a competitive back-and-forth encounter prior to Hellwig getting his hand raised. Levesque returned to Hellwig's locker room as he was showering, bringing Brisco alongside him for backup. He began outlining a number of ideas that he wanted to work into the script, but Hellwig cut him off immediately. Staring a hole through Levesque, he barked, "If there's anything you need to discuss with me then you come to me and discuss it man-to-man."

Even if Levesque had done that, Cornette attests it probably would not have made a great deal of difference. "Warrior wasn't going to hear of it; he wasn't going to let anyone get any offence in on him during his first match back. Helmsley wasn't important at the time so it didn't matter, but he didn't take it well." Levesque would later call Hellwig, "one of the most unprofessional guys I have ever been in the ring with," noting that his staunch refusal to show any weakness, "ruined the experience" of his first *WrestleMania* appearance.[24]

Realising that trying to argue with Hellwig was a lost cause, Levesque instead took stock of the situation and decided to comply with his opponent's demands. His subsequent professionalism in doing the potentially harmful job did not go unnoticed by his superiors. Levesque was told that as a thank you for going through with the bout without causing a fuss, he would be given the win in that year's *King of the Ring* tournament as a way of rebuilding him long-term.

There was also little in the way of grumbling from the notorious Kliq about the shoddy treatment of one of their own. Neither Scott Hall nor Sean Waltman were involved with the card, Kevin Nash was on his way out of the company, and Shawn Michaels was focused on his own career-defining moment. Hellwig avoided their ire, but Cornette sensed the faction knew better than to challenge him anyway. "They saw how high McMahon was on him upon his return and were deciding to pick their battles," he observes. "They probably realised the guy was going to flame out anyway. When you bring a guy back who can't work a lick, that no one backstage likes, the nostalgia factor of him being there is going to be brief."

Thus without any further opposition, the match transpired exactly as Hellwig wanted; The Ultimate Warrior decimated Hunter Hearst Helmsley in less than two-minutes. Judging by the reaction to his return that evening - which far surpassed anything else on the show - some observers felt his decision to squash the up-and-comer was justified. For one, Vince McMahon was thrilled with how the return of the Ultimate Warrior had come off. Following the show, he posed to Hellwig the same question he had asked following his return four years earlier, "Don't you miss it? Don't you miss all of this? The fame? The adulation?" Hellwig was non-committal in response, but the truth was he did miss it. He cherished playing the role of a real-life superhero who was an idol for millions, but he also knew he had other options. Unlike the majority of the roster, wrestling and the WWF was not the be all and end all for him.

UNFORTUNATELY FOR Iron Man Match main event stars Bret Hart and Shawn Michaels, a broad percentage of the California audience were casual wrestling fans in attendance only to see Warrior's return. Many were reared on the muscle monsters of the eighties and fondly remembered

---

[24] Fortunately for Helmsley, he would receive many opportunities to avenge the defeat. He appeared on a further eighteen (as of *WrestleMania 31*) *WrestleMania* cards, headlining six of them. Like Hellwig stated, his career wasn't harmed by the loss.

Warrior from their childhoods. They had no intention of sitting through an hour-long scientific wrestling clinic contested between two performers half his size. To those fans the WWF was about over-the-top razzmatazz, oversized physiques and overblown personalities, not trading holds and counters.

It was a stark contrast to the feelings of the hardcore fan base and students of the game. Many were expecting that Michaels versus Hart would go down as one of the great matches of a generation and be remembered as a bona fide *WrestleMania* classic. The WWF felt the same way too, practically promising that the pair would deliver the best match in the history of the annual extravaganza. It was a promotional strategy that *The Wrestling Observer Newsletter* felt came with risks:

> Riding the most momentum the company has had in four years, the World Wrestling Federation will present its biggest show of the year this weekend and potentially the best match in its history. The latter statement, which WWF has been using in hyping the Bret Hart vs. Shawn Michaels one hour Iron Man match for the WWF Title, puts tremendous pressure on the combatants. Never before has a major promotion basically told the fans they are going to see the greatest athletic match in the history of the promotion leading up to a PPV show. With expectations put at such a high level, if the two come through, it'll be a match remembered for years. But if they slip up just a tad, and going one hour with today's style of wrestling is asking a lot from both men, it'll be considered a disappointment.

The idea of the match, like so many others before it, came from the genius wrestling mind of Pat Patterson. "The Iron Man Match was a dream match that I had at one time proposed between Bret and Shawn," he recalls, "Vince was not really for it because he thought it would be too long of a match for a pay-per-view. Even some of the wrestlers laughed at me, but I really believed that Bret and Shawn could tear the house down." By the time Vince changed his mind and decided to go ahead with the bout, Patterson was on temporary hiatus from the company. For all intents and purposes he was retired. He was so burned out with wrestling that he was not even planning on attending the big show. Vince called and implored him, "Pat, you've gotta come to *WrestleMania!*" In the end he agreed to attend, and he was thrilled that he did.

Simply having two of his stars wrestling for an hour on any televised card, let alone *WrestleMania*, was a unique notion in itself for McMahon.

The last two wrestlers in the mainstream to do so were Rick Steamboat and Ric Flair in 1989, when they contested an intricate, gripping drama that was revered by many as the greatest professional wrestling match in history. However, that was seven years earlier in the wrestling-centric world of the NWA, not the sports entertainment circus of the WWF. In the past, McMahon had always filled his *WrestleMania* cards with so many matches that few even lasted beyond the ten minute mark. The longest to date had been the battle between Hulk Hogan and The Ultimate Warrior at *WrestleMania VI*, which was given twenty-two well-rehearsed minutes.

It was a significant shift in ideals for Vince to sell a show around an hour-long wrestling contest. While his father had regularly presented sixty-minute time limit draws during Bruno Sammartino title defences at Madison Square Garden back in the sixties and seventies, on televised events Vince Jr., hadn't even come close.[25] Hart had actually wrestled hour-long contests a number of times on untelevised house shows earlier in the decade opposite sixty-minute veteran Ric Flair, and his brother Owen Hart, so going in he had an idea of what to expect. Michaels had never wrestled a match that duration, but he had worked some tag matches when he was part of the Rockers team against the Rougeau Brothers that were billed as going an hour, though they actually clocked in at around forty minutes.

Nevertheless, Michaels was ready for the challenge. His ascent to the top of the Federation had been gathering momentum since he turned babyface the night after 1995's *WrestleMania*, where a favourable reaction to him in his match with best friend and fellow babyface Kevin 'Diesel' Nash at the supershow had forced McMahon's hand. That night, Michaels and Nash had been made to take a back seat and forfeit what they felt was their rightful main event billing in lieu of Lawrence Taylor's appearance. By 1996 though, there was no doubt that Michaels had earned and deserved his *WrestleMania* main event showcase.

While popular from the moment he shifted alignment, Michaels' momentum began to soar following a memorable angle with Owen Hart in November, in which he used injuries sustained during a well-publicised real life nightclub fight in Syracuse as a component of an inspired wrestling angle. To pull it off, Michaels let Owen kick him in the back of the head with a move called an enzuigiri. After initially showing no ill-effects he suddenly collapsed in the ring, apparently due to having suffered a complication relating to the prior concussion he had sustained. When *Raw* abruptly ended that night, teary-eyed fans worried that Shawn had collapsed and died in the ring from a brain aneurysm.

---

[25] At least in standard matches. Several *Royal Rumble* bouts surpassed the hour mark.

The way the whole story was shot and presented was so atypical for McMahon programming that people had instantly bought it as something real. A spot that had gone horribly wrong. It was exactly the reaction Michaels had been hoping for when he first pitched the idea. When he returned to win the *Royal Rumble*, the sympathy he received and the response he garnered as a result confirmed that he was receiving his moment of glory on well-earned merit rather than due to supposed political bartering. Following his victory in the annual thirty-man fracas, Michaels was given a limited touring schedule, restricted to television matches and a handful of house show shots with Owen Hart and friend Hunter Hearst Helmsley that served as a way of getting back into ring shape.

Michaels' reduced schedule was a cause of some vexation for Bret Hart. He was on the road every day battling goliaths The Undertaker and Diesel, wrestling matches that took an extra physical toll on his body due to the increased impact caused by each opponent's towering size. He also had to deal with an ailment known colloquially as "Bombay Belly" while he was on tour with the Federation in India, lamenting that while he was suffering from the runs, Michaels was at home training like a madman to get in supreme shape.

He also noted that in the months leading up to their big match, Shawn had been superkicking his way to victory over twenty-nine other men in the *Royal Rumble*. Meanwhile he was scraping past challengers The Undertaker and Diesel in pay-per-view contests, relying on interference in both bouts to retain his title. "I felt like I was being pushed aside, like I was just carrying the belt to *WrestleMania* so I could hand it to Shawn," he complains.

Hart was also bemused with a series of training videos commissioned by the WWF to promote the contest. While Michaels was shown performing upside-down push-ups on gym bars and running up stadium steps *á la* Rocky Balboa, Hart was seen jogging gingerly on a snow-covered Calgary roadside and getting beaten up by his eighty-year-old father in the famous Hart Family Dungeon. Intentional or otherwise, the message conveyed was of Michaels as the younger, and more in shape of the two, and Bret as the grizzled veteran desperately trying to get in condition simply to keep up with his foe.

IRRESPECTIVE OF the contrasting builds the pair experienced on television, come show day both were looking forward to their encounter. "We were excited about getting to do this marathon match for the first time," says Shawn, "I was psyched about going an hour for the first time, but I also knew it would be a real challenge to keep the fans interested for the duration. I was up for it, and we were two guys who management thought could deliver. We knew it was a big chance for us in their minds."

Unlike some *WrestleMania* headline bouts such as Taylor vs. Bigelow the year before, Savage vs. Hogan in 1989, and Hogan vs. Warrior in 1990, Michaels and Hart did not sit down and discuss anything about what they wanted to do in the bout until the morning of the event. They were both pleased when they realised they were on the same page creatively, and in only a few minutes had verbally laid out the majority of the contest. Michaels was pleased to hear the usually inflexible Hart suggest they change up their respective arsenals to fill the time, putting twists on their well-established holds and sprinkling some fresh moves on top.

They took it in turns calling ten and fifteen minute sections so they would not have to remember a full sixty minutes worth of content, knowing they could each lead the other through the parts they had memorised. It was made even easier with Hart's suggestion they should have no falls at all in the entire sixty minute contest; a way of showing that both were equally matched competitors. Then, when the bout proceeded to overtime as scheduled and Shawn beat him, Hart had an "out" - plus a way of staking a strong claim to a rematch at *WrestleMania* the following year. Michaels agreed with his logic, adding, "I didn't think Bret and I should be beating each other a bunch. If we were that easy to beat, we shouldn't be there wrestling for the championship." It would ultimately prove to be a decision that hurt the match.

Hart had been portrayed as the wily champion clinging to tradition and virtues like respect in the lead-up to the confrontation, and his entrance for the match with Michaels was suitably low key. He simply walked to the ring with a look of determined focus in his eyes and purposefulness to his stride. He was a professional wrestler; that was his gimmick, he did not need lavish pyrotechnic and laser shows like Warrior or many of the other guys. Shawn Michaels came from the opposite school of thought; he liked his ring entrances to be memorable.

Few introductions in history were as unforgettable as Shawn's that night, with the flamboyant superstar gliding to the ring on a zip line that covered half of the arena. McMahon, ever the thrill-seeker and a staunch advocate of his motto, "I wouldn't ask you to do anything that I wouldn't do," had already gleefully tested out the device earlier in the day. Shawn's mother, who was also in the crowd that evening, had been horrified when she heard the news. "I didn't want him to do it," she recalls, but Michaels had never been one for authority, and went ahead with the stunt. Fortunately, it came off beautifully; Michaels looked every bit the superstar that he was about to become as he parasailed into the ring.

Despite the build-up and the unquestionable talent of the two participants, for many the Iron Man Match did not manage to live up to the impossible hype. It was not helped when some fans in the arena - namely the casual crowd who had already gotten their fix from seeing Warrior and did not want to sit through such a long bout - started to leave once the clash started. Those who remained barely cared about the contest at all. It was the reason Vince had been apprehensive about running with the stipulation in the first place. After over a decade at the helm of the WWF he was well attuned to what his audience would tolerate, and he knew good old-fashioned wrestling would be a tough sell.

Those who did remain were presented with a slow-burning affair that peaked occasionally. Some spots were memorable, such as when Michaels inadvertently superkicked the timekeeper, but for the most part the pair grinded at holds and kept their energy in reserve for the final stretch of the ordeal. They even had a number system in place to let them know how exhausted the other was feeling. The lower the number, the better they felt, but if either man said "ten" then it would be the cue to grab a hold and take a breather. Around halfway through the match many fans cottoned on to the likelihood that there would be no falls in the contest, and began to loudly boo each subsequent close two count, knowing their interest would not be piqued by a pinfall.

For the duration of the encounter Michaels and Hart played a game of 'pass the potato'[26]. It began with an accidentally stiff shot from Michaels early in the contest, then led to a trading of 'receipts' and further intentionally stiff blows until it became a cycle with no possible conclusion. Hart would later dismiss what he described as a 'potato harvest' causing any issues, "Those things happened frequently in wrestling," he claimed.

Despite the laboured pace and some aspects of the match being a shoot, the pair's collective timing and execution of every hold, transition, and counter was otherwise practically flawless. That was exemplified in the final stages of the bout when Hart, knowing he needed to give the last five minutes over to Michaels, mounted the ropes ready for the agreed cut off spot and saw 4:59 remaining on the clock. He briefly smiled to himself before going into the final phase of the contest, satisfied they had hit all of their marks. The match was going exactly as they had talked about, right

---

[26] The term 'potato' is a wrestling colloquialism meaning a stiff, non worked shot. Sometimes potatoes are accidental, other times they are intentionally stiff. A *potato harvest* is a match where potato after potato is thrown intentionally.

down to the second. "I don't know of any other two professional wrestlers who could have done that so well. It was an amazing accomplishment to piece all of that together and then perform it on the same night without any glitches," he boasts.

The end of the scheduled sixty-minutes saw the contest reach the peak of its drama, with Hart tying Michaels in his trademark sharpshooter hold with only thirty seconds left on the clock. Michaels was permitted to survive the move until the bell, but the audience let out a collective groan at the lack of a decisive finish on the biggest show of the year. Hart grabbed his WWF Title belt and began trudging to the back, giving the impression that he was convinced the lack of a fall meant he had retained the championship by default.

Returning figurehead president Gorilla Monsoon was the man tasked with declaring the match must have a clear winner. He decreed that an overtime period would follow until one of the pair scored a fall. Hart grumbled about the decision, giving his character further perceived injustices to complain about when he made his return from a scheduled post-*WrestleMania* hiatus a few months later. The live audience should have been thrilled they were going to see a definite victor, but the response to the announcement of overtime was lukewarm at best. By now, most simply wanted to go home.

They did not have to wait long. Michaels hit two superkicks and pinned Hart clean in the middle of the ring less than two minutes into the restart. He had finally achieved his much-vaunted "boyhood dream". The emotion of the moment was too much for Michaels, who fought back tears as he grasped his newly acquired title belt, cradling it like a newborn baby. The sensitive moment was short lived. Mere seconds later he turned to referee Earl Hebner and instructed him, "Tell him [Hart] to get the fuck out of the ring. This is my moment." Hebner rolled his eyes at the impudence and relayed the message to Hart, who wore a facial expression stunned at the disrespect.

Hart would later attest, "I never had a problem with any of that really. Sometimes those things are said for the purpose of speed, and they don't quite come out right. It's not being rude, it's just one of those things." The boys in the back took a different view when they heard what Michaels had said. When Hart failed to shake Shawn's hand and stormed immediately out of the building into a waiting Lincoln Continental - as the pair had secretly agreed prior - the myth that they hated each other was further perpetuated.

All the talk at *Raw* the following day was about how Hart and Michaels had serious heat with each other following their bout. The story doing the rounds was that Bret had refused to lose to Shawn in the allotted hour, and had instead insisted on the deciding fall coming in the overtime period. Michaels later dismissed the rumour as mere fabrication. "It was just the other wrestlers coming up with their own storylines," he says. "People read so much into that, but we both wanted it to go an hour and then go into overtime." Even though Hart was now on hiatus from television and not at the building for *Raw*, he was pleased for stories about the enmity between him and Shawn to manifest. In his mind the perceived hostility helped their touted rematch. When his brother Owen called from the building and told him that word going around the locker room was that there was serious tension between the pair, Bret was delighted. "Good!" he exclaimed, "Let them keep thinking that."

The truth was - at that time at least - there was little if any animosity between Bret and Shawn. Contrarily, Hart left the bout with a greater level of respect for Michaels than he had before it, proud of both how hard he had worked to get where he was and how accomplished he had become. He had no problem whatsoever dropping the strap to Shawn. Even though Hart harboured some reservations about his attitude and various addictions, he was happy for him to be the leading man in the company.

Furthermore, Hart was personally thrilled with how the match had come off. "It was an absolute masterpiece," he boasts, "I don't know if I had that kind of match with anyone else in the sense that move for move, it was exactly how we talked about it." It was a sentiment echoed by the match concept's architect Pat Patterson, "Not too many wrestlers could have a match go an hour and hold the audience, and in that era there were only two guys who could do it - Bret and Shawn. I was so happy that they got to have the match that I expected them to have. They really accomplished something spectacular. I was there in the audience and it was one of the greatest matches I have seen in my career, it really was. I had tears in my eyes watching it and I cried afterwards."

While Michaels was generally a reviled figured behind the curtain, he was also highly respected for his wrestling ability. Nearly everyone on the roster congratulated him on having achieved his goal. He hugged his friends and cried tears of joy with them, while Vince reserved a hearty bear-like hug for him immediately after the match and told him warmly, "I want you to enjoy this!" Others in the company were more circumspect, with the likes of Jim Ross and Jim Cornette both worried about what Vince had let them in for. "I remember thinking, 'Boy, we've got our hands full here,'" says Cornette. His misgiving would be proven correct on a number of occasions for the duration of Michaels' turbulent eight month long reign.

FIVE

WHEN THE WWF WENT TO Madison Square Garden it was always a special occasion for Vince McMahon. The building, located deep in New York's central hub of activity had featured pro wrestling cards for over one hundred years, and the McMahon family had ran the arena for several decades. Vince strongly associated the Garden with his father, who had built his own legacy promoting the likes of Bruno Sammartino, Killer Kowalski and Bob Backlund in the golden days of the World Wide Wrestling Federation. For Vince, the Garden was more than merely a building; it was hallowed ground, and running there was a proud family tradition.

In March the WWF's first sell out crowd at the arena in seven years had given McMahon renewed optimism for the future. He was thrilled when the group repeated the feat on May 19, packing 18,800 fans into the building. The WWF had sold out the Garden on consecutive outings for the first time since way back in 1985 - the peak of Hulkamania. In addition the show pulled over $300,000 in revenue from the live gate - the first arena house show in company history to do so, and another $100,000 from merchandise sales. It should have been cause for celebration. Instead, it would go down in the annals of wrestling folklore as the day when the Kliq denigrated the McMahons' proud MSG legacy by committing the ultimate act of wrestling heresy.

That it was the final day in the company for both Scott Hall and Kevin Nash was not lost on the informed Garden crowd. It made for an unmistakable buzz in the air. Hall was originally scheduled to wrestle Goldust on the card, but the latter suffered an injury during the European tour and was replaced by Paul 'Hunter Hearst Helmsley' Levesque. With Nash going against fellow Kliq ally Shawn Michaels, right to the bitter end the group had once again managed to manipulate a situation to their liking. Nash and Hall had both been doing jobs on the road for weeks, complying with the time-honoured wrestling tradition of losing to everyone in the territory on the way out. Tonight would be no different, with both booked to lose to their friends in lieu of a victorious last hurrah.

Before his match Hall was beckoned over by Pat Patterson, who since returning to the fold at *WrestleMania* had resumed his role of chief house show agent. As per usual he was the one responsible for laying out the finishes to the matches at the Garden, and he had some ideas for Hall's final appearance. Because of where they were, Patterson wanted to change the match around from what they had been doing on the road for the past few nights. He suggested a different ending to their usual house show contest, which Hall had no problem with. He was pleased to be putting over his friend Levesque, and happily followed Patterson's instructions to a tee. The result was an absorbing clash that Hall would later claim was one of the most satisfying of his career.

When Hall stepped out of the curtain to play Razor Ramon for the final time, he was met with a rabble of conflicting emotions from the audience. Significant and vocal sections of the assembled throng were enraged by the sheer sight of him, and barracked him with venom-filled boos as he sauntered to the ring. A number of people leaned over the barricade to tell him directly that he was a sell-out. Some went even further; "You sold out to WCW, you faggot. Get the fuck out of New York!" bellowed one irate fan. Others - with Hall's well-known recent suspension fresh in mind - yelled that he was a drug addict.

However, many in the building were just pleased to be able to watch Hall lace up his yellow and purple boots for the last time. Others used the match as an opportunity to plead with him to rethink his decision to leave, chanting in unison, "Please don't go." Hall became swept away in the moment and stopped to look directly over at the Gorilla position[27] where Vince always situated himself at the Garden. He motioned to the chairman and the audience, mouthing, "Tell him to give me the money and I stay right here!". Vince remained stoic. He simply looked at his feet and refused to let anyone around see the vaguest hint of a crack in his stubborn demeanour.

The finish that Patterson had instructed Hall and Levesque to enact saw Ramon hook Helmsley up in his Razor's Edge finishing move, only for the momentum of the lift into the hold to send Hunter's heel directly into the referee's head, knocking him down so that he missed Hall's subsequent pinfall attempt. Wrestling parlance referred to it as a 'visual win', something to soften the blow of losing because it gave the man defeated the argument, "I had the match won, but the referee was unconscious." Sticking with convention, it was Helmsley who then scored the victory when Razor turned into a kick to the gut and was finished off with Hunter's Pedigree.

---

[27] The staging area just behind the entrance curtain, named after Gorilla Monsoon who made the position his own for a number of years. His presence became so synonymous with the location that it was named after him. The name "Gorilla Position" has since become part of wrestling lore, and is now as ingrained as terms that have survived for a century.

Following his clean pinfall loss, Hall was greeted with another round of boos from an audience who felt betrayed by his impending defection. Hall knew this was his last chance to respond so grabbed the house microphone, causing instant panic amongst officials. This was a deviation from the script, an act of rebellion not written into the show format. There was concern over what Hall - who was a notoriously renegade personality at the best of times - might say. He mumbled that he had not sold out, managing to utter, "Say goodbye to the 'Bad Guy'," before his mic was unceremoniously cut.

After the bout, Vince met with Hall backstage then ushered him into the private room doubling as his office for the evening. "Dammit, you still work for me," he implored, "Let's work this out." Hall was taken aback. "Gee Vince, I dunno... I didn't want to leave in the first place but it's a bit late for that now. I already agreed to work for Bischoff..." Hall once again outlined what it would take for him to stay with the WWF: given the concession to work fewer towns while getting paid on the same scale as a main event performer.

Vince still felt he was not in a position where he could compromise, and neither would Hall. It was something both men had known before they sat down to talk. It was an empty gesture from McMahon - a last ditch effort to get Hall to stay and take his old deal, which was inferred but never implicitly stated. With no agreement forthcoming the two simply shook hands. Vince begrudgingly wished Hall good luck in WCW, with Hall reciprocating the pleasantry by wishing McMahon continued success. At that moment, Shawn Michaels sauntered into the room with Paul Levesque and casually asked, "Hey Vince, do you mind if Raze' and Hunter come out after my match?"

McMahon was somewhat sidetracked dealing with Hall, and the request barely registered. He heard the words and understood what was asked, but he did not have chance to fully process it or consider the ramifications. He was slightly blindsided and somewhat hesitant, but such was his staunch refusal to show any vulnerability whatsoever that he acquiesced.

It was not an off-the-cuff idea from Shawn, rather something the Kliq had discussed while in Hamburg, Germany on a recent Federation European tour. They wanted to come up with something memorable to look back on as their last hurrah together, which included letting the fans in on the secret of their friendship. During a typically drunken night, one of the group suggested they should hug and pose together at the climax of Scott and Kevin's last show for a public farewell.

Everyone in the group had forgotten that the discussion had even taken place by the time May 19 rolled around. All except for Levesque, who didn't drink like the others and thus tended to remember far more from their late-night conversations. Michaels was confused when Levesque - still sucking wind following his match - panted to him, "Are we still doing that thing we talked about?" Michaels had no idea what his friend was referring to, and told him as such. "We talked about it in Europe!" pleaded Levesque, "Me and Scott coming out after your match. Are we doing it?" Michaels said he did not know, so Levesque implored him to ask Vince's permission.

What Shawn was ultimately proposing to McMahon was for him and the rest of the Kliq to drop the facade of kayfabe and lift the ever-thinning veil that allowed fans to suspend their disbelief in what they were watching. The Kliq's reasoning was that ninety percent of the people in the Garden were well aware that what they were watching was a show. They knew that the wrestlers did not actually want to rip opponent's arms off or gouge each other's eyes out. Many also knew that the Kliq were real-life friends, despite their conflicting babyface and heel alignments. It was one thing for them to be mildly aware of it, but a different matter entirely for the Kliq to transcend storylines by publicly admitting and acknowledging it themselves.

THE MAIN event of the show was Nash's final appearance, working in a cage opposite Michaels with the WWF Title on the line. Whereas in some cases it could have been considered a risk to put someone in a WWF Title match in their last night with the company, McMahon had no concerns.[28] He knew that Nash would never double-cross his friend Michaels, and even though he was leaving, Vince still trusted him to do the right thing for business. That did not stop Nash toying with the watching chairman a little during the bout by intentionally coming agonisingly close to escaping the cage and winning the title, but it was simply part of the show. Nash went down to Michaels' superkick as planned, then allowed Shawn to leave through the cage door and win the match.

It was after the contest that the evening's infamous incident occurred. Michaels returned to the ring and posed with the title belt while Nash acted

---

[28] Though unlikely, there was always the risk that someone on their way out could try something, especially if leaving for a rival. It was not out of the realms of possibility that Bischoff could have promised Nash a large kickback if he had walked out with the WWF Championship, as he had already proven that he was willing to deface WWF property with the Madusa angle on Nitro. There were stories too from back in the Hogan days, such as Verne Gagne offering to pay the Iron Sheik to break Hogan's leg in their WWF Title bout rather than drop the belt to him, and various promoters trying to convince Bruiser Brody and others to hijack WrestleMania. Realising bridges would be burned forever, these things never happened. But tensions were higher than ever in 1996 between WCW and the WWF, so in the back of his mind McMahon always suspected Bischoff could be up to something to try to take him down from the inside.

like he was knocked unconscious, not moving a muscle. Shawn's celebrations lasted for a couple of minutes as he wandered from corner to corner, waiting to see if his friends would arrive. For a moment he suspected that McMahon had nixed the whole thing, but then he saw Scott Hall walking down the aisle. Pleased, he turned to Nash and excitedly whispered, "They're coming down!"

When Hall stepped through the cage door, he and Michaels flashed their private Kliq hand signal to one another and embraced in a heartfelt hug. Both were babyfaces, so this was not the source of the controversy - it was what happened afterwards. Michaels walked over to Nash and knelt down over his prone body, then gave him a playful kiss to wake him. Dave Meltzer described it as akin to, "the frog kissed by the princess." Even this could have been construed as a typically cocky act from the swaggering Shawn Michaels persona, but the next occurrence could not.

Paul Levesque was standing beside Vince McMahon and his right-hand-man Jerry Brisco in Gorilla when Hall ambled to ringside. He turned to the chairman, asking, "Should I go out and join them?" Though McMahon had already approved the move, it remained unbeknownst to the rest of his team. With Brisco clearly already enraged by what was happening, and with others beginning to express their displeasure, McMahon did not respond. Levesque decided to take a chance and go through with it, figuring he would regret it more if he was absent. He wandered down the aisle flashing the Kliq sign with both hands, then upon entering the ring immediately hugged Michaels. Levesque had been a heel earlier in the night, and indeed throughout his WWF tenure, so the embrace was completely lost on any casual viewers. The more astute fans knew exactly what was going on; the Kliq were gathering to bid farewell to the outgoing Scott Hall and Kevin Nash.

Hall playfully slapped Nash on the backside before the four men embraced in a kayfabe-shattering group hug that left locker room veterans and Garden legends frothing at the mouth. The Kliq teased a fracas between the two staying and those leaving, but it was played for laughs. Soon they returned to embracing, mounting the four corners of the cage and giving one final parting pose.

"I remember standing in the ring and we were all there together. It was unheard of, but the people appreciated it. I looked at Kev - we were all hugging - and I remember thinking, 'We all made it,'" reminisces Hall. Everyone but Michaels then departed the ring, leaving the 'Heartbreak Kid' to do a final round of posturing before telling the remaining audience members, "The Kliq loves each and every one of ya!"

While in the ring there was celebration, backstage was a scene of chaos. Swarms of wrestlers, officials, and Vince's closest advisors were outraged by what they had witnessed. Few if any realised that Vince had unwittingly given the go-ahead for the group to pull the stunt, and a potent cocktail of confusion and fury swirled around the Garden locker room. "They just killed the fookin' business," bellowed Davey Boy Smith in his thick Manchester accent to anyone who happened to be in earshot. Devoted company man Jim Ross was livid, whilst road agent and veteran former wrestler Jerry Brisco was apoplectic, storming around the corridors and in the mood to stretch the perpetrators. Others, like Jim Cornette, threw public temper tantrums and hurled their gear bags around.

Steve Austin was in the locker room that night and witnessed the whole thing - which some were already dubbing the *Curtain Call* - from the Gorilla position. As he remembers it, "I jerked the curtain that night - I was like the second or third match - and I was at the curtain because that's what I did; I watched the matches. When that happened I was thinking, 'What in the fuck is going on?' Man, that's just something you don't do. Good guys and bad guys don't start hugging each other in Madison Square Garden. It was bullshit, I couldn't believe what I was seeing. I didn't know whether to shit or wind my watch."

THE SOURCE of ire was twofold. Primarily it was the violation of the sacred oath of kayfabe[29], a secret code old-timers valued so highly that some had been known to lie in courtrooms while under oath, swearing blind that what they did was real. Others did not even 'smarten up'[30] their wives and children, some of whom lived in genuine fear each time their loved one competed, worried they might be seriously hurt or even killed in the ring. Many had broke their backs and bled buckets to build the foundations of the business, much of the time in the Garden itself. It was the same building where the audience had been reduced to tears when Bruno Sammartino's record WWWF Title run ended at the hands of Ivan Koloff in 1971. It had rejoiced at the ascension of future industry greats, men such as Hulk Hogan, Bret Hart, and Bob Backlund, each of whom won World Titles in the famous arena. And it had just witnessed four upstarts drop a nuke on that rich history which could never be undone.

---

[29] The irony was that it was Vince himself who first publicly admitted that what he was presenting as sport was not all it seemed, and was in fact pre-scripted entertainment. The move was made to avoid athletic commissions imposing regulations on him that would cost him money.

[30] That is, let them in on the truth. Many perpetuated the belief that what they did was real, kayfabing even their own families in an effort to protect the integrity of the business.

That this kayfabe breach had occurred in the sacred grounds of Madison Square Garden made the transgression that much worse to many. As Jim Cornette later put it, "Whether you like Vince McMahon or not, MSG was his building at the time. It had been his father's building. He viewed that as his house. The Kliq went out and took a shit on the business in his dining room. Right there on his table. There was no reason for them to do that. There was no storyline purpose for it. It didn't sell any tickets and it didn't do anything for business. Smart fans were not widespread then, so only 1% of the people in the crowd even understood what the fuck was going on. It was just something for their egos. If they wanted to say goodbye they should have had a party in the locker room with a big fucking cake. In doing that they were saying, 'We are bigger than the business,' which was something they had been saying to each other all along."

Cornette was not alone in his mode of thought. "I understand how much those guys cared about each other," says Jake Roberts, "But you're on the grandest stage of them all and you're gonna piss on it? You're frigging wrong, man." Bruce Prichard concurred, "I felt that it was a slap in the face to the business. I felt it was a slap in the face to Vince McMahon. To his father. To his whole family."

Vince needed only to look at the commotion going on around him to realise that giving his half-hearted blessing to the Curtain Call had been a bad decision. Personally he had not been particularly offended by it. He knew the group were not trying to sabotage the business or disrespect the Garden; they were only intending to say goodbye to one another and their fans. He felt the audience had loved it (some in the crowd later stated that it was one of the best Garden moments they had ever seen) and that was ultimately what mattered. The Kliq had gone a little overboard with the hugging and posing for his tastes to the point that it became a self-satisfying ego trip, but Vince realised the instant heat they had generated from the rest of the crew was due to their reputations as much as the act itself.

As he would later state, "It was so shocking to everyone else in the locker room and the other performers. 'Wait a minute this is a sacrilege, you can't do *that*. And besides, these two performers are turning their back on us and going down to WCW. What are you doing?'" The complaints from the rest of his staff put Vince in a tight spot. He had agreed to let the Kliq do their public goodbye, but the rest of the roster were so livid about it that he realised he had to show similar sentiments lest there could be a revolt. The last thing he needed was his talent base turning on his new champion Michaels. He needed his roster to work together if they were going to win the war with WCW.

"I remember Vince came up to me afterwards and said, 'Was that important to you?'" says Michaels. "I said, 'Yes it was. I appreciate it. Thanks.' Vince just said, 'Then it was important to me to.' We hugged and that's how we left it that night. He was fine. It was fine that night. It wasn't a big deal until it became a big deal, and it didn't become a big deal to us until it became a big deal to Vince," he explains. As far as the Kliq were concerned, when they left the building on the evening of the show they did not realise there *was* an issue. They were oblivious to the fact they had even done anything wrong.

For a fleeting moment Kevin Nash had wondered why Vince was not at the curtain when he walked past after the match, the position he usually assumed in the Garden. When he then saw veteran agent Pat Patterson merely shake his head, he thought little of it. He simply assumed it was down to his leaving the company rather than anything else. He had no idea that the Curtain Call had caused such uproar. "What happened was the same thing that happened a lot of times: Vince was on the ride to wherever and getting [irate] phone calls," suggested Michaels, "Honestly, it was big to the old-timers in the locker room before it was a big deal anywhere else."

As it was Scott and Kevin's final show before bailing out on the WWF, many of the boys saw the Curtain Call as a final "fuck you" from the Kliq to Vince and the locker room, an act presumably perpetrated out of a lack of respect for their peers and superiors. Kevin Nash insisted that this was not the case, "That situation and those actions were never done with malice. It was just four guys that had spent a lot of miles, a lot of hours, and a lot of our lives together, saying goodbye."

Upon reflection, Hall when asked about it years later could see how the incident looked to the rest of the locker room. "I understand the talent that was still there thinking, 'What's with these dudes? They're leaving and they're trying to hurt us,' but that wasn't the way it was. We had permission. It wasn't some kind of outlaw renegade move to hurt the company, which is what everybody seems to think. For me, I felt the responsibility to go out there and say goodbye to the fans at MSG, to thank them for supporting me all those years. We stayed out there a long time because the fans were cheering. Had they not cheered, we'd have left. It became really emotional."

Michaels would come to see circumstances the same way, "I understand people's perception of it," he adds, "That's one thing that time and wisdom gives you. It wasn't done to stick anybody in the eye, it was just friends expressing their care for one another." Paul Levesque expressed similar sentiments, "We just wanted to say goodbye to our buddies," he defends, "They were our families, all we had was each other. We were told we killed the business, though it didn't sound like it listening to the crowd. If I was a kid sitting in that crowd then I had just seen an awesome moment in time."

Regardless of the Kliq's intentions, the excuses did not wash with the old-timers and traditionalists who wanted to see proverbial heads roll. There were demands from all quarters for McMahon to bring down the hammer, with many privately questioning whether he would dare do anything to the seemingly bulletproof Kliq. "The boys were saying we destroyed the business and that we didn't care," mulled Kevin Nash, "They dumped a ton of heat on us, but Scott and I didn't get any of it. Shawn didn't get any of it. But Hunter..."

AS VINCE watched the aftermath of the Curtain Call unfold, he knew that publicly he had to take a stance if he wanted to keep his team united and avoid losing respect. Ultimately, Paul Levesque was obliged to take the brunt of the punishment Vince was under pressure to mete out. As Jim Cornette explains, "He couldn't do anything to Diesel or Razor because it was their last night. Well, actually he *could* have - he could have taken money out of their payoffs for monies they were still owed. I was upset with Vince because he didn't do that; he said he didn't want them to be able to say he fucked them on their way out. He ended up giving Nash a six-figure payoff for *WrestleMania*, though he did bonus 'Taker an extra $50,000 to make sure he was still paid more than him. Vince couldn't do anything to Michaels either, because he was dumb enough to let an immature jack-off like him have his goddamn belt. He wasn't gonna punish the World Champion, so Hunter got spanked instead."

A week on from the Curtain Call, the WWF was in Florence, South Carolina for the latest instalment of the *In Your House* series, subtitled *Beware of Dog* thanks to the involvement of 'British Bulldog' Davey Boy Smith in the main event. On the afternoon of the show, Levesque and Michaels were called into McMahon's office, where the chairman laid out the situation he was in. "I know I kinda said okay, but it became something I didn't think it was gonna be. Now the image is out there. It's made me look terrible. I didn't know it was going to go that far. Normally I'd have no choice but to fire ya...," he said pensively, looking directly at Levesque. McMahon let the words resonate around the room and watched the wrestler's expression drop as the reality of the situation sank in. "But, I don't wanna do that," he finally added.

Despite what he intimated to the pair, Vince was never contemplating letting Levesque go. He was unwilling to let another top star leave his company and turn up in WCW, and besides, he rated the performer highly.

He was forced into disciplining Levesque to save face, but he felt it was not right to fire him over it. Instead, Vince was going to punish him by having his Hunter Hearst Helmsley character go back to square one. Long-term plans that were in place for him to win the annual *King of the Ring* tournament were dropped, and a subsequent program with Shawn Michaels contesting for the WWF Title was also nixed. McMahon told Levesque in no uncertain terms, "That's gone, you're not doing that. You go to the bottom of the pole. I mean the *very* bottom."

Michaels protested, both in defence of his comrade and due to concern that he would not be working his summer-long program with one of the few people in the company he actually trusted. Once again he pointed out that McMahon had permitted the Garden act. Vince repeated his stance that he did not realise it would go as far as it did, then tried to placate his sulking champion with an explanation. "Look Shawn, you are the champion so I can't punish you. Hunter I can punish, and I have to. If I don't do something about it, it's chaos. There's gotta be a punishment. If I don't show everyone that I am serious then I'll lose credibility." He glanced over to Levesque again, "You're going to have to learn to eat shit and like the taste of it. You're gonna have to learn to eat plates and plates and plates of shit. You're not gonna like it."

Levesque had little choice but to go along with the decree, despite how unfair he felt it was that he was getting punished for something Vince had authorised. He was also astute enough to realise that his boss was in a bind, and that ultimately it would be best for his career long-term to do as he was asked without complaint. "Vince kinda had his back to the wall and had to do something. Somebody had to pay the price for it," noted Levesque. "I took it all. I took the brunt of it. I went from winning the *King of the Ring* to getting beat by every guy, every week."

Michaels felt a sense of guilt about what was happening to his friend. While he was getting away practically unscathed, he could see Levesque's career getting derailed. For once he was powerless to stop it. "I felt bad for Hunter because he hadn't done anything wrong," he reflects. "Vince turned on us because he was getting a lot of heat and Hunter had to pay the price. Hunter was in a tough spot, but he never once left my side." McMahon too realised the punishment was harsh, later commenting, "Triple H was left holding the bag and he held it very well. He paid some heavy dues."

Bob Holly did not agree, "I don't think the punishment fit the crime. Sure, he lost a bunch of matches for a while, but he didn't do a job to me or any of the other guys who could have gained from it. If he'd been made to do a job to me, that would have made a statement - especially since I'd busted my ass putting him over so much the summer before."

To placate the situation, Michaels and Levesque were ordered to apologise to everyone on the roster, specifically the agents who remained the most offended about the whole ordeal. The boys were still furious too, but Shawn was not concerned about them. He knew that if it was not the Curtain Call, then it would be something else; they always managed to find a way to hate him. Prior to the pay-per-view the pair went around the entire staff and offered their strained apologies, forced to listen as each agent explained to them in painstaking detail why what they had done was so iniquitous.

Jim Cornette felt a sense of sympathy for Levesque and pulled him to one side, telling him, "Suffer under it because the heat will pass, you're still young, you're still talented, but you did the wrong thing. At least you apologised. Now just mind your own business and everyone will forget about it."[31] Levesque quickly had to learn to suffer, starting that same evening with a clean defeat to the recently debuted Marc Mero in the pay-per-view opener. Michaels watched the match on a monitor backstage and tutted at the outcome, but his night, and Vince's, was about to get a whole lot worse.

HURRICANE SEASON in the Carolinas officially started on June 1, but the bad weather came a week earlier to the city of Florence than the WWF expected. An electrical storm was raging through the locality and causing chaos, with Federation technicians battling bravely against the elements just to reach the building to erect the set for the show. Throughout the day, the ferocity of the weather had the production crew worried about the very real possibility that the power would go out on the pay-per-view. It was a storm that Michael Hayes later described as an act of God. "It was wicked," he recalls, "One of the worst storms I have ever seen in my life."

As the day developed and the weather worsened, concerns increased, but after the dark match and the opening Helmsley-Mero match went off without a hitch the worries alleviated somewhat. Following Mero's victory was a bout scheduled between Puerto Rican babyface Savio Vega and the former Ringmaster, Steve Austin. The two had been programmed together for the past few months and had been earning kudos for the quality and believability of their matches. Tonight would be a little different. The pair

---

[31] Cornette would later express disappointment when little over a year later Levesque and Michaels screened footage of the incident during a segment on *Raw* and admitted that they only apologised because they were told to, not because they felt they needed to.

were booked to wrestle in a "Caribbean Strap Match", a bout that saw the two combatants tied together with a leather strap, which they were encouraged to use as a weapon. By WWF standards it was a brutal concept; a stipulation that McMahon was unlikely to have signed off on twelve months earlier. It was another clear sign that the landscape in the company was changing.

Vega made his way to the ring looking determined, ready for the skin lashing that awaited him, then suddenly the lights went out in the building. Lightning had struck one of the transformers and killed the pay-per-view feed, leaving viewers at home staring at a blank screen and asked to stand by. Broadcasting partners *Viewers Choice* and *Request* were aware of the weather situation in Florence and knew that WWF officials were prepared for the possibility of an outage. What they did not suppose was that the Federation had neglected to have an emergency backup generator to restore power should it happen.

There was much commotion behind the curtain, with agents frantically scurrying around and adjusting match finishes in case the power failed to restore. Elsewhere, baffled technicians were at a loss as to what they could do to revive the feed. As soon as the lights in the building died, McMahon - who was situated at the commentary table - immediately realised what had happened. "Are we off, Jeff?" he asked the production truck, before thinking on his feet and taking charge of the situation. "Everyone was panicked, but not Vince," remembers McMahon's broadcast colleague that night Jerry Lawler, "Vince kept his cool and he talked everyone through it." McMahon ordered that the show continue in the dark for the benefit of the live crowd, and technicians managed to light the arena just enough via a low-power generator (one far from powerful enough to return the pay-per-view feed) to make the matches visible - only barely.

"Thankfully I was involved in a few matches that night so I had an excuse to be someplace else," says Jim Cornette. "I didn't wanna be in that line of fire because Vince was pissed. After the week we had just had with the Garden incident, the feeling was like, 'Fine time for this!' It had never happened on a major pay-per-view before. Naturally, they blamed the fact that we were in the south."

In the dark ring, Austin and Vega did as instructed, wrestling the same hard-hitting, bruising encounter they had intended prior to the outage. They fought hammer and tongs for fifteen minutes, losing themselves in the moment and ignoring the reality that most in the audience could barely make out what they were doing. Rather than taking it easy and working a token contest, they wrestled at full tilt in case the power was restored mid-match.

Avid WWF followers waiting patiently at home for the feed to be fixed were thrown a bone halfway into the blackout with a clip of Vince and Lawler telling them to stay tuned. McMahon offered hope they would still air an Undertaker-Goldust casket match, and the Michaels-Smith main event. It soon became apparent to Vince that it was going to be a long shot, which caused him consternation. "I was frustrated," he says, "And when I become frustrated, I am always thinking of our audience."

As luck would have it, the WWF had already scheduled a replay of the show to be broadcast on Tuesday evening. It was an agreement made not because of worries over the storm, but rather because the pay-per-view was airing on Memorial Day weekend. Thus officials already expected a low buy rate for the event, and intended to use the following night's live *Raw* show to encourage anyone who missed it to order the repeat. When the broadcast was plunged into darkness, Vince had instructed the crew to use archaic battery operated cameras to film the event, which in his hastily formed emergency backup plan would be slotted into the replay so no one missed anything. Unfortunately, the footage was nowhere near fit for broadcast. As time ticked on with no sign of power restoration in sight, McMahon made the decision to redo the missing matches live from Tuesday's North Charleston television taping and slot them in during the replay instead.

BEHIND THE scenes technicians continued to work diligently, and were finally able to get the broadcast fully operational again an hour after it went black, just in time for the Michaels-Smith feature attraction. However, with only twenty-five-minutes of air time left, there was no choice but to truncate the match. That was the final straw for Michaels on what had already been a bad day. The finish to the bout had been changed countless times already over the course of the evening to account for any possible blackout-related scenario, and Michaels was at the end of his tether.

So limited was the time between the feed's restoration and the main event going to the ring that Michaels did not have time to gather his patience prior to making his entrance. The result was the volatile champion taking his negative backstage baggage to the ring with him. As had been seen at *SummerSlam* the prior year when he was limited in his performance by a McMahon edict banning violence during his ladder match with Scott Hall, it was a recipe for disaster. Much like at *SummerSlam* that unhappiness manifested itself into clearly visible unprofessional conduct, as Michaels' temper erupted with the entire WWF audience as a witness.

There was an unusual atmosphere in the crowd right from the start of the match. They had just seen a bizarre card in the dark and were obviously distracted by it, spending much of the contest chatting amongst themselves. The lack of crowd participation gave the impression the bout was taking place at the end of a lengthy television taping rather than the main event of a pay-per-view. Furthermore, the relative quiet made the more vocal individuals in the crowd distinctly audible to the performers. One woman in particular could be heard clearly above the other 6,000 fans in the building, and she felt compelled to direct a tirade of abuse towards the polarising Michaels.

Usually he would have ignored the insults, but his simmering temper took over, and Michaels decided to respond in kind. "She had one of those voices that just grates on your nerves," he explains, "It was ruining the match. I yelled at her to shut up, which you could actually hear if you were watching on TV." Despite what he claims, Michaels did more than simply yell at the heckler to be quiet. While Smith had him prone in a chinlock, Shawn yelled over towards the woman, directing a foul-mouthed invective in her direction by demanding, "Shut up, ya fat skank!" Such was the vitriolic level of Michaels' response that fans sat around her who had otherwise been irritated by the catcalling were now on her side, turning on the supposed fan-favourite Michaels.

Referee Earl Hebner was visibly uncomfortable with Michaels' reaction to the fan. He was then given the unenviable task of duly informing the cantankerous WWF Champion that due to the earlier power outage, there was less time left for the match than expected and he needed to start taking it home. Upon being told the news Michaels, who was still nestled in Smith's mighty arms for the chinlock, immediately broke character and stopped selling. Instead he shrugged his shoulders and raised his hand in a gesture of resigning himself to defeat. His fit of temper spilled out in a further unprofessional way moments later. He purposely avoided a Smith knee that was supposed to look like it had hit him in the stomach, but still sent himself careening out of the ring where he lay prone on the floor. From behind the announce desk Vince McMahon was audibly at a loss to explain Michaels' purposeful sabotage of the match, stammering to find the words to cover for his actions.

Moments later the two grapplers went to the finish of the bout; a cheap double pinfall that resulted in neither man winning and served as a way to set up a rematch between the two the following month. So incensed was Michaels with how the match and his whole day had gone, that he let off steam at a hapless technician whose job was to cue the entrance music. He ranted at him because he happened to be there, rather than for any reason in particular. "I was frustrated and angry," he rationalised, "I was the champion and I had to deliver, especially at pay-per-views. But everything went wrong that day and it turned out to be the worst match of my career."

Usually Michaels' little outbursts would be quickly tempered by his friend Kevin Nash making light of the situation and keeping him grounded. But Nash was gone. Michaels looked around the locker room and found that his years of alienating the locker room left him with few allies. The Kliq had been broken up. Nash and Hall were in Atlanta, Waltman was taking time off to combat a pill addiction, and Levesque had his own problems to deal with thanks to his impending creative burial. Michaels was alone and he was miserable. "For the first time, I was starting to feel the pressure of being champion," he admits. It was a pressure that would cause his career-defining breakthrough year as WWF poster boy to consume him.

SIX

THE NIGHT AFTER BEWARE OF Dog, WCW presented its first two-hour episode of *Nitro*, live from Macon, Georgia. Scott Hall was scheduled to make his return to the company on the broadcast, though in what appeared to be a curious move, WCW did not promote his impending arrival at all. The reasons behind the tight-lipped tactics would soon become clear.

With their recent contract dealings handled through lawyers and agents, May 27 was the first time that Eric Bischoff and Scott Hall had seen each other since they had started negotiating back in February. Bischoff met Hall at the airport and personally drove him to the show, but he imparted some words of caution prior to unleashing him on television. With Hall's unsavoury reputation in mind and the news of the Curtain Call now widespread throughout the industry, the savvy VP warned, "Scott, we don't need it here. If you're gonna come here and you're gonna stir the pot and cause the trouble that I've heard you cause, I'm telling you; don't care, don't need it, don't want it." Hall was a little taken aback by the forthrightness of his new boss's remarks, but took them in his stride. He assured Bischoff that he was in WCW to be a team player and help the company grow, not merely for the money and cushy schedule.

Later that evening on *Nitro*, during an intentionally mundane encounter between former WWF midcard tag team wrestlers Mike Enos and Steve Doll, a commotion in one of the stands started diverting attention in the audience. The hullabaloo was caused by a denim-clad Hall, who calmly hopped over the security barrier and demanded a microphone. Announcers Tony Schiavone and Larry Zbyszko acted dumbstruck. They claimed Hall was an uninvited guest, subtly hinting that he was not supposed to be on the show because he worked elsewhere. Enos and Doll stopped wrestling and scurried out of the way, freeing the stage for Hall to address the *Nitro* audience. In his trademark Razor Ramon phony Cuban accent, he started:

Hey, you people, you know who I am, but you don't know why I'm here. Where is Billionaire Ted? Where is the Nacho Man? That punk can't even get in the building. Me? I go wherever I want, whenever I want. And where, oh where, is Scheme Gene? Cause I got a scoop for you. When that Ken doll look-a-like, when that weatherman wannabe comes out here later tonight, I got a challenge for him, for Billionaire

Ted, for the Nacho Man, and for anybody else in dubya-see-dubya. You wanna to go to war? You want a war? You're gonna get one.

The delivery and presentation of the promo in addition to the choice verbiage used were inspired. Hall was never referred to by any name, but with his slicked back hair, sham accent, ever-present toothpick and trademark swagger, it was clear to everyone watching that this was the WWF's Razor Ramon on *Nitro*. Ostensibly, he was representing the WWF in a hostile invasion of WCW. With the internet still in its infancy and the dirt sheets still an underground phenomenon that hit only a tiny fraction of the overall wrestling audience, few people even knew that Hall had left the WWF. His appearance on WCW television came as a complete surprise and created an instant, palpable buzz.

Bischoff wanted it that way. He was more than happy for fans to infer that Hall was a World Wrestling Federation vigilante, there to exact revenge on WCW for *Nitro* beating *Raw* so frequently. It was fantasy storytelling that many fans had dreamed about witnessing since the days of WCW's predecessor the NWA, and it instantly grabbed people's attention. Having Hall spout the same derogatory terms the WWF had coined to describe some of the players in the company during the Billionaire Ted spoofs was a perfect act of retribution for Bischoff, and it devilishly furthered the notion that Hall had been sent by Titan Sports. "It was brilliantly done," admits Michael Hayes, "Everyone in the WWF was glued to the TV watching the WCW show. It fulfilled the fantasy of every fan at that time who wanted to see WCW versus the WWF."

Soon Hall showed up again, confronting Bischoff directly at his announce booth and warning, "You want a war? You started it, we're gonna finish it." Following a minor fracas with WCW's top babyface Sting, Hall alluded to the introduction of someone else in his corner the following week, promising a "big surprise". It was of course Kevin Nash. Like Hall he turned up unnamed, playing a blatant facsimile of his WWF Diesel persona, missing only a black glove. "The perception was that we were sent by Vince to take over the company," admits Nash.

THE GALL of presenting the pair as invaders provoked outrage in the offices of Titan Towers. While it was never directly stated that either man was from the WWF, their wording and the way the announcers responded to their presence clearly suggested as much. With WCW referring to neither man by name, McMahon deemed it to be a scheme concocted to deceive his fans into believing the WWF had willingly sent Diesel and Razor Ramon to WCW for the onset of an inter-promotional war.

McMahon was already furious with the two wrestlers to begin with thanks to the manner of their departures and the parting gift of the Curtain Call. He had reached the end of his patience, so picked up the phone and angrily punched in the number of the company's chief attorney - the ever busy Jerry McDevitt. Vince could see that WCW's invasion angle was already working, so he desperately tried to prevent them from gaining any momentum by ordering McDevitt to file a request for a temporary restraining order on their use of Hall and Nash. His plan was to sabotage the forthcoming pay-per-view event featuring the pair as the headline attraction.

When that was rejected out of hand, McDevitt tried to sue WCW for anything he and Vince could dream up. He filed a lawsuit on June 20 that accused the Atlanta group of "verified complaint for unfair competition, trademark and trade dress infringement, and false designation of origin." McMahon simultaneously issued a press release expressing regret that he was forced into filing the suit at all, claiming that he had been, "pushed up against a wall," and "left with no other options to protect my company." In the case notes Titan claimed:

Plaintiff [WWF] contends that success in the professional wrestling business depends upon the development of interesting wrestling characters and storylines. Characters must have names, personalities, histories, relationships, personas, and visual appearances that appeal to consumers. Plaintiff alleges that WWF programming combines character -driven storylines with skilful wrestling while WCW has no reputation for creativity. TBS proposed inter-promotional matches in order to associate WCW with WWF, but Plaintiff rejected this idea.

After wrestling unsuccessfully with WCW, Scott Hall contracted to wrestle for Plaintiff. Plaintiff created a wrestling character for Hall called "Razor Ramon," alias "The Bad Guy," with a distinctive Hispanic accent, slicked back hair in a ponytail with a curl in the front, a toothpick in his mouth, a vest, and multiple chains around his neck. Plaintiff registered the service mark "Razor Ramon" with the U.S. Patent and Trademark Office. The contract provided that Plaintiff retained exclusive ownership of the character's name and likeness and the exclusive right to distribute copyrightable materials based on the character. Hall warranted that he would not enter other agreements conflicting with Plaintiff's contract rights.

Plaintiff developed Razor Ramon into one of its most popular characters. He has appeared in television broadcasts, live events, a two-hour videotape, several magazines, and is the subject of merchandise devoted to the character. He won WWF's Intercontinental Championship at least four times. The character is well-recognized by wrestling fans.

Plaintiff developed another character using wrestler Kevin Nash who wrestled unsuccessfully with defendant WCW. Nash and Plaintiff entered into a contract with provisions similar to Hall's contract. Nash's character was "Diesel," alias "Big Daddy Cool." Diesel's trade dress included a goatee beard and moustache, black leather pants, a black leather vest decorated with silver studs and tassels, a black low cut tank-top shirt, a black fingerless glove on the right hand, black elbow pads, black wrist bands, sunglasses, and black leather boots. Diesel is visibly different from the characters previously portrayed by Nash at WCW.

Diesel was added to Plaintiff's story lines and appeared in television broadcasts, commercial videotapes, magazines, and became the subject of merchandise. Like Razor Ramon, Diesel also became widely recognized and popular, winning the WWF Heavyweight Championship in 1995.

In 1993, Plaintiff promoted Razor Ramon and Diesel on its "Monday Night Raw" television program, which was broadcast weekly at 9:00 p.m. EST. In 1995, defendant TBS began broadcasting a competing program "WCW Monday Nitro" at the same time. Plaintiff alleges that TBS's broadcast continually disparaged WWF, while WCW agents circulated false rumours of Plaintiff's impending bankruptcy in order to lure wrestlers to WCW.

In 1996, enticed by WCW's promise of lucrative, guaranteed contracts, Hall and Nash contracted to wrestle with WCW. After the contracts were executed, Plaintiff alleges that defendant Bischoff planned to capitalize on the goodwill of the Razor Ramon and Diesel characters. Hall and Nash were to appear on WCW's broadcast as Razor Ramon and Diesel, supposedly representing WWF in an interpromotional battle. Before the broadcast, WCW's 900 hotlines told consumers that Razor Ramon and Diesel were considering leaving WWF for WCW, although in reality, they had already done so.

Defendants expanded the introductory broadcast to two hours, starting before Plaintiff's competing broadcast. Hall appeared in the persona of Razor Ramon, although the broadcast did not refer to him by name. The end of the broadcast falsely conveyed that interpromotional matches would thereafter air on TNT. Fans sent letters evidencing their presumption that Hall was performing as Razor Ramon for WWF on TNT. Plaintiff attempted to dispel the rumours by broadcasting that Hall and Nash were no longer associated with the WWF. Nevertheless, Hall appeared on two further WCW broadcasts, perpetuating the false presumption. Bischoff also indicated that the interpromotional matches would be seen on an upcoming pay-per-view program. Hall and Nash did appear on the pay-per-view program as the characters Razor Ramon and Diesel. Defendants, however, did not refer to them by any name.

As part of the suit Titan demanded that WCW cease and desist with a number of things they had been doing on television with the pair, in particular with regards to their apparent portrayal of registered WWF trademarks. The motions requested were:

1. WCW be prohibited from making any statements or visual indications that the WWF is affiliated in any way with this angle or that any wrestler appearing on the WCW programs are in any way affiliated with WWF.

2. Using any misleading description of fact that is likely to cause confusion or deceive the public as to the affiliation of any of the wrestlers appearing on any WCW programs.

3. Using any of Titan's trademarks for names or dress that would cause confusion among viewers.

4. Making references to Scott Hall as either "Razor Ramon" or "The Bad Guy" or presenting him with a Hispanic accent or being from a Hispanic background, with slicked black hair with a single curl in the front, with a toothpick in his mouth or behind his ear, gold chain or chains around his neck, wrestling shorts, wrestling boots, a vest, elbow and knee pads; razor blade jewellery or designs on his clothing or anything else used by Hall

during his WWF tenure that would cause consumers to believe he is portraying Razor Ramon

5. Making any references saying Hall is currently affiliated with WWF

6. Making any references to Kevin Nash as "Diesel" or "Big Daddy Cool" or presenting him in that character including a goatee-style beard and moustache, black tank-top, black pants, black leather boots, black vest, black fingerless glove or gloves, black sunglasses or anything else utilized by Titan during Nash's tenure with that organization.

7. Making any references saying Nash is currently affiliated with the WWF.

8. Presenting Hall, Nash or any other former Titan wrestler or personality without identifying that person by the character name they will use and explicitly stating which organization that performer is under contract to.

9. Prohibiting playing any videotapes on television or in commercials of Hall and Nash's appearances to this point on Nitro and the angle on the 6/16 PPV show.

10. State three times during every Nitro broadcast and on the preview show for the 7/7 PPV show that: "Scott Hall and Kevin Nash are both under contract to the WCW and all their actions since May 27, 1996 have been at the direction of WCW. Any statements made by us, or suggestion made by us, that Hall or Nash were affiliated with the WWF were false and misleading. The WWF was not, and has not been in any way affiliated with the portrayal of Hall and Nash since May 27, 1996 and there will not be any matches between WWF wrestlers and WCW wrestlers on Nitro, on any of our shows, or on any of our pay-per-views. Any statement or suggestion to that effect by WCW and TBS personnel was false. If you wish to view WWF wrestlers, you should watch the WWF's programs, including Monday Night Raw, which airs on the USA Network Monday nights at 9 p.m. EST.

Titan asked that WCW be forced to hand over all profits earned as a result of the so-called invasion angle. That extended to pay-per-view revenue from both the *Great American Bash* and the forthcoming *Bash at the*

Beach, which were heavily marketed around Nash and Hall appearing. They also demanded damages, and for WCW to cover all attorney fees.

Judge Peter Dorsey presided over a hearing with McDevitt and WCW attorney David Dunn on June 24, listening as the pair outlined their respective stances. Dunn rightly pointed out that scores of wrestlers had gone from WCW to the WWF and vice-versa without changing their personas significantly (with names such as Ric Flair, Vader, Arn Anderson, The Road Warriors and Jake Roberts amongst the many examples of that), yet this was the first time a lawsuit had ever been filed over it.[32] He pointed out that Hall was a WCW character before he turned up in New York as Razor Ramon, and that the Ramon presentation in itself was a fairly close approximation of Hall's WCW 'Diamond Studd' persona, having a similar look, hairstyle, and toothpick.

McDevitt's primary bone of contention was that Nash and Hall had so far appeared unnamed on WCW broadcasts, thus perpetuating a belief amongst viewers that they were playing Razor Ramon and Diesel. Sensing a simple resolution might be in the offing, Dorsey asked Dunn to have WCW tone down Hall's use of the Razor Ramon character traits. Dunn agreed, on the condition that Titan promised not to sue for anything that happened at the upcoming *Bash at the Beach* pay-per-view, correctly guessing that McDevitt would never agree to any such terms.

After listening to the lawyers argue for two hours, Judge Dorsey declared that he had no knowledge of wrestling - and no time for what he felt was a trivial case - until mid-July. That was music to the ears of WCW officials, as the date fell after the much-hyped *Bash at the Beach* pay-per-view on which Hall and Nash would make their in-ring debuts. The lack of a ruling meant Bischoff could proceed as planned, despite the WWF's best efforts afterwards to legally torpedo the entire angle.

Bischoff was annoyed by the lawsuit, though privately delighted that he was ruffling McMahon's feathers to the point that his rival felt he needed assistance from the courts. If McMahon was so moved as to draft in the judicial system to help him fight WCW, then what he was doing with Nash

---

[32] Ironically, the two companies were involved in a similar lawsuit in 1991, albeit with the roles reversed, following Ric Flair's jump to the WWF while still NWA Champion. The WWF gleefully promoted Flair as an outsider from a rival group, having him profess himself to be the "real World Champion". WCW took Titan to court and won, so Flair was forced to return the title. Undeterred, McMahon simply bought a new belt, an exact replica of the one Flair had returned, so WCW sued again. Once more they emerged victorious, with the precedent set that a title belt is the intellectual property of the group it represents. WWF were banned from using the title so McMahon digitized it on all television shows from that point on, until Flair became WWF Champion and McMahon dropped the angle.

and Hall was clearly having the desired impact. The higher ups at Turner were less amused. They admonished Bischoff, demanding he never pull any more stunts that could land them in legal hot water. He was issued with a formal warning, stating that he was to avoid any other potential copyright violations on all future programming. As Titan continued to pursue legal recourse and the lawsuit dragged on, Bischoff had little choice but to heed the warning and refrain from further violating WWF trademarks.[33]

Despite the WWF's attempts to quell WCW's momentum, the arrival of Hall and Nash in WCW and the fresh, edgy, and intriguing storyline they were part of would serve as the catalyst for *Nitro* to go on an unprecedented eighty three week winning streak against *Raw*. While the WWF won the ratings battle the night Nash turned up on *Nitro*, it would prove to be the final time they did for two frustrating years. The two companies had been neck-and-neck, with the war finely balanced and no clear winner emerging, until the Outsiders - the new name for the pair coined by Gene Okerlund - showed up and changed the game. The Kliq's proclamations of dominating the wrestling business on two fronts seemed to be coming true.

FOLLOWING THE Curtain Call debacle, the disastrous *Beware of Dog* pay-per-view, and the outrage at WCW's faux invasion, Vince McMahon's difficult week quickly turned into a fretful fortnight. On the Tuesday following Hall's *Nitro* debut, two days after the power outage in Florence, he received a fax from Wigan-born British grappler Davey Boy Smith, delineating that he was giving his ninety day notice.

---

[33] Eventually, WCW filed a motion to dismiss all the charges levelled at them by Titan, and an expensive four year long court battle ultimately ensued. By the time the case was settled in 2000, Bischoff was practically out of the picture and the WWF had long since surpassed the ailing WCW in all areas of business. Things were so bad for the Atlanta group, they were barely even considered competition anymore. The eventual ruling was a symbolic victory for Titan, however it did contain within it something that had future far-reaching implications: one of the more notable terms of the settlement was that should WCW ever be liquidated, then the WWF would have the right to bid on the company's assets. It was an "in" for Titan that they would not have otherwise had, but was considered such an unlikely scenario by the Turner legal team that it did not duly concern them - they willingly accepted the proposal. A year later WCW did fold, and Vince McMahon was right there to gleefully pick up the pieces. He bought the entire WCW tape library, a number of lower level talent contracts and the physical attributes owned by the group for a cool $2.5 million. It was a tiny sum for something with so much potential market and distribution value. As Chris Jericho later quipped, "If I had known how much WCW was available for, I would have bought it myself!" Upon buying WCW, Vince proceeded to destroy any remaining vestige of the company, presenting his own in-house inter-promotional war in which WWF wrestlers routinely hammered their WCW counterparts. In owning both WCW and the WWF, McMahon had become the selfsame monopolistic billionaire that he had lampooned Turner for so readily, and he could not have been happier about it.

It had been a trying few years for Smith. He had recently fought a lawsuit ongoing since 1993 that could have resulted in his incarceration for up to fourteen years, which had finally reached trial in January 1996. It stemmed from an incident that occurred on July 25, 1993 in Calgary. Smith and his wife Diana had attended southern Alberta's annual Rockyford Rodeo that day and were looking to unwind with friends in the evening. They decided to hit notorious Calgary hotspot the Back Alley Bar, a venue famed for playing popular rock music at ear-splitting volumes, and colloquially nicknamed "Crack Alley" by locals due to the drug and fight culture which defined it.

As Smith relaxed with a few beers and caught up with old acquaintances, Diana took to the dance floor with her friend's teenage son. The amity was broken when nineteen-year-old bar patron Kody Light, a student from the nearby Devry Institute, sidled up alongside Diana and made his move. Light had already been admonished by bouncers less than an hour earlier for harassing females in the club, but he did not heed the warning. Deeply intoxicated from having propped up the bar since the club opened that evening, he was obnoxious and belligerent in his discourse. Reaching forward, Light grabbed Diana's vest with his finger, "When a beautiful chick like you and a geek like that are screwing, who's on top?" he asked sordidly.

Diana was revolted by the line of questioning, but growing up in a household with eight brothers she felt she knew a thing or two about how to handle men. Deciding that the best course of action was to ignore Light, she turned her back on him. Unrelenting, Light lustfully thrust himself in Diana's direction. She remained nonplussed, dismissing him as nothing more than a sophomoric dolt unable to handle his liquor.

Davey had no idea that his wife had been accosted in such a manner when at 1:20 a.m. he strolled over to the dance floor tapping his watch, motioning that it was time to leave. "Hey, I'm talking to the lady," butted in Light, entirely unaware that the two were an item. "That's my husband!" yelled Diana. Davey Boy, still unsure what was going on, bewilderedly validated the statement, "That's my wife," he confirmed. "You've got a nice fucking wife!" smirked Light in response.

Smith was beginning to grasp what was going on, but decided that since no real harm had been done it would be best to leave the situation alone and forget about it. At that point the six-foot-three Light reached forward and grabbed Smith's hand, then began pumping it vigorously. It was not a respectful or even congratulatory handshake, rather a tough-guy grip designed to test how strong Davey was.

Sensing that Light was yet another opportunist pugilist looking to make a name for himself by brawling with a wrestler, Smith tried to diffuse the matter. "Thank you very much, I just want to let go [of the handshake] and leave," he told the teenager. In the heat of the moment, Light made a split-second decision that would cost him far more than he could have ever realised; he was going to fight. He lunged forward and tried to headbutt Smith, who immediately snapped into a defensive stance and snatched his assailant in a controlled front face lock. It was the standard go-to move for wrestlers in out-of-the-ring fights with intoxicated patrons, because it ensured the problem was instantly defused but did not leave them open for litigation for having thrown a punch.

Smith walked Light over to the building's rear exit door where some of the clubs bouncers were situated and told them, "This guy is trying to cause a problem, get him away from me." With that Smith released Light from the hold and turned around to find Diana so they could leave. When he turned around again, his heart sank. Rather than in the care of the bouncers, Light was sprawled out unconscious on the club's tiled concrete floor. Shards of broken glass from discarded drink vessels were embedded in his skull. The combination of a slick liqueur-covered floor, lack of coordination from the alcohol he had consumed, and a surge of blood rushing to his head after Smith released him from the face lock, caused Light to fall and smash his head.

An ambulance was immediately called. Davey and Diana decided to wait for it to arrive to make sure Light had not been seriously hurt, but by now word was starting to spread about the incident. Light's friends and other random drunkards looking to cause trouble had learned what had happened. They started to chastise Smith, with some challenging him to fights in the parking lot. The bouncers advised the couple that the best thing they could do was leave the club, which they did immediately.

THINGS BEGAN to spiral for Smith when he left his well-paid job with WCW a few months later due to a messy contract dispute. Smith had negotiated his initial deal with Bill Watts, but by the end of the year Watts was gone and pre-existing financial promises meant little. The issue of contention was that Smith felt he deserved to be compensated more for European tours than his regular U.S. payoff, due to his strong name value across the Atlantic. Watts had agreed, given that Smith was signing for the company less than six months after main eventing *SummerSlam* at Wembley Stadium in front of 80,000 people. Unfortunately for Smith, freshly sworn-in company Executive Vice President Eric Bischoff felt differently, refusing to adhere to the terms of the oral contract because he was desperately trying to save money across the board. He did not consider paying Smith anything extra to be worth the additional outlay.

With business in the United States at its lowest ebb, some cards in the country were struggling to draw even in the low hundreds. Meanwhile, WCW's October 1993 tour of England played before strong and sometimes sell-out crowds, and Smith felt he was primarily responsible for the packed houses. Bischoff disagreed. He argued that WCW was popular in the market due to a deal with terrestrial station ITV that covered the entire United Kingdom, believing it had little to do with Smith.

Thus Bischoff paid Smith at the same per-match rate as he received for his U.S. shots, resulting in the pair engaging in a heated verbal exchange at the Orlando Marriott hotel. Irate, Davey Boy threatened to no-show the company's upcoming television taping if the situation was not rectified. Not wanting to lose one of the few names on his roster with mainstream name value, Bischoff was about to concede and give Smith what he wanted. Then in walked company President Bob Dhue.

By late 1993, Bischoff and Dhue were locked in a power struggle, frequently clashing over the future direction of WCW. Dhue was sharp-witted, smartly-dressed, and intelligent in his dealings. He saw Bischoff as something of a loose cannon, too casual in his approach to business and overly eager to get along with the wrestlers instead of making bold calls that benefitted the company. Dhue refused to sanction the additional payment to Smith, reminding Bischoff that WCW was already haemorrhaging money. In response, Smith made good on his promise, failing to turn up for television and subsequently leaving the company.

Smith returned to his Florida home for the holidays with the intention of flying back to England to work for veteran promoter Max Crabtree, but then the Kody Light incident reared its head again. Smith had not heard much outside of a few rumblings regarding any potential fallout from the altercation for four months. It was only when Diana called home on Christmas Day to catch up with her family that one of her brothers informed her that the police in Calgary were looking for Davey and had a warrant for his arrest. Smith had suspected this might be coming and returned to the city to turn himself in, confident that he had done nothing wrong. He was immediately held in custody at Calgary's newly erected Remand Center on a charge of aggravated assault, then had to suffer the humiliation of his father-in-law - grizzled ring veteran Stu Hart paying to bail him out.

Light was pressing charges, suing Smith for $1.3 million as a result of the injuries he had suffered during the fracas. Light had ended up with a fractured skull, a loss of hearing on one side, and impaired motor, cognitive and speech skills, and was forced to spend over six weeks in hospital following the altercation. There was more to it than that: Light was claiming that the injuries came as a result of Smith attacking him for dancing with Diana, punching and choking him and then smashing him into a wall. This, he said, is what resulted in him falling on the floor and sustaining permanent brain damage.

Representing Light was Crown Attorney Gary Belecki, a long-haired would-be-cowboy with a blonde Fu Manchu and a boisterous, shouty demeanour. With an inherent disdain for professional wrestling, he was the ideal person for Light to have arguing his corner. Belecki's mode of attack was to suggest that highly trained athlete Smith had performed a wrestling move known as the piledriver on Light. Belecki intended to claim this as the cause of his client's extensive head injuries. It was a ploy designed to garner sympathy. Belecki was going to cast Smith as a dangerous trained fighter who had mercilessly pummelled a helpless teenager into a coma, simply for having accidentally danced with his wife.

It was such a departure from the truth that Belecki had a hard time finding any witnesses who would give credence to his story. He had initially lined up Alberta's former Chief Medical Examiner Dr. John Butt as his primary witness, but upon learning of the intended allegations Butt refused to concur with the story. He was adamant that a piledriver would not have resulted in the injuries Light had received, insisting they were more consistent with a slip and fall. It was a major blow for the loud-mouthed lawyer, and concerned that his entire case was in disarray, he requested that the June 12, 1995 trial[34] be postponed until January 1996, much to the annoyance of Smith's defence attorney Alain Hepner.

When the case finally did reach the courtroom, Belecki had managed to find a trio of patrons in attendance at the Back Alley Bar on the night of the alleged assault that were willing to back up Light's claims. Notably Peter MacKenzie, a friend of the defendant, testified that Smith had started the fight by punching Light and then caused his injuries by hurtling him head-first into a brick wall. The other two prosecution witnesses had stories based on a similar premise, but their respective accounts differed significantly to what MacKenzie and the other had described. The one shared thread was that each of the three suggested Smith had used a

---

[34] The trial had originally been scheduled for October 1994 but was pushed back.

wrestling move in the supposed attack, though the specifics explaining which move it was varied wildly.

The defence witnesses were far more consistent, substantiating Smith's original story that he had grabbed Light to control him and then handed him over to the club's bouncers. "He just fell down and hit his head," testified witness Robin Holstein. Another patron, Holstein's partner Melodie Braun told the same tale. "He just fell back on the floor, which was slippery from spilled drinks, and landed on his head," she insisted. Both refuted claims that Smith had pushed Light over or used any wrestling move on him at any point during the scuffle.

Realising he was struggling to win over the jury, Belecki decided to change tact by attempting to present Smith as a violent bully. He assumed that professional wrestling's inner workings were such a closely guarded secret that Smith would never admit it was all pre-determined. Sticking to the sacred oath of kayfabe would force Smith to admit that everything he had ever done in the ring was real. Belecki felt the admission, true or not, would give Smith a lengthy background of participation in real fights, making him come off as a brutal sadist who was fully capable of hurling someone across a room. "Every single thing in wrestling is fake," declared Smith reluctantly from the witness box, to the shock and outrage of far fewer than Belecki had expected, though to the obvious dismay of the near-beaten lawyer.

IT WAS hardly news. Vince McMahon himself had admitted as much in 1992 via Federation lobbyist Jim Tillman during a battle with the Florida State Athletic Commission. The FSAC were determined to regulate professional wrestling in the state, a move they argued would give fans better value for money as they would be offered immediate refunds if advertised performers no-showed. They also claimed it would help prove whether wrestling really was gripped by a drug culture - the hot topic at the time - as it would mean all WWF wrestlers taking drug tests three hours prior to performing in Florida. The third reason for pushing the bill was fiscal. Licensing fees incurred would be to the tune of around $140,000 per annum, which Titan felt was the real reason for the attempted legislation.

FSAC executive director Don Hazelton made his case to the committee. He asked that wrestling be regulated in the same way as boxing, thus potentially exposing the WWF's rumoured widespread steroid use. Much like Belecki four years later, what Hazelton did not expect was for the wrestling business to be so eager about opening its book of secrets. "Wrestling is not a professional sport, it is, purely and simply, sports entertainment," replied Tillman calmly. "Wrestlers are not professional athletes. They are no different from the Harlem Globetrotters, a circus, a rock band or Willie Nelson," he concluded. The bill was killed with an eight-to-one majority, and the WWF remained unregulated and untested. If Hazelton had done his research, he would have been aware that McMahon and his team had pulled the same stunt already three years earlier when fighting the New Jersey commission over similar attempted legislation.

It was something Belecki too probably should have been aware of before heading down the kayfabe route, but he was undeterred. He reasoned that if Smith was not a real-life bully then he was a phony, and theatrically called him as such. "To put it bluntly, you're a fraud," he roared with disdain. Smith remained calm, "If you want to put it that way," he coolly answered, refusing to be drawn into a slanging match. Belecki persisted with his zealous verbal assault, demanding, "You are putting on a show for Calgary and the world aren't you?", attempting to convey that Smith was also lying in his denials of having slammed Light onto the nightclub floor. Justice John Waite interjected, reminding Belecki that Smith was under oath. As had been consistent throughout the trial, Smith denied having ever performed any wrestling move in the brawl.

Smith further testified that the prosecution witness's claims of him having executed a wrestling hold were patently false, because the majority of moves involved a great deal of cooperation between both parties involved. Further lifting the lid on wrestling's secrets, Smith told the courtroom that the moves he was accused of doing to Light would not have been possible without his assistance. He was backed up on this point by local former Stampede wrestlers, though some were not as quick to jump to Smith's defence.

Long-time Stampede Wrestling announcer Ed Whalen, who had worked with the Harts for decades, turned down a plea from the family to write a character reference for Davey. Whalen intended on running for political office and did not want to get involved, which caused a permanent rift between him and some of the Harts. Another long-time Calgary wrestler, Karl Moffat, did show up as a witness. He was there on his own accord after calling Belecki to tell him he would happily rubbish Smith's assertion that a wrestling move could not be executed without cooperation.

Moffat had been at war with Smith and the Harts for years, stemming from a falling out seven years earlier. On July 4, 1989, Smith had been involved in a serious car accident while riding with Moffat, Ross Hart, Sumu Hara and Chris Benoit. Moffat shattered his leg and was out of wrestling for a year. He was never the same when he returned, so attempted to sue driver Ross. Realising he needed backup, Moffat had asked Smith to support the lawsuit, but given his family ties the request was swiftly repudiated. Moffat's appearance in court was entirely vindictive, and Ross Hart had to be brought in as a counter witness to explain the situation, rendering his appearance worthless.

More damning was a testimony from local Calgary Police Service officer Sydney Sutherland. He recounted an incident that he claimed to have been privy to where Smith grabbed a fellow officer by his belt and collar, then lifted him up and threw him six feet across the street. He stated this proved Smith did indeed have the strength to perform the wrestling moves he was accused of doing, without needing assistance from the person he was doing them to.

Whether cooperation was required to execute the moves the prosecution claimed occurred mattered little once Dr. John Butt took the stand. In a canny move, Alain Hepner had turned to the prosecution's one-time key medical witness and convinced him to testify for the benefit of Smith. "It is a classic injury for people falling backwards on a hard surface," he stated, adding that a throw would have likely resulted in Light landing on the top of his head. "I find it difficult to see how somebody is going to land that low on their head [from the wrestling moves claimed]."

On February 7, 1996 Court of Queen's Bench Justice John Waite returned with a verdict. He ruled that Smith had acted in self defence and was not guilty, and thus acquitted of all charges. He summarised, "Light's actions could be properly characterised as an assault on Smith. The rights of a professional wrestler are no different than any other citizen. The accused's conduct in placing Light in a front face lock is properly characterised as a legitimate act of self-defence. The accused's conduct throughout, in my opinion, was entirely justified."

Smith was overcome with emotion upon learning of the verdict. Even though he knew he had done little wrong throughout the ordeal, he also realised that as a celebrity wrestler there was the possibility he would be vilified. "This was the worst fight of my life," said a relieved Smith, before rashly lambasting Light for bringing about the lawsuit. "He thinks I make a lot of money so he tried to sue me," he snarled, before Hepner hurriedly took him to one side for a private consultation.

Realising he had spoken out of turn and that the throng of reporters might interpret his comments as heartless and uncaring, Smith added, "I feel really bad for what happened to Kody Light, but it wasn't my fault." Smith told the gathered assembly that he was worried about his reputation amongst children, noting that if he had been found guilty it would have ruined him. Light meanwhile was melancholy, expressing disquiet at the way he was portrayed in court as an aggressive drunk. When pressed, he was forced to admit that due to his brain damage he remembered nothing of the incident, or that he was even at the bar the night it occurred.

SMITH'S CONTRACT issue was yet another headache for Vince McMahon in a month that had been full of them. Unlike Scott Hall and Kevin Nash, Smith was not looking for a move to WCW after handing in his resignation. Rather, he was attempting to leverage a superior deal to the one he had been working with, because the trial had cost him around half a million dollars and he was verging on broke. Even though Smith claimed he was not planning to jump ship, McMahon had heard the same thing directly from Hall and Nash, and he was determined not to lose Davey Boy in the same manner. Smith was a key component in the WWF's European operations, and generally the most popular performer in the company when the WWF crossed the Atlantic. With U.S. business hit and miss, the European market was the WWF's one strong advantage over WCW, which by 1996 had a limited international presence outside of *Nitro* airing on basic cable channel *TNT* in the United Kingdom four days after it broadcast in America.

Smith had actually sent his notice prior to *Beware of Dog*, but due to Vince travelling on the road for the pay-per-view and the following night's live *Raw*, he was not made aware of the situation until the Tuesday, the night of the live *Beware of Dog II* replay airing. Smith was unhappy with a number of things in the Federation, namely the scale of his payoffs relative to his position on the card. He felt that as he had co-headlined a series of pay-per-view main events over the prior twelve months he should be recompensed appropriately, which he did not believe had been the case. He also wanted to be utilised better at non-televised live events, complaining that he should be wrestling in headline matches rather than working throwaway tag bouts and doing jobs for newcomer Ahmed Johnson.

Furthermore, Smith was unsatisfied with the creative direction he was booked in that saw wife Diana integrated into his storyline feud with Shawn Michaels. The long-term booking of the program called for Diana to make a pass at Shawn and try to bed him, only for Michaels to reject her advances. Jilted, Diana would then return to Smith and make claims that Michaels had come on to her first. Despite how Bruce Prichard and Jim Cornette tried to sell it as a great storyline, Davey loathed the idea.

"It makes me look like an asshole," Davey told them, pointing out that if his wife was trying to hit on Michaels then he should have a problem with her, not with Shawn. Smith didn't buy the justification that he would not be aware of Diana having initiated the affair, or that he would believe Diana over anyone else simply because he loved her. "Why wouldn't someone in the locker room tell me? Or why wouldn't I have seen what really happened on TV?" he asked logically. The Hart family did not much care for the angle either, primarily because Diana was playing herself rather than an overblown and obviously fabricated character. Her father Stu Hart was up in arms when he learned of the planned storyline, ranting and raving to Diana about how disgusting he found the whole thing, while threatening to stretch whoever was responsible. "Why would I want to watch my daughter doing a role like that?" he steamed.

Stu was so concerned about Diana's portrayal as a licentious trollop, that he contacted the WWF office to speak with Jim Cornette. The Hart family patriarch had a lot of time for Cornette. Knowing he was involved in the angle onscreen as well as working for the writing team, he wanted an explanation as to why Diana was, "made to look like some kind of whore." Having been handed the corded red phone (that he later noted, "looked like the phone that Commissioner Gordon called Batman on,") by notorious prankster Owen Hart, Cornette assumed that he was about to be on the receiving end of an elaborate rib. Like many of the other former territorial promoters, Stu was amongst the boys' favourites to imitate. Cornette knew that fellow booking agent Bruce Prichard did a particularly convincing impression of the esteemed Canadian, so assumed it was he on the other end of the line. It was not. It was the real Stu Hart, who spent the following five minutes listening aghast as Cornette ran down Prichard with revelations that he was a sexual deviant, and the man solely responsible for the offending Diana storyline. Stu took the information on board and expressed his surprise that Prichard was the apparent pervert that Cornette claimed he was, then decreed that he would speak with Vince about the situation. Suffice to say, the angle was dropped shortly thereafter.

As negotiations between Davey Boy and Titan rumbled on, over in Atlanta Eric Bischoff learned of Smith's contract situation and decided to offer him a deal. In a much stronger financial position than he had been in 1993, Bischoff promised Smith half a million dollars per year guaranteed - the same figure Smith had lost defending himself in the Light case - along with the significantly reduced schedule that had proven so popular with Hall and Nash when they inked their deals a month prior. Members of the office at Turner were privately confident that a deal with Smith was practically confirmed, and earmarked his debut for the September 2 edition of *Monday Nitro*. When Smith met with McMahon again on June 6 at Titan

Tower, he informed the chairman that WCW had offered him a big money deal to defect to Atlanta, but reiterated that he did not want to leave the WWF. McMahon assured him that no offence was intended to his family with the Diana angle and the pair put that ordeal behind them. Even so, Smith still did not give Vince any firm assurances that he was staying, simply that he was leaning in that direction.

Though he kept his cards close to his chest during negotiations, Smith's loyalties laid with McMahon, the WWF and his family who worked there. He was in a relatively strong position on the card, especially in Europe where he remained a huge star. Conversely, in the overcrowded WCW he realised he would likely be lost in the shuffle. Smith also remembered the way he had been treated the last time he was in the company and was reluctant to go back, despite assurances from friend Hulk Hogan that he would make sure he was well looked after.

He mulled over the respective deals, taking negotiations right down to the wire before finally putting pen to paper on a five year contract with Titan worth a minimum of $250,000 per annum. Even though it was not the main event money he had hoped from, the long-term security of the deal, the addition of substantial royalties, and pay-per-view payoffs meant Smith would be earning on par with, if not more than, what WCW had offered him. The addition of a promised lengthy Tag Team Title run with brother-in-law Owen Hart had also been enough to convince Smith that his future was with the WWF. Little over a year later he would come to regret that decision immensely, ending up in a situation where he had to pay $150,000 to buy out the remainder of his contract.

SEVEN

VINCE DID NOT HAVE MUCH time to sit and take stock of the past two weeks' tumultuous happenings; instead he had to focus his energies on finding a replacement winner for the forthcoming *King of the Ring* tournament. With Hunter Hearst Helmsley's scheduled ascension now off the cards, McMahon scanned his roster looking for an answer, determined not to err as he had done a year earlier in opting to put the cape and crown on blubbery midcarder Nelson 'Mabel' Frazer. He did not have to look far. McMahon decided to hand one of his famous brass rings to a rising star on his roster who had recently took stock of his lot and demanded a change in the way he was presented: 'Stone Cold' Steve Austin.

Earlier in the year the proud Texan, a gravel-voiced ring technician clad in plain black trunks and boots, was performing under the guise of The Ringmaster when he pulled McMahon aside during a television taping. Frustrated with his dead-end, ill-fitting gimmick, Austin requested that he be given a chance to come up with a different ring name and a fresh persona for himself. "Vince, I'm not The Ringmaster. I'm just not feeling it," he told the chairman matter-of-factly. "Well, okay. Who *are* you then? You're a master of what you do in the ring - it's logical," dismissed McMahon in response. Austin refused to back down, determined that he would rather lose his job for pushing McMahon than be forced to work as a character that he had no affinity with. He already had something else in mind having recently seen an inspiring documentary on serial killer 'The Iceman' Richard Kulinski. He wanted his WWF persona to be reborn as a similarly bald, bearded, ruthless, cold-hearted killer type, and he pitched the idea to Vince.

Admiring Austin's brassy determination, McMahon agreed to consider the request, telling him, "We'll give it some thought and maybe we'll come up with something else." Austin was dismayed when the WWF's creative team came back to him a few days later with a list of potential names that had missed the point entirely. They had interpreted the reference to 'The Iceman' as meaning Austin wanted temperature-based monikers, with suggestions including Chilly McFreeze, Fang McFrost, Ice Dagger and Austin's personal favourite: Otto von Ruthless.

"Those names came from a department in the WWF called Creative Services," explains Jim Cornette. "Whenever you would sit around a table with Vince and get ideas for new talent, Vince would ask for Creative

Services to come up with names for them based on what their M.O. was going to be. So if a guy was going to be a plumber, then they would write down names based on plumbers, which is where something like T.L. Hopper came from. Vince would get ideas for outfits and tell Creative Services to design him something that looked like the vision in his head. But they weren't wrestling people, they were trained monkeys."

Seemingly on an entirely different wavelength to his employer and the people tasked with driving his onscreen career, Austin grumbled about the situation to his English wife Jeanie. He admitted to being at his wits end, unable to bear the thought of having to go back to the office with no alternative to the names he had so vehemently shot down. As he paced around his Texas home struggling to come up with something, Austin began contemplating how he would go about trying to make one of the inane ideas the WWF had presented him with work. Then Jeanie said something that changed not only his career, but ultimately the course of the entire wrestling industry.

"Steve, calm down and give it a rest for a while. Don't worry about it, you'll think of something. Now come on, drink your tea before it gets *stone cold*." Unwittingly, she had stumbled across the perfect nickname for a character that would soon capture the zeitgeist of a generation. 'Stone Cold' fit the description perfectly. It was *exactly* what Austin wanted. Sure enough, Vince let Austin go with the name, although it was not because he was particularly enthused by it. In fact, he barely even cared. As Cornette remembers, "Vince didn't give a shit about Steve Austin anymore. Nothing was working and all else had failed, so Steve was told to just go out there and fucking do it, do whatever he wanted. He got to be himself, and the rest is history."

DESPITE A name change, Austin - noted for his oratory skills during his brief ECW run prior to signing with Titan - remained hampered by an onscreen association with mouthpiece Ted DiBiase. Because McMahon's first impression of Austin was that he was a bland ring technician lacking in charisma, he paired him with DiBiase, who did all the talking while Austin stood in silence and grimaced, attempting to look menacing.

It was only DiBiase handing in his notice that allowed Austin to break free of those shackles. Once one of McMahon's top hands in the late eighties, the 'Million Dollar Man' had become jaded with life on the road. His passion for the wrestling business had long since faded, and after a twenty year career he wanted to go home to be with his family. He had been with McMahon for nearly a decade and wanted to leave him the right way, but he also wanted to make sure that his resignation fit the legal requirements of his contract. He decided to have his attorney draft the letter to make sure it was officially in writing.

Vince received word of DiBiase's intention to leave the day after the original cursed *Beware of Dog* pay-per-view show during a live *Raw* taping. He was upset that yet another one of his talents had lacked the fortitude to approach him face-to-face. When he encountered DiBiase at the taping he told him bluntly, "I got your letter. You finish tomorrow at the pay-per-view." DiBiase was disappointed that his departure was not entirely amicable and apologised for how his WWF tenure was ending, then the two shook hands and parted ways.[35]

Later that day, DiBiase was asked to shoot an angle in which he declared that should Steve Austin lose to Savio Vega in the second run of their strap match, then he would leave the WWF forever. Suffice to say, Austin lost a blistering rematch and DiBiase was gone for good. It was an inglorious way for him to end what had been a stellar career in New York - one that had even seen him given a brief albeit 'unofficial' run as WWF Champion in 1988. For Austin it was great news. While he had no problem with DiBiase personally, who had always been there to offer advice during his first few troubled months with Titan, his departure allowed him to finally fly solo and start building momentum on his own.

Despite intending to leave the business, like most others who left the WWF during the Monday Night Wars, DiBiase soon wound up in WCW once his ninety day non-compete clause had expired. He was introduced to the fans as 'Billionaire Ted', an obvious nod-cum-dig at Vince's *Wrasslin' Warroom* skits. An even more blatant shot at Titan was WCW's hiring of DiBiase's one-time WWF man-servant Mike 'Virgil' Jones[36], who was given the name 'Vincent' (after McMahon) to amuse Eric Bischoff. Jones was accustomed to being the butt of the joke. His Virgil moniker in the WWF in the first place had been a jab at then NWA booker Virgil 'Dusty Rhodes' Runnels. Jones did not mind: he was just grateful to have a regular job on television again.

---

[35] DiBiase returned to the WWF in 2004 as a road agent and occasional onscreen cameo performer, but he despised the agent job and by his own admission was not cut out for the role.

[36] The post-wrestling career of Mike Jones was one of the business's strangest tales. Following the demise of WCW in 2001, Jones found himself out of a job. He decided to try to live off his past glories by hitting the convention circuit, hawking his signed apparel wherever he could. But interest was low due to his overexposure, and he became an internet wrestling meme; the sad, lonely ex-wrestler who no one cared about anymore. Jones became so desperate that he began trying to flog his wares in increasingly unconventional areas, from subway stations to trailer parks.

WITH DIBIASE gone, management deemed that Austin using the Million Dollar Dream sleeper hold as his finishing manoeuvre was no longer appropriate, nor did it fit the mentality of his new 'Stone Cold' persona. They felt Austin needed something explosive and impactful that he could hit without warning, and road agent Michael Hayes had exactly the move for him to try.

It was during a *Raw* taping in Fayetteville, North Carolina on May 27, 1996 that Hayes came up to Austin and asked, "Hey kid, you got a minute? I wanna show you something." As a child, Austin had grown up idolising Hayes, watching in awe as he tore up the famous Sportatorium in Dallas, Texas week after week in Fritz Von Erich's World Class promotion. He held the former Fabulous Freebird in high regard, so was happy to listen to any advice he had to offer. "I think I have come up with a better finishing move for you," Hayes told him as they walked to the ring. In fact Hayes had not come up with the move at all, but rather had recently watched a tape sent to him by John 'Johnny Ace' Laurinitis, featuring him blowing the roof off Japan's Budokan Hall on April 3 in a classic tag team match alongside Steve Williams. Titan turned down Ace's request for work, but the match stuck in Hayes' memory - and in particular a move he used called the Ace Crusher; the manoeuvre he presented to Austin.

It was brilliant in its simplicity, with the executor reaching back and grabbing his opponent's head in a three-quarter face lock, then dropping down to a seated position to give a whiplash type effect. There was nothing else like it in the WWF, and Austin was instantly sold. Not only was it possible to perform the hold on any member of the roster - one of the key components of a successful finisher, but it also fit the disposition of the burgeoning character down to a tee.

Austin remembers the day well, "We were assisted by several willing volunteers that were around ringside. These guys let me experiment and get the hang of it. I was sold. This would be my new finish from that point on. When I first started using the Stunner - as it would come to be named - I simply went into the manoeuvre without a setup. It was delivered with no anticipation. I'm a little fuzzy on this, but I'm almost positive that Michael and I were talking about the move happening too fast, and that the crowd could not anticipate the action because it happened out of the blue. I needed some type of setup move *á la* Jake Roberts' signature short-arm clothesline that he delivered before unleashing the DDT. An easy and quick solution to this was a kick to the gut, which perfectly set the victim into an effective "ready" position. Not only was the kick effective as a weapon to neutralize my opponent, it was also a visual signal to the crowd that the Stunner was next."

Without DiBiase filching his limelight, and with the 'Stone Cold Stunner' finisher turning heads, Austin built up so much momentum in the four weeks between his former manager's departure and the *King of the Ring* tournament, that Vince McMahon deemed him worthy of being booked to win the coveted crown. His route to victory started nearly a month before the pay-per-view event when on that same fateful night in Fayetteville he was given a victory over Bob Holly in a first round qualifying match. Because Austin did not have chance to clear the use of the Stunner as his new finish with McMahon, he won the contest via the outmoded Million Dollar Dream. Later in the night, during another *King of the Ring* bout opposite Savio Vega, he used the move for the first time to score victory. It was a perfect fit for him.

THE FOLLOWING three-and-a-half weeks saw Austin's stock rise as he headed towards the pay-per-view. He was determined to take full advantage of the opportunity he was afforded as a result of the Curtain Call fallout. He worked hard, wanting to prove to Vince and the fans that he was the right choice to wear the proverbial and literal crowns. He wanted both to see that he could be a main event player in the WWF. "Steve started finding that character," remembers Mick Foley, "On a weekly basis you could see it growing."

By the time the live pay-per-view from Milwaukee rolled around on June 23, Austin was ready. He opened the show in a tournament semi-final opposite Marc Mero, who after only three months with the company was already seeing his push stall. He was not connecting with an audience who were more preoccupied with Sable - exactly as Jim Cornette had predicted. Austin dealt Mero his first television loss in a hard-hitting fifteen minute scrap following the Stunner. However, there was a problem: Mero had bust open Austin's lip with an errant boot. He would need stitches to close the wound otherwise he risked being left with an unsightly scar. Austin was rushed off to the emergency room at a local hospital to have sixteen stitches inserted into his mouth, then whisked back to the building for his second match of the evening.

With practically no time to prepare, Austin wondered precisely what he could say in the customary post-victory coronation speech upon defeating final opponent Jake Roberts. As he rushed to the curtain from the ambulance his head was racing with ideas. Then he bumped into Hayes. The former Freebird would be conducting the interview after the match, and he had already talked with Roberts earlier in the show. "What did Jake say?" asked Austin, to which Hayes informed him that Roberts had brought up his religion, saying he wanted to win the tournament as an act of personal redemption.

Instantly an idea began to formulate in Austin's mind. When watching college football he had noticed that there was always a giant "John 3:16" sign in the end zone, clearly visible and obviously memorable. It was at that moment he realised "Austin 3:16" had a pretty nice ring to it. He didn't have time to run the idea past anyone, but figured it likely would not be an issue anyway. He had also learned from his experience in the industry that sometimes pleading for forgiveness after the fact was better than asking for permission in the first place. In the match with Roberts, Austin was allowed to make short work of the veteran in something of a torch-passing moment, then adlibbed a career-changing interview with Hayes:

> The first thing I want to be done is to get that piece of crap out of my ring. Don't just get him out of the ring, get him out of the WWF, because I proved, son, without a shadow of a doubt; you ain't got what it takes anymore! You sit there, and you thump your bible, and you say your prayers, and it didn't get you anywhere. Talk about your Psalms, talk about John 3:16 – Austin 3:16 says I just whipped your ass! All he's gotta do is go buy him a cheap bottle of Thunderbird and try to get back some of that courage he had in his prime. As the King of the Ring, I'm serving notice to every one of the "WWF superstars". I don't give a damn what they are, they're all on the list, and that's 'Stone Cold's' list, and I'm fixin' to start running through all of 'em. As far as this championship match is concerned, son, I don't give a damn if it's Davey Boy Smith or Shawn Michaels. Steve Austin's time has come, and when I get the shot you're looking at the next WWF Champion. And that's the bottom line, because 'Stone Cold' said so.

With that one interview a star was born, at least in the eyes of the fans. "Austin 3:16" captured the public's imagination, and his "Because 'Stone Cold' said so..." sign off line became another instantly memorable trademark catchphrase. "I shit out two winners in one promo," laughs Austin. "I only wrapped it up with the 'bottom line' spiel because I could hear Vince trying to take the segment home because they were short on time."

Michael Hayes remembers the response to Austin's promo well. "There was a lot of buzz backstage after hearing that initial interview," he says,

"When Steve said that, it just caught fire." On that night in Milwaukee, when Austin first spouted the "Austin 3:16" phrase it was met with some cheers, but as the weeks passed, support for 'Stone Cold' swelled. Soon fans started bringing homemade placards to live events emblazoned with the Austin 3:16 slogan. "Middle card guys didn't get a whole lot of signs back then," notes Cornette, "It was clear that something was happening."

Suddenly, Austin's ruthless serial killer heel persona was receiving vehement support from the WWF audience as a babyface anti-hero. The 'Stone Cold' character was resonating with the fans, though Austin 3:16 was not the overnight onscreen success story that WWF revisionist history would later claim it to be. Certainly, McMahon was conflicted by the crowd response to Austin. He had always believed in good versus evil as a hook to drive his storylines, with clearly defined wrongdoers and heroes but nothing in-between. As far as Vince was concerned, wrestling was a simple black and white world. It had always been that way; it was the way his father's business had been too, years before he took over the company reins.

In McMahon's world, foreign wrestlers, flamboyant outcasts and those guilty of committing dastardly deeds were designed to be booed, whereas All-American babyface cherries were supposed to be clean shaven and cheered. The former Dynamite Kid, Tom Billington, told the story of having briefly grown a moustache and beard during his babyface run with the British Bulldogs tag team in the eighties. He recalled how Vince berated him, then forced him to shave it off due to his firm belief that babyfaces should not have facial hair, only heels. "I'm not being funny, Vince, but what about Hogan?" asked Dynamite. The response was swift and final, "Shave it off immediately." McMahon was set in his ways, because his ways had always worked for him in the past.

Austin wanted to ride his wave of momentum and cut loose from that worn-out norm. He attempted to break the mould by delivering interviews that appealed directly to the edgy model that McMahon was cautiously beginning to implement. Austin soon became frustrated. One evening he was at home watching a taped episode of *Raw*, only to find that some of his better moments - many of which had amused the boys and people in the production staff - had been cut out of the show completely. When it happened again a week later, Austin decided to take his grievances straight to the source.

Austin knew he had found something special with his new persona, so was again forthright in dealing with the situation. He asked Vince why he was getting censored when everyone had nothing but praise for his work. McMahon declared that Austin was supposed to be a heel but he was getting a babyface response for his actions, which he felt was the wrong response. It was his long-standing belief rearing its restrictive head again. Austin argued that it did not matter which way the fans reacted - as long as he was getting a reaction one way or another, what he was doing was working. "Vince, if you take my personality away from me then I can't compete with anyone here," he declared, baffled by Vince's apparent willingness to stifle something unmistakably connecting with the audience.

The reality was that underneath a public corporate mask in which he expressed reluctance to venture too far down the paths of bad taste, Vince simply was not yet sure what he had stumbled onto with the 'Austin 3:16' phenomenon. He remained reluctant to go ahead with Austin's renewed push, though it was obvious to practically everyone else that 'Stone Cold' was the WWF's answer to WCW. He was one of the scant few members of the roster that the jaded fan base actually cared about and were willing to rally behind. As Jim Cornette remembers it, "We all knew it was something special. We told Vince, 'Hey, this guy we have been telling you about? Just leave him the fuck alone.' We said it much nicer than that of course."

Under pressure from his advisors, Vince kept coming close to pulling the trigger on 'Stone Cold', only to get cold feet as his dated predilections about how wrestling should be presented returned to the fore. He was locked in an internal battle; forced to choose between his principles and the almighty dollar. Some close to the situation privately wondered if Eric Bischoff's biting quip earlier in the year that Vince was, "the modern day Verne Gagne,"[37] did indeed ring true. They worried that the WWF would ultimately collapse due to McMahon's refusal to change with the times or present professional wrestling in a different way to his tired, safe, and played-out ideals.

ELSEWHERE ON the *King of the Ring*, Tony Norris was undergoing the promotional push of his career as Vince McMahon's latest pet project 'Ahmed Johnson'. The granite-chiselled, perma-oiled grappler, a Florida native billed as hailing from Pearl River, Mississippi, was being marketed by McMahon as an everyman hero. In pushing Norris, Vince was following the

---

[37] It is often erroneously repeated in wrestling circles that Verne Gagne and his American Wrestling Association could have been as big as the World Wrestling Federation had Gagne not been "behind the times" and refused to change his promotional methods. Many pointed at his refusal to pull the trigger on Hulk Hogan before losing him to Titan as his downfall, claiming if he had done so then the AWA would be fronting the wrestling monopoly rather than WWE. Credible wrestling historians tend to view this as WWE-led revisionism rather than the truth. The reality was more that Gagne's stars got old, and McMahon undercut him with TV stations then overpaid for his talent to lure them away.

advice of his former booker Bill Watts by utilising Ahmed Johnson as the WWF's black success story. Although not publicly stated as such, it was a direct counter to WCW's lilywhite main event scene.

At the pay-per-view, Ahmed Johnson was booked with Goldust in a match for the Intercontinental Title, though Norris was not especially keen to be in the ring with the controversial champion. As had been the case with Scott Hall earlier in the year, the Goldust character made Norris uncomfortable and he did not want any part of the character's envelope-pushing "histrionics". Norris was not the only one unhappy with Goldust. For different reason, parent groups and gay rights movements continued to barrack Titan over their use of the character. GLAAD had made life uncomfortable for the WWF in February when they received significant press coverage in the *Stamford Advocate*, expressing their concerns that Goldust portrayed all gay men as predatory homosexuals. They believed that the WWF were knowingly presenting a message that glorified gay bashing and homophobia.

Titan's local newspaper *The Connecticut Post* jumped on the bandwagon a few weeks later with a scathing article that attacked the WWF for promoting a blatantly homophobic gimmick. With the powerful media giving further text to the increasing protests from various gay groups, Vince felt he had to act. The reams of negative press eventually caused him to rethink his strategy after months of having turned his nose up at the negative publicity. He instructed the gimmick's portrayer Dustin Runnels to pull back a little with some of his actions, telling him to refrain from caressing opponents in the ring and instructing him to tone down some of the more overtly sexual aspects of the role.

"Things were changing, I could feel it," remembers Runnels. "Vince was getting a lot of criticism from different groups. Parents were calling WWF headquarters and complaining about Goldust. Some of them didn't want their kids watching if I was performing. An article in *New York Times* came out saying gay rights activists were upset over the character. As far as I was concerned, it wasn't my problem. I was having fun doing my job. I couldn't see the larger picture and I am not even sure how much I cared to."

McMahon's agitated flitting between promoting risqué adult content and wholesome family viewing was highlighted again when he introduced thirty-six-year-old New Jersey independent wrestler Jim Heaney as 'Cloudy', a tattoo-covered, heavily muscled transgender manager for the Body Donnas tag team. Elsewhere on Federation television, Goldust's valet and real-life wife Marlena engaged in the first throes of a quasi-lesbian relationship with Sable. Some worried that McMahon was going too far whereas others egged him on, welcoming the direction the company was taking. However, as was becoming a running theme for the year, McMahon pushed the boat out and then quickly hauled it back into dock, concerned about the repercussions of turning his mom-and-pop wrestling program into a sordid free-for-all. Neither Cloudy nor the lesbian angle lasted more than a few weeks as a result, and McMahon decided that his product needed cleansing to prevent the WWF from becoming a sexual freak show.

As with pushing Steve Austin, Vince was conflicted, caught between keeping his sponsors and associates happy, and wanting to forge a new creative direction for the WWF. That manifested into further confused edicts, such as where one instant he would tell Dustin Runnels to calm down some aspects of Goldust, then at television had him shoot a pre-taped interview naked and covered from head to toe in gold paint. With only his Intercontinental Title belt to protect his modesty, Goldust rather obviously - and graphically - implied via crass innuendo that he wanted to commit forced sexual acts on Johnson. The segment drew the lowest quarter hour rating for *Raw* since the Monday Night Wars had began.

Another skit that left little to the imagination saw Goldust give Johnson unnecessary mouth-to-mouth resuscitation against his will, which served as a unique way to jumpstart a program between the two. Norris recalls the segment well, "I was really pissed off about that kiss. We had practiced it and he was supposed to put his hand over my mouth and kiss his hand, because the way it was shot no one would ever know. We had rehearsed and rehearsed it. Dustin knew it was gonna be live television, so instead of doing what we talked about he decided to have a little ha-ha and do it for real. So I'm lying there with my eyes closed and the part is coming up, and then I feel his motherfucking lips [on mine], and man, I lost it.

"To me, another man's lips touching your lips is the grossest thing in the world. I didn't find any humour in it. I went hunting for him, but they told me he already had his car running during the angle, and as soon as he got to the back he jumped in it and took off. After that I disappeared for like a month because I was so pissed that I quit. I knew I was gonna hurt him real bad if I stayed, so I quit. When I came back I was still heated up, so Vince sat us down and made us talk and shake hands, but inside me I couldn't put the fire out. Every time I saw him I couldn't let it go." [38]

The tension between the two going into *King of the Ring* was a positive thing as far as Vince was concerned, because it added a layer of realism to

[38] Despite what Norris professes, this is a false claim. The segment in question took place on May 27, and Norris worked the following night's *Superstars* taping before hitting the road, going over Vader, Davey Boy Smith and Owen Hart on a nightly basis.

the contest. McMahon was all but imploring his viewers to tune in so they could see Johnson get his revenge and beat up the gay guy. The Goldust bashers were duly satiated at the pay-per-view when Johnson smashed through the champ and lifted the coveted title belt, firmly establishing him as one of the top babyfaces in the company.

The way Johnson had been protected with smart booking since his debut at *Survivor Series* the past November had given him the aura of a superstar, and Vince seemed to believe that he was the future of the WWF. Others who cared about actual wrestling ability noted that he was unpredictable, sloppy and a risk to himself and others in the ring, not to mention unintelligible in promos. McMahon hardly cared about minor details like that. Wrestling skill was right towards the back of the list of qualities he looked for in talent - and it appeared Vince was convinced he had found his next big babyface star. The reaction backstage to the title change was not as enlightened, with Norris infuriated to discover that someone - he presumed one of the boys or someone working behind the scenes - had keyed the words, "Congratulations nigger," into the side of his car.

Entirely justified in his outrage, Norris confronted Vince about the slur and was promised that immediate action would be taken. However, Norris had worked himself up about the ordeal to such an extent that he decided to confront the chairman about something else that was playing on his mind. Norris' query concerned his feel-good television storyline of being the first ever black singles champion in the WWF. "Why did it take the WWF so long to have a black champion anyway?" he fired incredulously at a startled McMahon, then pointed out that there had been a host of talented black performers in the company in the years prior to his arrival, many of whom he argued would have made strong cases for the role.[39] Vince recoiled in shock at the brazenness of the questioning, upset at the insinuation he was in any way a racist.

According to Norris, his actions that day meant the *King of the Ring* was both the peak of his WWF run and the night his career in the company effectively died. He was perturbed that nothing was done about the car vandalism incident, and convinced that his questioning had irked McMahon to the point where his push was affected. He would later claim he had heard via others that in meetings behind closed doors, McMahon had commented

---

[39] Butch Reed was nearly that man in 1987, at one stage scheduled to win the Intercontinental Title from a departing Ricky Steamboat. He lost the opportunity after missing a number of dates. McMahon lost patience with him, so on the recommendation of Hulk Hogan he gave the title win and a record run with the belt to cocky Elvis-alike heel Wayne 'The Honky Tonk Man' Ferris.

that his audience was not ready for a black champion, and he was only promoting one because he felt obliged to.

Norris' failure to live up to the impressive hype that McMahon had surrounded him with was more down to his frequent injury problems than anything else. The first came prior to a heavily touted WWF Title match that was scheduled to air in September - three months after his career apparently died - thanks to a kidney injury that caused him to miss four months of action. In those four months, the WWF metamorphosed into a completely different animal, and Norris was no longer McMahon's flavour of the month. Steve Austin had quickly usurped him as the "people's choice", the everyman nine-to-fivers could rally behind, leaving him somewhat lost in the shuffle. Vince persevered with Ahmed Johnson regardless, but with each clunky performance and each additional injury, his lustre dimmed. A heel turn and scheduled match for the WWF Title in mid-1997 seemed to have achieved the goal of revitalising him, then almost immediately Norris was injured again during an in-ring scuffle and once more missed out on the opportunity. With Vince feeling Norris was too unreliable due to his injury proneness, he was released in 1998.

STEVE AUSTIN and Ahmed Johnson were not the only rising stars in the WWF who made names for themselves at *King of the Ring* - the event was also a banner night for Mick 'Mankind' Foley. After finishing up his commitments with ECW, Foley had made his Federation bow the night after *WrestleMania*,[40] defeating Bob Holly in an awkward match. Foley was not yet comfortable in his Mankind skin after nearly a decade playing Cactus Jack, and the exchanges between the two were fumbled and uninspired. Other than a smattering of "ECW" chants from a minority in the audience, the reaction to the persona was lukewarm at best.

Perceptions changed later on in the show when Mankind was thrust into a program with WWF custodian The Undertaker, the script calling for him to burst through the ring and deliver a brutal beating to the 'Dead Man'. He duly obliged with a vicious-looking assault that ended with him diving ten feet off the ring apron with an elbow drop. It was rare that Undertaker was allowed to be shown in perilous situations, so immediately the program gave Mankind credibility. Leaving Undertaker looking so vulnerable also served as a way to begin a much needed "humanisation" of Mark Calaway's

---

[40] This was his television debut. His in ring debut was a few weeks earlier on March 10 in Corpus Christi, as he was asked to work a few untelevised shots because of thin cards. In an historic twist, it was also the same day Dwayne 'The Rock' Johnson made his WWF in-ring debut, and the first time the prefix 'Stone Cold' was used in conjunction with Steve Austin.

character, bringing it more in line with the WWF's shift towards reality-based melodrama.

Calaway appreciated the chance to work with someone like Foley, because after years of programs opposite giants and stiffs in plodding matches, he was finally able to do something creatively satisfying. Mankind was the perfect choice of antagonist for the Undertaker character. He was able to challenge him mentally with creatively booked "mind games" rather than pure physicality, as had been the case in years prior with towering monsters like Giant Gonzales, Kamala, King Kong Bundy, and Yokozuna.

It was a significant step up for Foley to go from competing in bingo halls and bloody barbed wired matches in Japan to the WWF marketing him as a feature performer on pay-per-view. Some privately wondered if he would be able to live up to the task. While his initial television showing may not have been particularly memorable, Foley threw himself into the role of Mankind and soon began to feel the character. Shortly, he was playing the role with such aplomb that even the cynics in the locker room were impressed. "He rose to the challenge," admitted Shawn Michaels.

Foley may have been unconventional in style and appearance, but his willingness to give his body to the cause won him many friends, not least Calaway. In return, Calaway was willing to let the Undertaker look more vulnerable than he ever had before, an act that raised the stock of both performers in the eyes of the fans. "I sometimes think about where my life would be if Undertaker had chosen to be a complete asshole, but he was completely the opposite. His professionalism was beyond reproach, and, as a result, both of our careers benefited," says Foley.

The two held little back in their *King of the Ring* scrap, utilising hard chair shots and wild brawling uncharacteristic for the WWF. That Mankind was allowed to inflict a rare pinfall defeat on Undertaker made it even more memorable. So strong was their program that the WWF continued to book them in matches opposite each other for the remainder of the year, then rebooted the rivalry in 1997 and again in 1998.

Victory over the Undertaker served as strong vindication for Foley that he was right to have given up blood and guts wrestling for a much safer existence inside of WWF rings. He had defied the odds, overcoming the negativity that his friends in ECW greeted him with when he informed them that he was making the jump to New York. They had implored him to reconsider, warning that he would be thrown into a program with a top name and routinely beaten, then tossed aside with less value going out than he had coming in.

Foley's performance at *King of the Ring* and in subsequent months proved them all wrong. In any other era they might have been right, and Mankind may well have gone the way of other contrived gimmicks of the past had he shown up a year or two earlier. But in 1996, he was the key proponent of brutal hardcore style wrestling in the WWF. He managed to elevate nearly everyone he worked with - no matter how big a star they already were - without damaging his own persona or reputation in any way.

Mick Foley's mere presence in the WWF personified the loose terrain of shifting ideals underfoot. Soon the man considered the antithesis of what Vince McMahon wanted a WWF Superstar to be became one of the most integral cogs in the New WWF machine. Foley was the group's workhorse; someone who could be relied upon to put his body on the line for the cause. It was a trait that helped him overcome what he lacked in physique and finesse. Eventually Foley would be rewarded for his consistently selfless work when Vince McMahon afforded him a trio of brief runs with the WWF Title in 1999. For a short time at least, he became the least likely figurehead in the history of the promotion.

EIGHT

WITH VINCE STILL STRUGGLING TO give the WWF a clearly defined identity, his conflicted ethos was typified by a series of paradoxical talent acquisitions made in the middle of the year. At the same time that McMahon had hired a number of journeyman veterans, rebranding them as dated banal stereotypes, he agreed to terms with the most talked-about and controversial free agent in the industry: Brian Pillman.

During a typical spring day sat around Vince's pool at his lavish Connecticut home, Jim Cornette and the rest of the creative team were trying to write an episode of the group's weekly television. It was proving problematic: the roster was the thinnest it had been in years and there was little to work with. Wanting to avoid the inevitable creative dead end they were wandering down each week, Cornette proposed a solution to McMahon. "Vince, there's a bunch of talent out there not working now, since there are no territories any more. Why not bring some of them in, give them some wins on TV, pay them a little more than the underneath guys, and sprinkle them in to put the top guys over? That way we can make some part time guys who are at least partway credible, give them a little push and then beat them a time or two."

McMahon was interested, willing to try anything to get the edge back over WCW. He too realised that his talent pool was limited so agreed to the proposal. "Make me a list," he told Cornette and Bruce Prichard, who both immediately turned to guys they knew and trusted from their years in the business. "Immediately I thought of Tracy Smothers and Dirty White Boy (Tony Anthony)," recalls Cornette, "Bruce thought of Bill Irwin, and Tom Brandi who worked in the North East. We had done a lot of TV there so we had seen Tom a few times already, and he looked good."

Irrespective of WCW's recent ascent as a direct rival to Titan's reputation as professional wrestling's des res, the WWF's name value still carried plenty of weight. Not to mention the journeyman wrestlers stood to earn at least four times what they could earn anywhere else by working for Vince. Consequently, the grapplers were eager to accept the offer of regular work with the long-time market leaders. Cornette was pleased, believing he had done a worthy service to a group of talented performers who had earned their jobs through years of hard work. His mood soon soured when McMahon began to remodel all the new-starters in typical WWF fashion.

"Wait until you see some of the gimmicks we have come up with!" yelped Prichard excitedly. Cornette recoiled aghast when he saw that seventeen-year veteran 'Wild' Bill Irwin had been convinced into letting Vince repackage him as a rogue hockey player (loosely based on Irwin's legitimate collegiate hockey past) supposedly kicked out of the NHL for being too violent, and rebranded as 'The Goon'. Bruce Prichard argues the case for the gimmick, "Bill was a talent who had a lot of different gimmicks, but what do you do with him? One thing Vince was excellent at was talking to guys and finding out what they did. Irwin played hockey, he was a big hockey fan from Minnesota. He *was* "the goon" in his hockey days - the guy sent out to start fights. I loved it. Sometimes reality and believability get messed up in there somewhere, but you have to take things to the extreme."

FOURTEEN-YEAR veteran Tracy Smothers suffered a similar fate, given the name Freddie Joe Floyd (as a rib on Freddie Joe "Jack" Brisco and Floyd "Jerry" Brisco) and asked to depict a dim-witted southern yokel. Tony Anthony, who had been working part-time at his father's plumbing business was brought in as 'T.L. Hopper', a wrestling plumber. He was instructed to show his butt crack and wear filthy, ill-fitting vests that made him look pudgy and slovenly. To further ramp up the supposed comedy factor, Hopper was given sound effects of flatulence and toilet bowls flushing as his ring entrance music.

Smothers and Anthony had been regular fixtures for Cornette's own Smoky Mountain Wrestling group prior to it folding in late 1995, and the former promoter was embarrassed that he had played a part in the WWF hiring them to be portrayed as fools. However, Smothers did not help his own career with Titan thanks to two separate, seemingly trivial backstage incidents, which due to the hypersensitive disposition of the locker room were blown out of proportion.

The first came while he was sat getting dressed in the locker room beside Mark 'The Undertaker' Calaway on the night of his debut. As Smothers remembers it, Calaway was troubled by the presence in the WWF of the Body Donnas' recently debuted transgender manager Cloudy. Sharing his disdain with the rest of the boys, he grumbled, "Some guys will do anything to get in this fucking business." Immediately Smothers quipped in response, "Yeah. I hear ya man. So, how long you been dead now?"

Smothers had known Calaway since the latter had first started out in the business back in 1984 with Fritz Von Erich's Dallas-based promotion WCCW, and the two had crossed paths a number of times after that. He had always known Calaway as someone he could share a joke with, and his comment was intended as an innocent jibe, a friendly bout of ribbing between old acquaintances. Calaway did not the funny side. He felt Smothers was trying to make a name for himself and 'get over' with the boys by making a fool out of him. As one of the unofficial leaders of the locker room, it was something he could not tolerate. Calaway did not reply, instead he shot Smothers a glance that said far more than any words could have, then returned to getting dressed. "He got pissed off and went red all over," recalls Smothers, "I had been there for two hours. I was fucked."

He became even more convinced that the gig was going to be short-lived two months later when he butted heads with WWF Champion Shawn Michaels during a *Monday Night Raw* taping in Wheeling, West Virginia on August 19. Smothers was pulling double duty that evening, with Vince attempting to cut costs by grouping four episodes of *Raw* into a single night's worth of tapings. These were typically tiring for the exhausted crew, and frayed tensions usually tore in a moment's notice at the slightest incident. Smothers was already unpopular with Michaels anyway due to his friendship with Kliq enemy Chris Candido, in addition to an apparent snub a decade prior that Smothers had long since forgotten even took place. Since Smothers had joined the WWF, Michaels had been waiting for an opportunity to right the perceived wrong. That night in Wheeling it finally happened.

In his first match that night, Smothers was working against Leon 'Vader' White, the man who had worked with Michaels for the WWF Title at the prior night's *SummerSlam* pay-per-view. As had been the case with Calaway, Smothers had known White for years and he was pleased to be finally sharing the ring with someone more complimentary to the rough and ready southern brawling style that he favoured. Going into the bout, Smothers was expecting to have a fairly competitive match with White before doing the job for him, given that he had himself picked up a few wins on television of late against John 'Justin Hawk Bradshaw' Layfield.

Prior to the two squaring off, Smothers first had to wait out an angle the WWF were shooting to debut Olympic weightlifter Mark Henry, Vince's recently signed real-sports acquisition. Henry had eagerly penned an unheard of ten year contract that guaranteed him $250,000 per annum, a figure that far eclipsed most on the roster outside of the top names. It was yet another source of contention for the underappreciated and underpaid opening match talent, especially as Henry proved to be cumbersome and a danger to himself in the ring for at least the duration of his first contract.

Henry's appearance in the Smothers-Vader match exemplified once more that McMahon was heading down two opposite creative paths at the same time, with credible athlete Henry about as far removed as one could be from Smothers' prosaic Freddie Joe Floyd persona. Having waited out the segment, which saw Henry and Vader engage in a staring contest but little more, Smothers realised that time was quickly ebbing away. They only had three minutes to work with and Smothers reasoned that the start of the match would belong to him before Vader overpowered and beat him. He decided to jump Vader as soon as he entered the match, mounting some quick fire offence before getting routinely squashed.

Shawn Michaels had not seen the bout playing out that way. He tore into Smothers backstage, telling him in no uncertain terms that his job in the WWF was to make others look good by getting beat, not to - as he put it, "take liberties and try to get yourself over." Michaels was of the opinion that the deficient Floyd character getting any offence against a monster like Vader hurt his credibility, and thus would harm his own reputation when he worked with Vader on the road. The ever volatile 'Heartbreak Kid' was further riled that Smothers had inadvertently bust Vader's lip during his match-opening flurry, which again he determined would be perceived as a weakness by watching fans.

What Shawn did not realise was that Smothers had unfortunate timing: the only part of his offence that aired on television was a handful of punches, at which point the show cut to a pre-allotted commercial break. Smothers was somewhat taken aback by the tirade. White had not expressed an issue with the content of the bout, so he did not believe Michaels had any right to dress him down in such a manner. Despite having a fearsome reputation amongst the boys as a dangerous fighter, Smothers also knew that to lay out the WWF Champion would result in his immediate dismissal from the Federation. Instead he wisely turned to Michaels and simply stated through gritted teeth, "Okay, Shawn, I got it. It won't happen again."

It was too late for Smothers to save his WWF career. He had managed to annoy the two most influential members of the locker room in only a few short months, and resultantly a proposed program teaming with Savio Vega was immediately nixed. Instead he wound up staring at the lights in opening matches for such luminaries as T.L. Hopper, Crush, and The Bushwhackers. Despite further attempts at rebuilding the bridge with Michaels, his time was up. The WWF released him from his contract in early 1997 having barely used him for months prior.

In reality, Freddie Joe Floyd would have died a dismal death regardless of political sabotage. Like many of the other new characters in the Federation, the persona harked back to Vince's earlier mindset of rebranding wrestlers as overblown cartoon characters. It was something he had refrained from doing following an infamous Indianapolis hotel room meeting with the Kliq in late 1995, in which they had expressed their distaste for the childishness of the WWF product and advised him to change the way he presented wrestling. For a while at least, it seemed that McMahon had turned a corner and caught up with the times following the utilisation of a host of more realistic characters, but his latest anachronistic splurge had plunged the WWF back into the grip of hokey preposterousness.

By now, Jim Cornette was regretting even pitching the idea to use the journeymen in the first place. "It was more of that fucking "funny" shit that Bruce and Pat Patterson liked so much. Everything always had to be silly with them," he complains. "I was embarrassed. I got those guys jobs and then they had to go out there and look like buffoons. It ruined their image, and it ruined our chances of bringing in part-time guys with credibility who were good workers and could get our main event guys over."

THAT THE cartoonification of one-time respected industry veterans coincided with the rise in popularity of the vulgar, beer-drinking and cussing Steve Austin persona caused Vince's entire organisation to become a baffling juxtaposition. "Vince just kind of backed into the edgier stuff slowly," offers Cornette. "It's not like Vince didn't *like* The Goon, T.L. Hopper, etcetera, because he did, but it was always Bruce Prichard who would defend those gimmicks publicly, even when Vince wasn't there. Bruce would be the one handling those guys, and it was easy for him because it was all funny shit that Vince wouldn't get mad about. It was only later in the year when Vince saw the crazy things the top guys were doing getting over that he decided to fully go in that direction." Hiring Steve Austin's former Hollywood Blondes tag team partner Brian Pillman in June only further clouded the perception of Vince's long-term intentions about where he wanted to take the WWF creatively.

Having suffered through the trauma of thirty-six operations to treat the throat cancer he had suffered from since the age of two, Brian Pillman sensed his career had an earlier expiration date than most. With five children to feed at home, he realised that time was running out for him to make enough money from wrestling so that his family would be comfortable for the rest of their lives. At merely five-foot-nine in stature, the former Cincinnati Bengals linebacker was determined to overcome similar odds to the ones he had been fighting his entire life.

Pillman had been wrestling in the middle of the card at WCW for six years, working primarily as a high-flying aerial specialist. He observed

WCW's main event scene and saw aged, reliable company hands Ric Flair, Lex Luger, and Arn Anderson mixing it up with New York imports Hulk Hogan and Randy Savage, noting they were doing the same routines that had brought them to the dance decades prior. With his contract soon up for renewal, he devised a masterplan that he intended would increase his value exponentially and catapult him to the top of the company. He wanted to think outside of the restrictive box that had contained wrestling storylines for as long as anyone could remember. His plan was to pull off a "shoot angle", something to shatter the norm and make him the hottest name in the business.

Brian was astute enough to see that the industry was changing. A keen student of the game, he felt he had witnessed the future when he glimpsed the likes of Rey Misterio Jr., and Eddie Guerrero wowing audiences with innovative aerial ability unlike anything he had seen before. Once acclaimed for his own high flying skills, Pillman's body was beginning to suffer from the effects of the style and he knew he could no longer keep up with the new breed. As a high flying style was one of the few options available to him because of his small stature, Pillman recognised that he needed something brazen; a completely different approach to wrestling that would help him overcome the same size handicap that he had so successfully battled in professional football.

His frustration with the big man bias prevalent throughout the industry was the catalyst for what would become known as his "Loose Cannon" persona, but the idea was actually born from the mind of someone outside of wrestling: his football coach and life mentor Kim Wood. Wood sat with Brian at his kitchen table and offered an outsider's perspective on the business. He outlined the entire gimmick, shooting ideas back and forth about what he thought would work, and how Pillman should go about doing it. The idea behind it was to get Brian enough notoriety that he would receive what he had termed a "Luger deal", as in Lex Luger, a man Brian felt was a fraction of the performer that he was, but had received his countless breaks in the industry based on his physique. The only other people he confided in were his trainer Bruce Hart, wrestling mentor Terry Funk - who he felt had seen and done it all and could advise him properly - and eventually, close friend Dave Meltzer.

The premise was simple: Pillman would start acting erratically both onscreen and behind the curtain, tricking even the boys in the back into thinking he had lost his mind. Thinking ahead of the curve, he wanted the dirt sheets, conspiracy theorists and newsmongers to get wind of his eccentric behaviour and drum up intrigue in him by theorising that he was on the verge of a breakdown. He let Eric Bischoff in on the plan and the WCW head was eager to enable him, though insisted that booker Kevin Sullivan also be in on the act too.

"Brian came to me and we talked about the evolution of his character, and turning him into somewhat of an unpredictable loose cannon. He wanted to portray a character that could do anything at any moment. A character totally unpredictable, on the verge of snapping, who might just be a little crazy," remembers Bischoff. "That was all Brian, and it was something that I liked because it was different. Oftentimes when you try to be better than somebody else you copy them. The magic with Brian is that he found a character that was so different to everyone else that it was easy for that character to stand out."

ON TELEVISION Pillman slipped seamlessly into the role, and soon began acting in a manner that appeared to be off the script. With the rest of the locker room oblivious to the fact it was an act, Pillman's actions seemed awfully real to those around him. Many assumed he had started abusing drugs and was simply displaying the side effects. Becoming increasingly unpredictable, Pillman began to rub some people in the company the wrong way. During a live broadcast of WCW's regular television special *Clash of the Champions* on January 26, 1996 from Caesar's Palace, Las Vegas, Pillman even managed to get under the skin of the usually unflappable Bobby 'the Brain' Heenan.

Heenan had been around the wrestling business since 1960 and thought he had seen everything, but realised he had never met anyone as obviously insane as Brian Pillman. For the *Clash* special, Heenan was situated at ringside as part of the show's two-man broadcast team alongside Tony Schiavone. Heenan had recently undergone surgery to correct a long-standing injury that left his neck fragile, so he informed Bischoff that he was strictly off-limits when it came to doing anything physical. He was wary about anyone even coming near him, because even something as innocuous as a simple shove could cause him further irreparable problems.

As Pillman made his entrance prior to a match with Eddie Guerrero, he wandered behind Heenan and grabbed his jacket, pulling it over his head and removing it. Heenan did not have any idea what was going on; Pillman's actions were completely unscripted. Shaken up, the announcer broke character and yelled, "What the fuck are you doing?" directly into his live mic, then threw down his headset and stormed up the aisle. He mostly wanted to get away from the unpredictable Pillman, but a sizable part of him was fed up with life at WCW in general. He was tempted to keep walking and leave the company completely, but halfway up the aisle he calmed down enough to see sense and return to the broadcast table.

Heenan would later claim he did not realise that it was Pillman who had grabbed him. His mentality as an announcer had always been to "call what you see" and watch the monitors rather than what was going on around him. As a result, Heenan thought the attack was by a fan. It was something he was familiar with after years of suffering attempted assaults on a nightly basis during his years working in the territories, back when people still thought wrestling was real. When he discovered it was Pillman who had committed the act, he was no less furious. Still enraged after the show, he confronted Eric Bischoff about it backstage. "What's he touching me for?" Heenan demanded. The VP pleaded innocence, but Heenan accusatorily fired back, "Hey, *you* hired him!" Eventually the situation was calmed when Pillman took Heenan aside and privately apologised for getting carried away.

Pillman was so committed to the character that he even played it to the hilt outside of the ring. One night, when checking into a Las Vegas hotel, he spotted Eric Bischoff sat at the bar having a drink with his wife, Loree. Even though Bischoff was obviously well aware his character was an act, Pillman instantly slipped into performance mode and began making a scene. The reasons were twofold: partly to impress Bischoff, but also to sell his act to anyone else who happened to be watching. His rationale was that if a fan saw him causing a disturbance in front of the WCW boss, then it added credence to the unhinged disposition of his persona and fuelled rumours that he was on the verge of getting fired.

Despite what many of the boys would later claim to save face, Brian had them all fooled. Even the long-time veterans who had seen everything, and his close friends who knew him best, began to question whether what he was doing was an act or if his life really was spiralling out of control. "He was either the smartest crazy guy I ever met, or the craziest smart guy I ever met. I don't know," admits Pillman's former Four Horsemen stable-mate Arn Anderson. Even Hulk Hogan was once heard commenting, "What the hell is wrong with Pillman?" though he became wise to what was going on a few weeks later. When he figured it out he was incensed that Bischoff had not let him in on the secret. He felt it violated the clause in his contract that gave him creative control over not only his own programs, but everyone else's as well. He passed a message to Bischoff through the VP's personal secretary Janie Engle, "Tell Eric he can go to hell."

THE REAL genius to Pillman's scheme was not so much what he did onscreen under the authorisation of Bischoff and Sullivan, but the situation he was able to wrangle for himself behind closed doors. Pillman was not only fooling everyone else, but the two men in WCW who thought they were working with him. He was playing a canny confidence game, the ultimate wrestling long con. In a move of bold inspiration, he convinced Bischoff to give him an official termination notice two months prior to his contract expiring so he could go and work for ECW, the perfect place for his renegade Loose Cannon character to flourish.

Pillman explained to Bischoff that if he turned up at ECW whilst under WCW contract the news would get out that it was a work, and the knowledgeable ECW fan base would kill the whole thing by calling him on it. He argued that it had to be legitimate. If he was given a termination notice that served as an official release from his contract then everyone from the company's legal team outwards would be fooled into believing that his 'firing' was real rather than part of an angle. That information would then filter down throughout the company, and any sceptics would believe the whole thing again.

Bischoff was always eager to pull one over on everyone and naively agreed to go through with the plan. Under the impression that Pillman would be back with WCW after six months, he consented to him brokering his own deal with ECW head honcho Paul Heyman. It was a no-lose situation for Heyman, who would enjoy access to one of the hottest names in the industry for free, as Bischoff would still secretly be paying Pillman his contract. What Bischoff did not realise was that Pillman had been covertly negotiating with Heyman anyway. Though he did not yet know it, he had been tricked into giving Brian exactly what he wanted, and let him leave with his blessing.

Pillman's final "official" WCW act came at pay-per-view *SuperBrawl* on February 11, where he was scheduled to have a "Respect Strap Match" with company booker Kevin Sullivan. Sullivan had been smart in programming himself with Pillman, because as one of the few people in on the work he could play along in letting Pillman showcase his creative magnum opus to the world. The two had been embroiled in a bitter feud on television over the past few months, which included working a match on *Nitro* that even the boys were convinced had gotten out of control and turned into a legitimate confrontation. During one moment in the contest, Sullivan had seemingly become so angry with his opponent that he had tried to gouge out his eye.

It was simply part of the façade, but there was still a buzz backstage prior to the encounter at *SuperBrawl*, with those not in the know anticipating a legitimate situation developing in the bout. In keeping with the way their program had played out, the pair did not even get to the stage of being tethered together with the leather strap. Instead they rolled around in a fake shoot, before Pillman broke away seconds later and grabbed a microphone. It was what he said next that convinced any remaining non-believers that he had genuinely lost it: "I respect you... booker man."

The words meant little to the majority of the audience, but to the attuned members of the crowd and the boys in the back, it was earth-shattering. Pillman had outed Sullivan as the booker of WCW, the puppeteer which wrestling doctrine denied existed, which in turn made the rest of the angles on the show seem like hokey theatre in comparison. Even the people who knew wrestling was not real were *convinced* that this was. Pillman immediately dropped the microphone and headed to the back. He was shouted out of the building by Bischoff - as they had prearranged - with the apparent act of disrespect for the entire industry serving as the catalyst for his mutually agreed upon, yet legitimate, firing.

PILLMAN SHOWED up in ECW six days later at *Cyberslam*. He made his bow to a rousing response from the Arena crowd, but then did a shocking about turn and ripped them and the organisation to shreds:

[Joey Styles:] "What the hell are you doing here?!?"

[Brian Pillman:] Haven't you heard? I like you as an announcer, Joey Styles. You know why? Because I just had an announcer in Atlanta, Georgia take away my constitutional rights. I have been fired by Eric Bischoff. He's a pretty popular guy these days. He's also pretty popular with my legal department as well. Bischoff - or should I say jerk-off - you can't take away my constitutional rights, because I'm in Philadelphia where the fucking constitution was written! Now Mr. Gopher, Mr. Nineties Whizz Kid, the great success story of '96. Former Coffee Gopher for Verne Gagne is now leading the show in the big time. You are a piece of fucking shit!

[Joey Styles:] On that note we're gonna go to commercial. A bombshell has been dropped here tonight, Brian Pillman is...

[Brian Pillman:] No, no, no, Joey Styles you're not running this interview. I am, 'cause I'm Brian *fucking* Pillman. Let me tell you a little more. You know what Eric Bischoff is? Eric Bischoff is each and every one of you motherfucking smart marks sons of bitches rolled up into one giant piece of shit! Oh, I guess you guys didn't get that huh? Smart marks? What's a smart mark? A mark with a high IQ? Okay smart marks, you know what a mark is? A mark is a guy that spends his last twenty dollars on crack cocaine. A mark is a guy that believes that O.J. didn't do it. And a mark is every one of you sorry sons of motherfucking bitches. So you know what I'm gonna do? The only appropriate thing Brian Pillman should do. I'm gonna jerk out my Johnson and piss in this hell hole.

[Paul Heyman:] Stop this! This is not a part of the deal. Brian it's not a part of the deal.

[Brian Pillman:] Deal? What deal? I do whatever I want, whenever I want and I don't give a fuck about you and your smart marks, booker man!

During his performance Pillman had managed to turn the entire building against him with one cutting promo, delving into each deep-lying insecurity the audience members held about the way they were perceived. To put an exclamation mark on the point, Pillman spat in the face of a fan that had been 'planted'[41] at ringside, hurled him over the steel barricade and then viciously assaulted him. It was some way to make a debut. Pillman was thrilled with how well it had worked. His antics cut close to the bone, but fully achieved his goal of keeping him hot and generating further interest in what he would do next.

Paul Heyman was in constant contact with WCW's Kevin Sullivan for the duration of Pillman's tenure in ECW, firmly of the belief that his presence in the organisation was simply a way to further an angle. He did not mind; Pillman was white hot and generating considerable talk, which was exactly what ECW wanted. Like the WCW management team, he too was none the wiser about Brian's real agenda in getting his WCW release: double crossing Bischoff and opening negotiations with Vince McMahon and the WWF, then playing the two heavyweight corporations against each other to secure a lucrative contract.

---

[41] Intentionally placed by the promotion specifically for use in an angle

THE CHANNELS of communication between the WWF and Pillman had initially been opened while Pillman was still working at WCW, thanks to an off-chance social phone call between Pillman and Titan's head of talent relations Jim Ross. Ross was an old friend of Brian's who had taken it upon himself to contact Pillman at his Cincinnati home after catching sight of some of his antics and hearing industry scuttlebutt regarding his backstage demeanour. He was genuinely concerned for the wrestler's wellbeing. His fears that Pillman was on the verge of a mental breakdown were hardly assuaged by the first five minutes of their conversation, in which Pillman masterfully suckered Ross into the work. Eventually Pillman dropped the act and confided to Ross that it was simply a new character he was running with. "Isn't it good?" he asked him. "It's *very* good," cooed an impressed Ross.

So affected was Ross with Pillman that he suggested Brian should consider coming to work for the WWF in order for his skills be utilised more readily. He promised he would talk to Vince about offering him a contract should he become available to jump ship, though Pillman was noncommittal. McMahon too was initially sceptical, worried that Pillman was living far too close to the edge with his gimmick and that the work had manifested itself into reality.

His concerns only increased when he met Brian for the first time at a NAPTE convention in Las Vegas, the day after the *Clash* altercation with Heenan. As he had with Ross, Pillman turned on the showbiz and put on a display for McMahon. After firmly convincing the WWF chairman that he was out of his mind by brazenly hugging him and taking pictures with him, he briefly dropped the pretence and flashed a wink at Ross, effectively admitting that everything he had been doing was a work. He later told Ross that he would like to enter negotiations with the WWF.

Vince still had reservations due to the convincing and extreme degree of Pillman's portrayal, but Jim Ross and Jim Cornette both went to bat for him. As Cornette tells it, "You have to remember that at the time, everybody was fucking nuts. JR convinced Vince that Pillman was a genius - which he was." After McMahon had Pillman's various attributes pointed out to him, not to mention that he was a perfect fit for the 'New WWF', he finally agreed to enter serious talks with the renegade performer.

At that time, Pillman had no intention of actually signing with the World Wrestling Federation. He simply wanted to use them as leverage in getting a WCW deal that would offer him job security, long-term career advancement and a half million dollar guarantee that would see him set for life. He theorised that Bischoff would be so pleased he had spurned the WWF that he would be well looked after, especially as they had pulled off such a creative and elaborate angle together. Not to mention that if he was paid main event money then it only made sense that he would be given a main event level push to go with it too.

As discussions between the two sides took place, Pillman continued making waves in stopgap home ECW. His plan to create a name for himself was working, so much so that Hulk Hogan learned of the buzz surrounding him and demanded that Pillman be brought back to WCW to work opposite him in the main event of *Uncensored*. The scheduled bout was an absurd concept: a three-tiered cage match that would see Hogan and partner Randy Savage taking on no less than eight of the company's top heels. It was obvious to Pillman that Hogan's motivations were entirely selfish; the Hulkster wanted him back in the fold only so that he could get over on his newfound reputation by beating him, rather than because he saw him as a main event level talent whom he wanted to work with.

Under orders from Bischoff and Sullivan, Pillman made a surprise, supposedly unscheduled, appearance during *Nitro* on March 11 from Winston-Salem, appearing in the crowd and receiving a huge reaction. He showed up again the following week to beat down Hogan and Savage at the end of the show, but it would turn out to be his final WCW appearance. Wise to Hogan's transparent machinations, Pillman had undergone another bout of throat surgery at Vanderbilt University on March 13, eleven days before the pay-per-view. He claimed he was fit enough to be involved in the show-ending beat down on *Nitro* but was unable to wrestle, thus meaning he could not work *Uncensored* and do the inevitable job to Hogan's leg drop.

The recurring manner of Pillman's condition meant he could have scheduled the surgery for another time and not missed the pay-per-view - a fact WCW booker Sullivan was secretly aware of - but Pillman had no intention of having his hard-earned momentum extinguished by Hogan in such a selfish manner. That did not stop a deceitful WCW from using the promotional tactic of making allusions that Pillman would be at the event. They even plugged him on the *Main Event* show held prior to the pay-per-view, even though they knew for sure that he would not be involved. It was a ploy to drum up a little more interest in the product, riding Pillman's momentum to generate last minute buys. Bischoff's explanation the following evening on *Nitro* that Pillman had refused to team with Sullivan was seen as a lame copout by those in the know, and the WWF had no qualms about pointing out the disingenuousness of WCW on *Raw* that night.

LITTLE OVER three weeks after *Uncensored*, Brian Pillman's wrestling career took an abrupt backseat to reality when he almost lost his life in a horrific motor accident. On the evening of April 15, Pillman was returning home from handing in his yearly tax return, driving 70mph in a 45mph zone on the deserted Kentucky Route 338. Exhausted from having spent the previous night filling in the forms, he fell asleep at the wheel of his brand new $85,000 open-top Humvee. Immediately the vehicle veered off the road and into an adjacent field, where it careened into a ramp-shaped tree stump. Brian, who was not wearing a seatbelt,[42] was flung forty feet from the wreckage and left in a pool of his own blood, while the truck flipped repeatedly before coming to rest. Pillman suffered a catalogue of injuries, the most serious to his face - which was unrecognisable - and ankle - which had turned 180 degrees in the wrong direction and was crushed to the consistency of egg shells.

Pillman spent the following few weeks laid up in hospital in a critical but not life-threatening condition. While there he underwent surgical procedures to rebuild his damaged face using steel plates and screws. He also had rods inserted into his shattered ankle to set it in walking position. Though his accident was undoubtedly real, Pillman had worked himself into a shoot and few in the industry believed he had been in a car wreck at all. They assumed it was yet another elaborate strand of his intricately weaved stratagem. Even Kevin Sullivan, who had been closer to the truth than most, did not believe the story. He became utterly convinced that Pillman was in hospital because he was getting plastic surgery to make himself look like Shawn Michaels, so he could work a program with him in the WWF.

Pillman spiralled into a deep depression. He was angry with himself for letting the accident happen, but also with the situation he now found himself in. He felt he had finally been on the brink of the success he craved and the crash had ruined his chances. "That wreck just tore him up. He was consumed with guilt over it," recalls his then-wife Melanie. His state of mind deteriorated further when doctors told him that the damage to his ankle was so severe he would likely never wrestle again. He reacted to the news with typical defiance, telling anyone who asked that not only would he wrestle again, but he would make a complete recovery.

Fortunately for Brian, the groundwork with the character had been enough that the road accident only added to his intrigue, and he remained the hottest free agent in the business. As Dave Meltzer noted, "Under

---

[42] He would later state that not wearing the safety device had ironically saved his life. "The vehicle was like a pancake; it was crushed because it had flipped over so many times," he told PowerSlam magazine.

normal market conditions it would have killed what little negotiating leverage he'd have had, but since the WWF wanted him, that meant WCW wanted not to lose him every bit as bad, if not worse." Thus Pillman reopened negotiations with both WCW and the WWF, and soon returned freelance to ECW and independent shows. Turning up in a wheelchair with crutches, he managed to be so good at being bad that even with his condition he did not elicit any sympathy.

PILLMAN'S INJURIES had done little to quell his thirst for controversy. On June 1 he returned to the ECW Arena and delivered a scathing interview from his wheelchair, expressing defiance in the face of his injuries. "It took an act of God to stop a runaway train," he barked, "Because nobody in wrestling can slow me down or stop me from being successful." Pillman continued his embittered rant with few safe from his vitriol. During a tirade against ECW wrestlers, he turned his attention to controversial tag team the Gangstas (Jerome 'New Jack' Young and Terrence 'Mustafa Saed' Ladd) and referred to them as, "these niggers with attitude," instantly infuriating Young.

Young, a black former bounty hunter with four justifiable homicides to his name, was performing a gimmick that repeatedly veered over the line of what was acceptable in an enlightened modern society. So intense was the heat he and Ladd generated, they had been forced to leave Jim Cornette's Smoky Mountain Wrestling in 1995 because their racial-hatred fuelled gimmick had caused so much uproar. When he heard Pillman say the word "nigger", he was incensed and ready to fight.

Pillman later defended his comments, insisting they were not intended as a racial slur. "I made a reference to the rap group N.W.A.[43] (which stood for "Niggaz Wit Attitudes") and he took it out of context," he claimed. Young, who was watching and listening from a stage above the audience, did not see it that way. "He was talking about us. He wasn't talking about no fuckin' rap group. When he said it, everybody there looked at him and they turned around and looked at me. Every fuckin' head in the whole goddamn building was looking at me, shocked," he remembers.

Young blew a gasket. Storming downstairs to the locker room he confronted the wheelchair-bound Pillman as he came through the curtain. "What did you say? I don't think I heard you...," asked Young

---

[43] It is a common misconception amongst wrestling fans that 'Natural Born Killaz' was an N.W.A. song. It was actually a collaborative effort from Dr. Dre and Ice Cube, both members of the N.W.A. group. The song was originally earmarked for N.W.A. album 'Heltah Skeltah', but was scrapped. By the time of the song's release in 1994, the N.W.A. had been split for almost three years.

provocatively. Pillman played it cool, telling Young he did not say anything, and was only doing his promo as instructed. "The fucker denied it," steamed Young, "But I would have knocked his fuckin' teeth down his throat if he had admitted it."

By now many of the boys were in the vicinity, though some were sceptical that the commotion was not merely another well-crafted Pillman brainchild designed to work everybody. Others who knew Young well realised he was serious; there was a real chance he would attack the crippled Pillman. "I didn't give a fuck that he was on crutches or in a fucking wheelchair," says Young, "He didn't care no more about me than to go out there and call me a fuckin' nigger!"

Paul Heyman realised that he had a problem on his hands. He ran up behind Young and grabbed him around the neck to pull him away, and was instantly flanked by a number of the other wrestlers. "Come on, Jack, it ain't worth it!" bellowed Heyman, "Think about your career!" Pillman went on the defensive, telling Young it was simply a work and a misguided attempt to generate heat, but Young would not accept the explanation. "We weren't even running an angle with him," he says, "I barely knew him, I hadn't even spoken to him before that. He had no business doing that shit."

The tension increased when Young stormed off and threatened to walk out of the show, potentially torpedoing the planned main event he was scheduled in. Young's Gangstas partner Ladd had not heard Pillman's promo and was frantically trying to find out what had happened. Upon learning the situation he was conflicted, caught between wanting to support his partner and wanting to keep his job. "What do you want to do, Jack?" he asked his irate teammate. "I don't give a fuck," came the hostile response, "Do what you want to do. Don't base your decision on what I do. If you want to stay, stay. If you want to quit, quit." Eventually Ladd decided to stay. He then apologised to Pillman for the whole ordeal, telling him he realised his comments were not intended as a racial attack. Ladd felt that Pillman had done nothing more than use a misguided choice of words and that the situation had been blown out of proportion.

Young was eventually talked into retuning and working the show on the proviso that he was allowed to respond with a promo of his own. He was granted his wish and delivered a tirade aimed at Pillman, running him down before going into explicit detail about homosexual acts that he alleged Pillman had engaged in with former tag partner Tom Zenk during their time in WCW. Many remained convinced that the whole thing was an elaborate ruse, especially as it turned out to be Pillman's final act for the company.

Pillman's own comments on the incident dispelled the theory. "When I get criticised for talking about a rap group... You know, that ruined what I enjoyed about ECW. I went up there purely for my passion for the art form, because I knew I could truly express myself. The fact that I made a reference that someone in the dressing room took out of context, and tried to turn into a racial injustice, is just a complete joke. If I can't be Brian Pillman in ECW, I'm wasting my time there..."

In actuality it was simply circumstance dictating that Brian never returned. At that point, he remained scheduled to blow off a conflict with Shane Douglas once he was fit enough to wrestle again later in the year. Once that was no longer possible however, hearsay and misconception turned the incident into something it was not, and it became attributed to the reason Pillman was "fired" from ECW.

AWAY FROM Philadelphia, Pillman continued talks between the WWF and WCW, with both companies vying for a turn with wrestling's prettiest girl at the dance. Pillman's life-threatening auto accident left Eric Bischoff feeling sorry for him. He sympathised with Brian's plight, but in light of the injuries he had sustained and with no indication about whether he would ever be able to return to the ring, Bischoff refused to remove the ninety day termination clause that was written as standard into all WCW contracts. It was the same deal-breaker that had caused Marc Merowitz to leave the Atlanta group earlier in the year. Pillman viewed WCW's bid as a ninety day offer that would potentially recur, rather than the three-year, $400,000 per annum guaranteed contract that Bischoff was selling it to him as. He also knew for a fact that many of the top stars in WCW did not have the clause written into their contracts, making him question Bischoff's commitment to pushing him. If he was going to be used as a main event talent, then he felt he should be treated as one.

Despite the pair orally agreeing to provisional terms on June 1, Pillman for the first time was also beginning to seriously consider defecting to the WWF. Though he would never admit it, he knew that he was not going to be the same physically following his accident, and would be severely limited with what he could do in the ring. Over in Stamford, Jim Ross assumed as much too. However, because of his admiration for Pillman's oratory skills and engrossing personality, he was able to convince McMahon to offer him a substantial contract featuring the no-cut clause that Bischoff was refusing to give.

The WWF offer was for $250,000 per year, a far lower guarantee than Bischoff was promising, but crucially, it was genuinely long-term. Unlike

WCW's deal it also offered job security, which was now even more essential to Pillman than ever. While he mulled over the respective offers, Bischoff jumped the gun and assumed that a deal was all but confirmed. He began hyping Pillman's WCW return on the June 3 episode of *Nitro,* wrongly assuming that he would eventually back down on the contentious ninety day cycles issue. He was arrogantly over-confident, believing that Titan could not come close to matching the contract he was offering.

What he did not expect was for Pillman to go back to McMahon and sign a three year deal, which is exactly what happened on June 7. Bischoff was furious about losing such a hot commodity to the WWF in the middle of the Monday Night War, but there was nothing he could do about it. He had waived the right to exercise a ninety day right of first refusal clause that would have allowed him to match the offer when he gave Pillman his official termination notice as part of the angle. Bischoff - who thought he was working with Pillman in fooling everyone else - ended up the one who was fooled the most.

TITAN CHAMPIONED their signing of Brian Pillman as a major coup, gloating on their television shows about acquiring the hottest free agent on the planet. At a mock press conference, Pillman acted the picture of humble, graceful sincerity. He talked about how happy, privileged and honoured he felt to be part of the World Wrestling Federation. Then, when the cameras were supposedly off, he launched into a tirade:

> I think this press conference is now Brian F'N Pillman's press conference, and we're really gonna find out what all you yes men... what all you obsequious lapdogs that are telling Monsoon and J.J. Dillon what they want to hear, when they want to hear it! Well, ladies and gentlemen, the "Loose Cannon" is here, at your disposal.

Unlike Messrs. Smothers, Anthony, Irwin, Foley, Austin, and a whole host of other established performers that the WWF had signed over the years, Brian Pillman was allowed to simply be Brian Pillman. Instead of Vince McMahon and his creative team moulding him into something else, they recognised that with Pillman there was no-one who could write the Loose Cannon better than Brian himself. After his initial caution, McMahon was thrilled with his new acquisition. He saw that Pillman would serve as perfect foil for Steve Austin, and felt that his risky, unpredictable persona was a perfect fit for the New WWF that he was slowly building.

Despite Pillman being nowhere near recovered from his injuries, McMahon wanted an immediate return on his investment. He rushed Brian onto WWF television in a non-wrestling role as a desperate attempt to claw back some ground in the bitter ratings war with WCW. It did not work. WCW retained their lead, and Pillman suffered further damage to his ankle due to the strains of travel. He would be forced to undergo surgery again as a result, but before he was written off television and allowed to convalesce properly, he had one last hot angle left in him. It was a stunt more controversial and influential than anything he had done prior in WCW or ECW, and ultimately set the tone for what would become known as the WWF Attitude Era.

NINE

THE WWF WAS BREAKING NEW ground with the likes of 'Stone Cold' Steve Austin, Brian Pillman, and Mankind, but meanwhile over in Atlanta, WCW was staging a business-changing revolution of its own. One month after Austin 3:16 was thrust into the public consciousness, Eric Bischoff unveiled his own masterplan: the New World Order.

The seeds of a hostile takeover angle had already been sewn by the returns to WCW of Scott Hall and Kevin Nash. "One of the things that clicked was the reality of the situation," noted Bischoff. "I'm not going to lie and say that I didn't want to walk that fine line of making it look like they were from the WWF, but that wasn't the real motivator. The real motivator was that both Scott and Kevin had worked at WCW before, felt that they were misused, mistreated and abused, went over to the WWF to become big stars, and they were coming back to exact their revenge." Now Bischoff wanted someone else to join the duo, with the intention of rebranding them as an alternate company that was looking to destroy WCW from within.

It was a creative idea but not a unique one. Introducing a disgruntled, invading faction to wage an uncivil war with the home promotion was inspired by an angle Bischoff had witnessed firsthand while visiting with New Japan Pro Wrestling that spring. At the time New Japan were embroiled in an inter-promotional battle with the Union of Wrestling Forces International, a shoot-style group founded by Nobuhiko Takada on May 10, 1991. It was a continuation of the second incarnation of the UWF group founded three years earlier by Akira Maeda (a Korean grappler born Go Il-myeong). Ironically enough, Maeda had been dismissed from New Japan after fracturing Riki Chōshū's orbital bone when he kicked him in the face as Chōshū held Osamu Kido in a sharpshooter.

It was not the first unprofessional act of Maeda's career; he had once thrown shoot kicks at Andre the Giant during an infamous April 1986 match which neither wrestler would agree to lose. Similarly, a real-life feud with New Japan booker Antonio Inoki resulted in Inoki flat out refusing to work with Maeda. The incident with Chōshū was the final straw for Inoki, but with the business still shrouded in secrecy, it gave Maeda a fearsome aura amongst fans and turned him into one of the hottest names in Japan. His supporters fervently followed him to his newborn UWF start-up. Such was the success of the promotion they became only the second organisation to promote wrestling at the Tokyo Dome, headlining their November 29, 1989 *U-Cosmos* card at the venue with a Maeda vs. Willy Wilhelm bout to the tune of 60,000 fans, outdrawing New Japan's *Super Powers Clash* the previous April by over 16,000.

The UWF's success was short-lived. Shinji Jin, a non-wrestler who had taken over from Maeda as company president had wanted to co-promote with other federations, including Super World of Sports, but Maeda resisted the idea, averred to other forms of pro wrestling. This disagreement, coupled with a general economic downturn in Japan, led to the closure of the UWF. Maeda instead opted to strike out alone with his new Fighting Network RINGS group. Other former UWF competitors such as Yoshiaki Fujiwara, Masaharu Funaki, Minoru Suzuki, and Yūsuke Fuke splintered to establish the Pro Wrestling Fujiwara-gumi outfit, while the rest of the main roster (Takada, Kazuo Yamazaki, Yōji Anjō, Tatsuo Nakano, Kiyoshi Tamura, Masahito Kakihara, and Shigeo Miyato) put together the UWFi, with Takada as company president.

As the UWFi's first champion, Takada continued to push Maeda's fabrication that this brand of wrestling was wholly legitimate, in contrast to worked organisations like New Japan and All Japan Pro Wrestling. Unlike Maeda however, Takada was willing to link horns with outsiders, leading to WCW World Champion Leon 'Vader' White cutting a deal with the group for a series of main events with Takada. Unfortunately for Takada, monetary issues led to White abandoning the UWFi, along with Takada's other main opponent, Gary Albright. Left with a lack of credible challengers, and with interest in the promotion beginning to wane, Anjō and other bookers proposed co-promoting with New Japan. They even agreed to New Japan booker Chōshū's demands that he have full control over the outcome of all inter-promotional matches, such were the dire financial straits the UWFi were in.

CHŌSHŪ WAS no stranger to invasion angles himself. In 1984 he had 'defected' from New Japan to lead the Chōshū's Army stable in a three-year run against the likes of Bruiser Brody, Harley Race, Ric Flair, Nick Bockwinkel, Terry Gordy, and others, before switching back to his original home as a genuine main event player. It also was not the first time New Japan had rumbled with an upstart group of martial arts-inspired grapplers performing under the UWF initials.

The inaugural incarnation of the UWF existed from 1984 to 1986, and had its roots not in the ambitions of a group of would-be martial artists, but in the failure of Antonio Inoki's bio-ethanol business in Brazil. Inoki and

New Japan business manager Hisashi Shinma were found to be using New Japan's money to cover Inoki's debts, resulting in the enforced resignation of Inoki as company president and Seiji Sakaguchi as vice-president, with Shinma expelled from the promotion outright. Shinma's response was to form his own promotion, the Universal Wrestling Federation, taking New Japan talents Maeda, Rusher Kimura, Ryūma Gō, Gran Hamada, and future MMA star Hayato "Mach" Sakurai.

Intriguingly, Shinma turned to All Japan impresario Shohei "Giant" Baba to assist the UWF in booking overseas talent, apparently to "avoid another promotional war", such was the fierce rivalry between New Japan and All Japan. Similarly, New Japan loaned a young Takada to the UWF for their first card on April 11, 1984, before he joined the promotion permanently two months later, along with his and Maeda's trainer, Yoshiaki Fujiwara.

Further expansion of the group's talent roster occurred with the addition of Belgian-born grappler Karl Isatz, known professionally as Karl Gotch, whose presence greatly influenced the more realistic style of the promotion's bouts. Alongside Isatz the group pulled off another marquee capture with the signing of Satoru Sayama, the former Tiger Mask. Sayama had quit New Japan and gone into early retirement the year before, and a student of his, Kazuo Yamazaki, a former rookie with New Japan, came as part of the package. Ironically, it was the presence of Sayama that led to the departure of Shinma from the UWF, as Sayama had requested the dismissal of several office employees as a condition of his joining the group.

Unfortunately for the UWF, a series of events led to their downfall. Among them, a scandal involving company president Noboru Urata, Kimura and Gō leaving for All Japan after office disagreements over the sources for the foreign talent, as well as the murder of a key sponsor. Philosophical problems also arose. Sayama, a former kick boxer, wanted more emphasis placed on kicks and suggested rule changes to accommodate that, while Maeda pushed for a focus on submissions. It all came to a head during an infamous September 1985 match between the pair in which both are alleged to have stopped pulling their punches, referred to by fans as 'going cement'. A second similar meeting took place later that same month, the bout ending when Maeda failed to adequately restrain a kick, which Sayama claimed caught him hard in the groin, causing a disqualification.

The in-fighting led to Sayama leaving the promotion, while Baba offered the now-suspended Maeda an escape route to All Japan. He declined the invitation when he discovered there was room in the promotion for him and Takada, but none of his other colleagues. That in turn led to them joining Yamazaki, Fujiwara, Kido and the remaining rookies in a return to New Japan to begin an inter-promotional angle in December 1985.

Known as, "the battle of ideologies", the first major meeting between representatives from both sides saw Inoki defeat Fujiwara on February 6, 1986 at Tokyo's Ryōgoku Kokugikan, after Fujiwara had downed Maeda in a "qualifier" the month before. Despite New Japan taking the lead the first night out, the presence of the former UWF names was a huge boost to the popularity of the promotion after the departure of Chōshū and his Ishin Gundan stable. Interest in the angle peaked for a five-on-five elimination match between the two groups at Tokyo Gym on March 26 of that year, and a singles battle between Maeda and Tatsumi Fujinami at Osaka Castle Hall on June 12.

Despite being a critical and commercial smash in the ring, real tensions boiled backstage, leading to an infamous shoot bout between Maeda and Andre the Giant at Tsu City Gym on May 26, 1986. A year later, the return of Chōshū led to a "new vs. old" feud with Chōshū, Maeda, Fujinami, Takada, Kengo Kimura, and Super Strong Machine uniting as the 'New Leaders' to square off with Inoki and his 'Now Leaders', comprised of Fujiwara, Seiji Sakaguchi and Masa Saitō, which resulted in the phasing out of the UWF brand.

Bischoff witnessed the second version of the feud firsthand. It was a supremely hot period for New Japan, which saw them pull crowds in excess of 50,000 supporters to no less than three Tokyo Dome stadium shows in the span of six months, beginning on October 9, 1995 with *New Japan vs. UWFi*, headlined by IWGP champion Keiji Mutoh submitting Takada. *Wrestling War in Tokyo Dome* on January 4, 1996 saw Mutoh return the favour with Takada winning New Japan's top prize, which he in turn passed on to Shinya Hashimoto at *Battle Formation* on April 29 of that year. The card also boasted many of WCW's top names, hence the presence of Bischoff. As he recalls, "The arena shows were inspiring. Sixty or seventy thousand people were watching wrestling. At the time, we were lucky if we could draw eight or ten thousand. I began studying and thinking about what was going on around me, trying to find elements I could bring back to WCW."

The principal element Bischoff brought back to the States with him was the idea of the inter-promotional conflict between two groups. Realising that Vince McMahon would not be open to the idea of lending him a helping hand - even if it would be beneficial to both organisations - he decided to create his own in-house faction of "outsiders".

CURIOUSLY, IT was not even the first time WCW had attempted to promote such an angle. In March of 1986, Bill Watts rebranded his regional Mid-South Wrestling promotion as the Universal Wrestling Federation in an attempt to go national and compete with McMahon's burgeoning WWF, and Jim Crockett's NWA-affiliated Jim Crockett Promotions (rebranded World Championship Wrestling after it was later purchased by media mogul Ted Turner). Unfortunately for Watts, he was third out of the starting blocks in a two-horse race. Despite a critically acclaimed television product, the UWF struggled to gain traction with many of its biggest names having left for the bright lights of New York, including Watts' number one draw, Sylvester 'The Junkyard Dog' Ritter.

Worse still for the UWF was a crippling depression in their home base of Oklahoma that autumn, with a price war against Saudi Arabian oil providers leading to a 67% plunge over the course of four months that saw oil drop to just over $10 per barrel. The U.S. oil industry collapsed, with a production decline that lasted nearly a quarter of a century. Significantly for the UWF unemployment in Oklahoma rose to 8.9%, with many struggling to make ends meet. For most, money was being scrimped to put food on the table rather than blown on a night out at the wrestling.

Seeing the writing on the wall, Watts opted to sell the UWF to Crockett on April 9, 1987, along with the promotion's championships and many of its remaining star names, including Rick Steiner, Shane Douglas, Steve "Dr. Death" Williams, Eddie Gilbert, the Fabulous Freebirds, and a young, up-and-comer named Sting. Though all would later go on to varying degrees of success under the WCW umbrella, initially it seemed like Crockett and JCP booker Dusty Rhodes felt their already-established stars were superior to the newly-acquired UWF ones. Despite the presence of two UWF title matches on Crockett's annual *Starrcade* supershow on November 26 (Williams defeated Barry Windham in less than seven minutes to retain his UWF Heavyweight title, and NWA Television champion Nikita Koloff downed UWF Television champion Terry Taylor to unify both titles), the UWF name was dead come December, less than nine months after it was purchased.

CROCKETT WOULD have done well to learn from the lessons set by Jerry Jarrett and Jerry Lawler in Tennessee and Kentucky some three years earlier. At the time, the Jarrett and Lawler-led Continental Wrestling Association was the undisputed king of the south-eastern United States, during a period when promotional boundaries were still strictly adhered to. At various points they also boasted links with both the National Wrestling

Alliance conglomerate of territories, and Verne Gagne's American Wrestling Association out of Minneapolis.

In contrast to the CWA was the somewhat rebellious International Championship Wrestling group, helmed by Angelo Poffo and his two sons, 'Macho Man' Randy Savage and 'Leaping' Lanny Poffo. The ICW promotion had been founded in 1978 after a nasty split from Ron Fuller's Knoxville, TN and Dothan, AL based Southeastern Championship Wrestling. It was immediately considered an 'outlaw' promotion, one filled with wrestlers blackballed from the established monopoly that was America's promotional patchwork.

Without any support, the Poffo clan felt their best option was to go on the offensive, and did so by having Savage - their principal star - routinely appear on ICW television to cut disparaging promos against the CWA's top names. He threw out grandstand challenges left and right to Memphis bookers Jerry Lawler, Bill Dundee, and Jerry Jarrett, going so far as to blast Jarrett, Dundee, and Tojo Yamamoto as "cowards" for not accepting a challenge to fight him three-on-one for a $100,000 payoff.

Savage of course knew that there was no way anyone would take him up on his outlandish offers. The threats soon turned nasty. Savage declared that Lawler's late father would be "turning over in his grave" if he knew how scared his son was of him, decried him for having not yet retired (though Lawler was still only in his early thirties), even going so far as to knock on Lawler's front door with a camera crew in tow to demand a fight, safe in the knowledge that 'The King' was out of town that day. As Lawler recounted, "They'd go on their show and challenge all the guys on our show. They wouldn't talk about their own matches, Savage would just rip into me; 'I went to Jerry Lawler's house in Memphis and I threw a rock through the window and he was too scared to come out.' Stuff like that."

Most wondered whether Savage's words were hollow, and the question came close to getting answered in January 1980. Savage arrived at a CWA event in ICW's home base of Lexington, Kentucky and told Lawler's on-screen manager Jimmy Hart that he was there to take Lawler out. That night, the threat was real. As fate would have it Lawler was not in the building, having broken both bones in his lower left leg during a touch football game. Savage was fuming; suspecting the boys would be convinced he'd intentionally picked his moment to strike and would label him a blowhard.

Figuring he needed to save face, Savage turned his attention to Dundee, the number two babyface in the promotion. He purchased tickets at the box office for the entire ICW roster, with the intention of causing a disturbance during Dundee's main event match that night. Incredibly, fate would play another wildcard to prevent that, as a CWA fan, entirely unaware of the tensions around him, legitimately attacked Hart during the penultimate match of the evening and caused a riot unrelated to the ICW wrestlers. With the police quickly arriving to calm the situation, nobody from Savage's crew dared make a move, and Dundee's bout eventually passed without incident.

Despite that narrow escape, Dundee was not about to get off scot-free. His number came up after he unexpectedly crossed paths with Savage, Angelo Poffo, Pez Whatley and Thunderbolt Patterson outside of a local diner. Following a verbal exchange Dundee reportedly produced a gun, which Savage soon wrestled control of before pistol-whipping Dundee, leaving him with a broken jaw. Savage bragged about the attack relentlessly on the ICW television show, and with Dundee out of action for six weeks it was tough for the CWA to deny it. Dundee later claimed to have been sucker-punched, maintaining that Savage fled when he produced his Smith & Wesson.

THE LANDSCAPE had changed by 1982 and the Poffo family were struggling. ICW limped along under the spectre of dwindling fan attendance, brought about in part due to a raft of star names vacating the promotion over a short period of time. The argument could also be made that ICW were not helped by Savage and co's obsession with wasting so much of their valuable TV time slandering performers from a rival organisation instead of pushing their own matches. Even so, the bitterness that festered between the two leagues still was not enough to dissuade Jarrett from doing what he felt was right for business. He and Lawler soon purchased the assets of ICW, bringing their noisy neighbours into the CWA fold.

"Four years, eight months, thirteen days!" bellowed Savage as he strode onto the set of the CWA's live Saturday morning television broadcast of *Championship Wrestling*, flanked by his father Angelo to interrupt a match featuring the masked A-Team. "Do you know who you're talking to right now?! Where's Lawler?! Don't call me nothing, man! I'm the World Heavyweight champion! Get 'The King' out here!" Savage followed his words with actions, smashing a framed photograph over his head, tearing up a picture of Lawler and obliterating enhancement workers Henry Rutledge and the Pink Panther with piledrivers and flying elbow drops. He was soon dragged out of the studio by police under orders from CWA booker Eddie Marlin, though not before Savage could throw out a challenge for Lawler to meet him in a steel cage match.

Although not strictly an inter-promotional battle in the truest sense, with Savage, Angelo, and later Lanny becoming part of the established CWA roster, the initial rivalry was certainly grounded in that implication, much as Bischoff intended to achieve with Hall and Nash. The first meeting of Savage and Lawler was actually something of a test run, only advertised locally to fans in Lexington without any TV hype or on-screen angle to support it. Despite that, it still pulled a remarkably strong house of 8,000 fans to what would have otherwise been a routine Rupp Arena spot show. That was followed with their first properly advertised bout on December 5, 1983, a match which doubled the CWA's average attendance at the Mid-South Coliseum that year and drew 8,000 fans, making it the fourth-highest attended card of the year. The only cards that beat it were two gimmick celebrity appearances from renowned performance artist Andy Kaufman in handicap matches with Lawler, and Lawler's challenge of AWA World Heavyweight Champion Nick Bockwinkel.

If Bischoff knew the ghosts of wrestling past, and could learn from the triumphs of New Japan and the CWA, in addition to the mistakes of his predecessor's handling of the truncated UWF invasion, there was no way he could fail. If booked correctly, two diametrically opposed organisations presented on equal footing but espousing conflicting ideologies, could be box office gold for years, if not decades to come. Of that there was no doubt. WCW vs. nWo was going to be the biggest angle in wrestling history, and best of all, as the puppeteer pulling the strings of both factions, Bischoff knew he was guaranteed to end up on the winning side regardless of the storyline outcome.

The introductions of Nash and Hall on television had been a strong starting point for Bischoff's adventurous storyline, but he knew that he needed to align them with someone even bigger to fully capture the public's imagination. Any potential targets over in New York were now tied up in long-term contracts, and there was not anyone on the independent scene with the level of mainstream appeal that he coveted. He needed to look closer to home, and it so happened there was someone on his roster who ticked all the right boxes: Hulk Hogan.

MONTHS EARLIER, when the nWo was still an un-popped kernel of an idea nestled deep in the recesses of Bischoff's mind, he had visited Hulk Hogan at his Tampa home to discuss his WCW future. Bischoff was also in town looking to float the idea of Hogan turning heel for the first time in over fifteen years, since before the days of Hulkamania. He had heard the negative reactions aimed at Hogan from the WCW audience of late, which in truth had been there from the start but were beginning to intensify. Hogan's career was so intrinsically weaved in the tapestry of the WWF and the New York style of wrestling, that the long-time WCW fan base had a hard time accepting him as one of their own. Hogan had flirted with the idea of a turn briefly in October 1995 when he donned all-black, shaved his moustache and made distasteful allusions to O.J. Simpson, but a few weeks later he changed his mind, dropping the look completely and pretending it had never happened.

With Hogan earning an unprecedented salary, Bischoff expected him to justify what he was paying him. He wanted him to contribute something meaningful to the company, rather than simply turning up and apathetically sleepwalking through his well-worn routine. He decided that a Hogan heel turn would be groundbreaking, a perfect way to establish *Nitro* as the only 'can't miss' wrestling show on television. When he outlined his idea for Hogan as a villain, playing up potential future programs working with fresh opponents such as Sting or a rebooted run with perennial rival Randy Savage, Hogan did not respond. He barely even looked at the executive, such was his displeasure at the suggestion. After remaining silent for several minutes, Hogan stroked his famous Fu Manchu before turning to Bischoff and telling him, "Brother, until you have walked a mile in my red and yellow boots, you have no idea."

Realising it was a lost cause, Bischoff left the idea alone and vowed never to suggest it again. The next time the notion of Hogan turning was proposed, it was the man himself who made the suggestion. He had been watching at home as Scott Hall and Kevin Nash turned up on WCW television and began making serious waves, generating much interest in themselves and the WCW product. In typical Hogan fashion, he was eager to be a part of it.

WCW had been advertising that The Outsiders would be debuting a third teammate at the *Bash at the Beach* pay-per-view in Daytona Beach, Florida on July 7. In the weeks leading up to the event, Bischoff was unsure who the third man would be. The one thing he knew for certain was that it had to be someone from within WCW. His original idea was for Lex Luger to join the pair - given his recent WWF past, but word of the plan leaked to the dirt sheets so he decided to rethink. Eventually he settled on Steve 'Sting' Borden, a lifetime babyface with a brightly painted face. He was a strong candidate, someone many fans considered the face of WCW due to him never having worked for the WWF. Bischoff felt that turning Sting heel for the first time would get people talking, making the sort of instant impact he was looking for.

Borden was somewhat reluctant. As much as he knew the Outsiders had momentum and his career would benefit from an association with them, he was also apprehensive about throwing away the fan support that he had amassed over the past nine years. As Bischoff tells it, "Sting was receptive, not knock-me-over enthusiastic, but receptive. Everyone could see the power this storyline was developing. Only a few weeks old, it was already one of the most interesting stories in the last five or ten years." As the pair discussed potential ways for the invasion angle to develop with Sting's turn, a call from Hogan out of the blue changed everything.

Bischoff had not seen 'the Hulkster' in months, not since he had been shown the door from his home for daring to suggest a heel turn. Since then, Hogan had been taking some time off to film his latest direct-to-video B-movie in California, family comedy *Santa With Muscles*. When Hogan asked Bischoff to fly to L.A. for a meeting on June 26, the executive vice president dubitably agreed. The pair shot the breeze while drinking beer and smoking expensive cigars, before Hogan finally made his intentions clear. "Brother, who's the third man?" he asked in his deep, distinctive voice. "Erm, I'm not sure yet," replied Bischoff semi-truthfully. "I think you're looking at him," declared Hogan.

Bischoff was interested in the proposal, but he was also taken aback and confused. He pointed out the only way that could possibly work would be if Hogan turned heel, the same thing he had been so vehemently opposed to earlier in the year. Hogan knew that was coming, but had already resigned himself to what had to be done. Bowing his head, he admitted to himself as much as to Bischoff, "Brother... I'm already there."

"Hogan had the business acumen to watch that money train leave and think, 'It's not moving that fast, I can still jump on it.'" remembered Kevin Nash. While his words dripped with cynicism, it was true that Hogan's timing was no coincidence. He only had two pay-per-view shows left on his lucrative contract and he knew that his leveraging position had been severely weakened with the arrival of Nash and Hall, in addition to the strong ratings that *Nitro* had generated in his absence. As business-savvy as any wrestler in history, Hogan had made a calculated call to ensure he maximised his potential worth to WCW, or indeed the WWF, once his deal expired in October.

"It was around this time I realised that Hulk Hogan was a master negotiator," admits Bischoff. "He had seen the Outsiders story unfold, and he wanted to be part of it. If anyone can smell an opportunity and turn it to his benefit, it's Hogan." While Bischoff recognised that the motivation behind Hogan's change of heart was entirely self-serving, he also realised the performer fit the profile of what he wanted the third member of the invasion group to represent down to a tee. Not only was Hulk Hogan the most recognisable wrestler in the world, possessing a charisma and aura that could carry the angle to unforeseen heights, he was also *the* face of Titan's glory days.

As much as Vince's lawsuit had forced Eric to have Nash and Hall admit on air they were not working on behalf of the WWF, having Hogan join the duo would inevitably further that notion in the minds of the fans. Bischoff figured viewers would weave their own narratives as to who was representing who, thus adding a legitimacy and extra layer of intrigue to the storyline without him having to violate any further copyrights. Bischoff knew he could always argue that he was not encouraging that belief directly, he had simply - unintentionally - enabled it.

Bischoff was excited at the prospect of what he and Hogan were about to do, but still erred on the side of caution. He knew that while the plan was only an angle to him, it was going to be genuinely life-changing for Hogan. For Steve Borden to turn Sting heel after nine years would have been risky. For Hogan - who was far more popular at his peak - to turn on his loyal band of "Hulkamaniacs" after nearly fifteen years was practically unthinkable.

Worried that Hogan would change his mind at the eleventh hour, Bischoff talked again with Borden, who agreed to be on standby if for any reason Hogan felt he could not go through with it. If Hogan did not want to do it then there was nothing Bischoff could do; the creative control clause that Hogan had negotiated for himself meant he had the final say over everything that he was involved in.

HOGAN REMAINED torn in the days leading up to *Bash at the Beach*, second guessing his decision numerous times and internally wrestling with the consequences. He was a hero to millions, he had talked to dying children whose one last wish in the world was to meet him, he had championed a strong set of moral principles of saying prayers and eating vitamins to an entire generation, and now he was going to give all of that up to spike interest in a scripted storyline. His mind was made up; he was going to tell Bischoff that it was a bad idea and instead suggest that he be the hero of the piece; the man to stand up and fight for WCW against 'The Outsiders'.

When he and Bischoff talked again, the executive was able to convince him to rethink his decision and go through with the turn. He reminded Hogan that it was his idea in the first place and he was simply getting cold feet as the day grew near. Hogan agreed, but remained in such a state of distress about the entire ordeal that Bischoff, even on the day of the show, did not know what to expect. To ensure Hogan remained calm, Bischoff kept him holed up away from the rest of the crew at booker Kevin Sullivan's house. He did not want anyone on the roster getting in his ear, self-servingly telling him it was a bad idea, and that he should not go through with it.

Bischoff finally began to relax when Hogan sidled up to the arena in his blacked-out limousine an hour before the show began. Satisfied that Hogan's presence meant he was going to execute the angle, Bischoff once again talked to Steve Borden and thanked him for his professionalism, telling him that he appreciated his willingness to step into the breach if needed. Privately, Borden was somewhat relieved that Hogan was the one selling out his principles for money rather than he. As much of a boost as the storyline would have been for his ailing character, Borden still felt that being a slightly less popular babyface was better than becoming a traitorous heel. He mused that once the proverbial black hat had been donned, there was no coming back from it.

He did however harbour the slightest resentment towards Bischoff for not having faith in him to fully deliver on the angle. He noted that as soon as Hogan had bustled in with a selfish political power play, he was pushed to the side without any second thought. This real life resentment eventually grew to manifest itself on-screen. Soon Borden took advice from Scott Hall and reinvented himself as a darker variation of his persona, a brooding guardian inspired by cult movie *The Crow*. It would eventually lead to him co-headlining *Starrcade* with Hogan in 1997, a show that drew the highest WCW pay-per-view buy rate in the company's history.

Meanwhile, backstage in Daytona at *Bash at the Beach*, Hogan secretly discussed with Bischoff the post-match interview that he was set to deliver following his dastardly deed. It was here that Bischoff - realising that the 'Outsiders' moniker would no longer fit with Hogan involved - threw out a name for the movement for the first time: the New World Order. It was a handle plucked straight from the world of politics, with the connotations of the name implying dramatic change. It perfectly captured the ethos of the hostile takeover that Bischoff was presenting, and to his pleasant surprise Hogan agreed.

Kevin Nash and Scott Hall headed to the ring that night for what had been advertised as a three-on-three encounter against Sting, Lex Luger and Randy Savage. The bout became a three-on-two handicap match, without Hogan - whose big introduction was saved for the conclusion of the bout. As Scott Hall would later reveal, the pair were not even one-hundred percent sure who the third guy was, as Hogan's presence in the building had been kept a secret. "We had no idea who it was going to be," he remembers, "We wanted it to be Hulk, but he had creative control in his contract so he didn't have to do anything he didn't want to do. We went to the ring and we hadn't even met Hulk yet - I met him briefly at *WrestleMania IX* but I didn't know him. Bischoff wanted it to be Hulk, but before we went out he told us, 'If Hulk doesn't show, I'm gonna go with Sting.'"

The match unfolded with the Outsiders negating their numbers disadvantage by eliminating Luger from the contest with a worked injury that saw him taken away on a stretcher. It was a relatively humdrum affair for the most part, until a low blow from Nash to Savage sixteen-minutes in served as a cue for the watching Hogan to make his move. Behind the curtain the iconic wrestler said a final prayer and crossed himself, before stepping out to do the one thing he had always swore he never would.

When Hulk sauntered down the aisle, everyone watching assumed he was poised to slip back into the same familiar role that had acted as his calling card for years. That of the ultimate babyface hero, there to save the day. No one, not even the announce team trio of Bobby Heenan, Tony Schiavone, and Dusty Rhodes could imagine for a second what was going to happen next. That in itself was not unusual though; Bischoff preferred it that way, much to the annoyance of the veteran Heenan.

"Bischoff would never tell us the finishes of the matches or the angles that were supposed to air," Heenan would complain, "He justified it by saying, 'I want you to react like it was a shoot.' I told him that if it was a shoot we wouldn't say anything, because we had never seen one actually happen in the ring. I told him that it would be better to just tell us what was happening so that we could enhance the product."

There was a little more to it according to Bischoff, who felt the announcers had a troublesome habit of giving away what was going to happen when they were aware of the outcome. He wanted their responses to come across as organic and genuine, as if viewed through the eyes of the watching fans. Unfortunately, on this occasion it backfired for him when Heenan unknowingly yelped, "Whose side is he on?" as Hogan made his way down the aisle. The announcer was not trying to make himself appear insightful by foreshadowing the angle, he simply never suspected anyone would be gutsy enough - or perhaps stupid enough - to turn Hogan heel in the first place. He was merely posing the question to play devil's advocate. On this of all occasions, he happened to be dead on the money.

Even though Heenan had asked the question and planted a seed of doubt in viewers' minds, still no-one *really* believed that Hogan would be the third man. Then in an act that shook the sturdy foundations that modern professional wrestling had been built on, Hogan shoved the referee out of the way to ensure the camera was focused only on him, and dropped his famous legdrop on perpetual rival Savage. He stopped briefly to take in what he had done, before snarling menacingly towards the crowd and dropping the legdrop twice more to hammer his intentions home: Hulk Hogan was now a bad guy.

"A career of a lifetime right down the drain. Enjoy it my friend, you've gotta stand and look yourself in the mirror," howled a contemptuous Dusty Rhodes, summing up the thoughts of everyone at home. The response in the building was one of similar shock and anger, with the Daytona audience as close to rioting as a mainstream pay-per-view audience had even been. Immediately a shower of debris hit the ring, with Styrofoam cups, popcorn, Hogan merchandise and crumpled up flyers hurled into the ring in a display of unilateral anger. One fan was so enraged by what had transpired that he charged the ring to take matters into his own hands, only to be knocked unconscious with a single punch from an alert Kevin Nash.

Mean Gene Okerlund, a long-time onscreen ally of Hulk Hogan, stepped into the garbage-strewn ring and conducted the iconic performer's first heel interview in decades.

[Gene Okerlund:] Hulk Hogan, excuse me. Excuse me! What in the world are you thinking?

[Hulk Hogan:] Mean Gene, the first thing you need to do is to tell these people to shut up if you wanna' hear what I've got to say. The first thing you gotta' realize, brother, is this right here is the future of wrestling. You can call this the 'New World Order' of wrestling. These two men right here came from a great big organization up north and everybody was wondering who the third man was. Well, who knows more about that organization but me, brother? Let me tell you something. I made that organization a monster, I made people rich up there, I made the people that ran that organization rich up there. And when it all came to pass, the name Hulk Hogan, the man Hulk Hogan, got bigger than the whole organization. Billionaire Ted wanted to talk turkey with Hulk

Hogan, well Billionaire Ted promised me movies, brother. Billionaire Ted promised me millions of dollars. Billionaire Ted promised me world calibre matches. As far as Billionaire Ted goes, Eric Bischoff, and the whole WCW goes, I'm bored brother. That's why these two guys here, the so-called "outsiders", these are the men I want as my friends. They are the new blood of professional wrestling. And not only are we going to take over the whole wrestling business with Hulk Hogan and the new blood, the monsters with me, we will destroy everything in our path, Mean Gene.

[Gene Okerlund:] Look at all of this crap in this ring. This is what's in the future for you if you want to hang around with this man Hall and this man Nash.

[Hulk Hogan:] As far as I'm concerned, all of this crap in the ring represents these fans out here. For two years, brother, for two years I held my head high. I did everything for the charities. I did everything for the kids. And the reception I got when I got out here - you fans can stick it, brother. Because if it wasn't for Hulk Hogan you people wouldn't be here. If it wasn't for Hulk Hogan, Eric Bischoff would still be selling meat from a truck in Minneapolis. And if it wasn't for Hulk Hogan, all these Johnny-Come-Lately's that you see out here wrestling wouldn't be here. I was selling out the world, brother, while they were pumping gas in their car to get to high school. So the way it is now, brother, with Hulk Hogan and the New World Organization of wrestling, me and the new blood by my side, whatcha gonna do when the New World Organization runs wild on you.

Backstage Eric Bischoff wiped the sweat from his brow and breathed a sigh of relief. Despite a couple of gaffes regarding the group's name at the end of the interview, he was thrilled with how the plan had unfolded. The turn had worked perfectly, generating the exact response that he had hoped. "I knew it had not only worked, but it had gone over big. Really big," he boasted. "Congratulations," one member of his staff offered, "Now you will *always* be remembered as the guy who turned Hulk Hogan." Bischoff allowed himself a private moment to bask in his triumph with a cold beer, before contemplating what he had pulled off.

Turning Hogan had been his riskiest move to date, more so in many respects than going live with *Nitro* each week opposite the WWF. Hogan - despite his waning popularity - was still considered by Turner brass to be a significant factor in moving television ratings, pay-per-view numbers and merchandise. He was also genuinely considered a hero to millions of children who would potentially be turned off by the move. Bischoff's hope was that the loss of the younger fans and their families would be offset with the return of the adult males who had otherwise shunned his product. As *The Wrestling Observer* assessed:

> For older and long-time fans, seeing the biggest name in American wrestling do his first turn on a national scale is going to spark interest in a big way, particularly short term.

A few days later the ratings came in for the *Nitro* immediately following *Bash at the Beach*. Bischoff was thrilled; the show had pulled a 3.5, one full ratings point more than *Raw*. People were clearly interested in the Hogan turn, though Bischoff knew the real test came the following week. Piqued interest was one thing, but sustained viewership was the key. To his delight, the following week was much the same, with *Nitro* again beating *Raw* convincingly. At that moment Bischoff knew he and Hogan had made the right decision. People were genuinely interested in the 'nWo' angle, and where it would go next.

AS VINCE McMAHON looked to counter the impressive lead that WCW was forging in the Monday Night Wars, he was hampered once again by yet more departures of his top stars. The first major fallout was one entirely expected within the industry, when Jim 'The Ultimate Warrior' Hellwig's position in the WWF became untenable after less than four months back with the company.

Problems had started brewing in June while Hellwig was working a stretch of house show matches opposite Leon 'Vader' White. The two had been delivering bouts that lasted less than a minute due to respective injuries that both performers were carrying, with Warrior going over each night. However, White was getting riled because he felt Hellwig did not show any gratitude for what he was doing for him, and that the losses were hurting his own once mighty aura.

After doing the match and the job for three nights straight in front of meagre crowds in Rockford, Peoria, and Moline, White was taken aback when the respected Japanese wrestling press began reporting on his increasingly frequent defeats. He had reasoned that losses on small-time shows would not resonate outside of the towns in which they occurred, and as a former headline attraction in Japan the stories were bothersome to him.

He knew they would damage his strong reputation in the country, and potentially hurt his future prospects working there should his relationship with the WWF fall apart.

When he turned up at the much larger Rosemont Centre in Chicago, he was surprised when the agents told him to do the same twenty second match in front of a 13,650 strong crowd. Already carrying an enormous chip on his shoulder because he was rushed back early from surgery in January, White decided to take matters into his own hands. Following a series of Warrior clotheslines he refused to stay down as per the plan, instead rolling out of the ring and walking away. Officials stopped him as soon as he walked through the curtain, warning that if he did not finish the match then he would almost certainly be fired once Vince learned of the incident. White duly agreed, but still refused to lose via pinfall again, instead allowing himself to be counted out after a second barrage of Warrior's blows.

White was not the only one who resented Hellwig steamrolling over everybody on the roster, a privilege many felt he did not deserve due to his ingratitude. It caused a toxic environment backstage, which was a headache Vince did not want to deal with after finally seeing the notorious Kliq disband. He knew he needed a locker room with high morale, one with everyone pulling together to fight WCW, so the mass resentment towards Hellwig was of some concern to him.

On the other side of the fence, the main source of contention on Hellwig's part related to his staunch insistence on protecting his own trademarks from the WWF's eager marketing team. It was an agreement he felt was violated at a trade show a few weeks following the Vader walkout, where his slogans and iconography were used by Titan without consultation. It was a simple misunderstanding. The blunder came about because Hellwig's deal was confirmed at the last minute, with the marketing team unaware of the strict terms written into his contract that forbade the usage of some of his catchphrases and imagery.

The WWF had known for months in advance they had a booth at the licensing show, and they had already built the stall for it prior to Hellwig's return. Upon the Ultimate Warrior's reappearance on the screens, Titan wanted him to be represented at the convention because they were promoting him as one of their biggest stars. Those responsible for taking care of the event hurriedly slapped the trademarked Warrior face paint logo and "Always Believe" slogan on the side of the stall, simply as a way to have him involved. They had no idea that using them both was strictly prohibited, nor the trouble it would ultimately cause.

WWF Marketing Executive Jim Bell did. After seeing the modified booth he knew there was going to be a problem, realising immediately that the company were in direct violation of the terms outlined in Hellwig's contract. He decided that the best mode of defence was ignorance, reasoning that if Hellwig did not find out then no harm would be done. There might not have been an issue had he not prevaricated to such a degree in trying to prevent Hellwig from attending the show that it immediately made the highly-strung wrestler suspicious. Hellwig decided to investigate. He turned up at the expo with his girlfriend and was horrified when he saw his trademarks exploited. "Warrior went ape shit," recalls Jim Cornette, "He said, 'You've used my trademark and my logo, but all will be okay if you buy a million of my comic books for a dollar apiece.' We were all like, 'What the fuck? The guy wants a million dollars because we slapped his fucking logo on the side of a booth? Fuck him.'"

As betrayed as Hellwig felt by what he believed to be an act of disparagement, he put on a brave face and represented the company professionally. Once he returned to his hotel he tried to call his mediator Linda McMahon but was unable to get in touch. As a result he was still simmering when he arrived in Indianapolis on June 28 for the start of a house show loop. It was there that he and McMahon engaged in a heated telephone conversation, where Hellwig informed the chairman that he was furious his trust had been violated and that he had been lied to. McMahon - who was increasingly tiring of what he felt were Hellwig's unreasonable demands - dryly responded, "Hey, shit happens. People lie to me every day." When McMahon again refused to purchase the Ultimate Warrior comic books at the inflated price requested by Hellwig, the wrestler decided he had heard enough. He stormed out of the Market Square Arena, contravening one of McMahon's golden rules that if you are advertised and you are physically able to compete, then you work. "It's the single biggest no-no in our business," McMahon would say, "You cannot refuse to show up when advertised."

When it soon became apparent that Hellwig was also going to no-show his scheduled bookings in Detroit and Pittsburgh over the following two days, McMahon realised he would need to replace him. He had already been forced to give out hundreds of dollars worth of refunds in Indianapolis due to Hellwig's absence, and he wanted to minimise the deficit in the other two cities, both of which were key WWF markets. Vince initially asked Bret Hart to appear as a one-off, but he was unable to attend at such short notice due to other commitments. Getting desperate, McMahon punched in the area code for Arkansas and dialled the number of Sid Eudy, otherwise known as 'Sycho Sid'.

EUDY HAD not worked for the WWF since January, having left on poor terms due to a boiling over of frustration about the way he felt the Kliq had harpooned his career. When headlining with Kevin Nash back in 1995, he had frequently butted heads with his opponent over how their matches together should transpire. As the veteran in the bouts, he was unwilling to back down to Nash's whims, even though he was the WWF Champion at the time. The Kliq did not like it, using their stroke with McMahon to have Eudy shunted down the card and into opening matches. Tensions climaxed on January 6, 1996 in New Haven, Connecticut when Sid, thanks to manoeuvrings from the Kliq, was told he would be losing to real life friend but company jobber, Bob Holly.

Eudy felt that someone in his position being asked to put over a character long portrayed as a perennial loser was an affront. He decided to go through with the vindictive booking only for Holly's benefit, then walk away from the WWF altogether immediately afterwards. The first time Holly learned he was winning the match was when a bewildered Eudy came into the locker room where he was changing and asked, "So, how do you want to beat me?" It was so inconceivable that Holly assumed he was joking. Eudy confirmed he was not - they really were wrestling each other and Holly was getting his hand raised. Holly supposed his friend would be annoyed with him personally, but Eudy assured him he was not. "It's them," he snarled, meaning the Kliq, "They're fucking with me. Fuck this place, I'm done after tonight."

Even Holly felt that it was an insult for him to win the match, because he realised that Sid was a main event calibre star and had been pushed as such, while he was a lowly jobber on the totem pole who otherwise lost to everyone. He was uncomfortable about the whole situation and tried to stay out of the way while Eudy blew a gasket and rampaged around the locker room.

In the match, there were no problems. Sid put Holly over clean following a fluke crossbody, then came backstage acting like he had injured his neck. According to Holly, it was a lie; Eudy was feigning injury so he could walk out of the WWF and away from the politics of the Kliq. He flew home to Arkansas, then a few weeks later called up J.J. Dillon and Vince McMahon to tell them his doctor had advised he could never wrestle again. He then publicly announced his retirement live on a local Memphis wrestling show on March 2. He soon scored a job working in agriculture, and was content with the relaxed lifestyle away from the grind of the wrestling business.

When he picked up the phone six months later on June 29 and heard Vince McMahon's distinctive voice on the other end of the line, he was surprised to say the least. "How you doing, pal?" asked McMahon, and Eudy immediately knew what was coming. "Look, I need you to do me a favour. Warrior has pulled out of some shows and left us in the shit. Can you help me out and do two shots for me? I'll owe you one..." Eudy had genuinely intended to never wrestle again, but McMahon was a hard man to say no to. He also realised that with the Kliq now working across two different companies, their hold on the WWF was lessened significantly. The political minefield he had struggled to negotiate last time was no longer an issue. Sid agreed to help McMahon out, then asked the question he should have probably asked earlier in the conversation. "So Vince, when are the dates?" McMahon gave his trademark 'hyuk-hyuk' laugh and told him, "Well, the first one is in Detroit tonight, and the next one is in Pittsburgh tomorrow!" It was too late for Eudy to back out, so he agreed to jump on a chartered plane and fly to Detroit for the show. He was soon coerced into a full time return to the WWF, with the promise of yet another major push as a thank you for bailing McMahon out.

As much as Eudy provided an adequate short term solution to the star-power chasm left by Warrior's disappearance, some in the locker room were unhappy about his return and immediate push to the top of the card. To many of the underneath talents it felt like a slap in the face. They saw the Warrior situation as an opportunity for the WWF to take a risk and elevate one of them instead as a gesture of appreciation for their hard work. Instead McMahon had simply reverted to type and pushed the biggest guy he could find, even though Eudy was equally notorious for having many of the same character flaws as Hellwig.

Not a strong worker to begin with, Eudy was now even more limited than before because of his neck issues.[44] For those saddled with the task of putting him over, it would mean having to work even harder to get a respectable match out of him. Many looked at the status of Owen Hart as an example of why the Sid situation was so galling to them. Hart was a smooth ring general, one most felt deserving of another shot at the top of the card, but he was modestly built by WWF standards. He had been given his big shot in 1994 and then was shunted back down the card when it was over, whereas the limited but imposingly-built Eudy was given chance after

---

[44] Even though Eudy had not actually injured his neck during the January house show match with Holly, he did have recurring neck problems as a result of a cage match with Kevin Nash in 1995.

chance. Instead of working on top, Owen had been reduced to getting squashed by Eudy on house shows in under a minute.

At the Detroit event, the WWF decided to smear Warrior's name through ring announcer Bill Dunn. In his opening spiel he informed the audience that, "The Ultimate Warrior is not here because [in his words] he refuses to wrestle in a town like Detroit," shifting the heat for the no-show directly onto Hellwig and away from the WWF. Dunn promised that the "craziest wrestler in the WWF" would take Warrior's place, referring to the returning Eudy. Due to the limitations caused by his injuries and having been away from the ring for six months, Eudy was unable to physically do a great deal. As a result he worked only short, impromptu matches, but the response to him was enormous.

When Hellwig learned of the way his name and reputation had been sullied by Titan, he was shocked. He soon made an appearance on Bob Ryder's *Prodigy* online chat (which irked company officials no end as the WWF had an exclusive online deal with *AOL*), and expressed his surprise at the burial. He offered the explanation that his father Tom Hellwig had been sick on the 28th and 29th and had then died on the 30th, which he claimed is why he missed the shows. The WWF immediately protested the excuse, because Hellwig had not informed anyone of the situation with his father during any stage of their discourse. The last McMahon heard, Hellwig had been estranged from Tom since the age of three, and had repeatedly noted what little time he had for the man. The timeline did not match up either. Hellwig had been at the Indianapolis event on the 28th, only walking out because of the issues with McMahon over the licensing show, again without a single mention of his sick father.

Hellwig also told Ryder that he intended to return on the WWF's July 11 show in Albany, but McMahon was not so readily willing to accept him back into the fold. "[Hellwig missing dates] was the straw that broke the camel's back for me," said McMahon, "I finally learned my lesson. I would have been doing a disservice to the audience if I had kept promoting him." On July 8, McMahon officially suspended Hellwig. He demanded the performer pay a $250,000 bond to ensure that a similar situation would not happen again, which he would then forfeit if he pulled out of any future dates. He was fed up with Hellwig's constant demands, no shows, and unprofessional behaviour, so the bond was a way of either ensuring his commitment, or would serve as a valid excuse to get rid of him if he violated it.

In a somewhat surprising turn of events, McMahon decided to blur the lines of truth and fiction when he had Gorilla Monsoon announce Hellwig's suspension and bond stipulation on *Raw*. As the show had already been taped it left the WWF with little opportunity to make changes, though somewhat fortuitously they had already shot an angle that saw Warrior getting beaten down in a three-on-one attack by Jim Cornette's trio of Owen Hart, Davey Boy Smith, and Vader. It would have been a fairly simple task to claim he had been injured in the assault as a way to write him off television, then not air the already filmed follow-up segment on the following week's show where he exacted a measure of revenge. Such was the changing nature of the business that Vince felt too many people already knew the truth, so he decided that for once he would tell it to everyone else as well.

Hellwig's suspension also caused problems with the main event of the forthcoming pay-per-view *International Incident*, where Warrior had been scheduled to work alongside Shawn Michaels and Ahmed Johnson against Camp Cornette. McMahon decided to resort to his successful recent house show strategy, and brought in Sid Eudy as Hellwig's replacement. He flew Eudy to Titan Tower and had him hurriedly film some promos to promote his involvement in the bout, then had his production team slot them in to the upcoming *Raw* broadcast.

McMahon did not run down Warrior on television as many expected he would, because he still held out hope that Hellwig would post his bond and that the two could get back to business. In his commentary that night on *Raw* he sent out what appeared to be a direct plea to Hellwig as the Ultimate Warrior made his way to the ring for his pre-taped match with Owen Hart. "Hopefully we are not seeing the Ultimate Warrior for the very last time here on *Raw*," he told the audience, perhaps more hopeful than anything else.

Hellwig thought their issues could be worked out too, but Vince quickly became frustrated with the wrestler's failure to make the payment he was demanding. Under constant pressure from those around him to let Hellwig go, Vince called up the stroppy worker and flat-out told him, "We're not doing this anymore." After yet another heated row between the two over the licensing disagreement, McMahon turned on Hellwig and snarled, "I didn't sign that contract anyway, Linda did!" With that, Hellwig's deal was terminated and the two parties were back in their familiar position of being at loggerheads. It was the exact endgame scenario to their troubled relationship that many had predicted from the start.

Little over a month later, Hellwig filed lawsuits against Titan for unfair termination of his contract and trademark infringement[45], claiming the

---

[45] The trademark infringement related to the trade show situation, with Hellwig claiming a violation

WWF owed him $1 million for reneging on their agreement. He also claimed wrongful dismissal, again naming the death of his father as the reason he missed the June dates cited as the official reason for his firing.

Titan lawyer Jerry McDevitt dismissed the lawsuit as vague, stating that the suit had no merit because it did not mention specifics regarding the trademark infringement claims. Hellwig had pulled a similar trick after he was fired in 1992, but quickly withdrew the suit when the WWF responded. With this case, Titan expected the same, but Hellwig refused to back down. Eventually, he beat them in court and won the right to use the name "Warrior", as well as the gimmick, costume, face paint, and mannerisms of the character. Despite that, McMahon still offered him yet another chance in late 1997 when he made a desperate big money play to resign Hellwig in an effort to stop him from going to WCW. Hellwig rejected the deal, and wound up working for Turner in 1998.[46]

THE NEXT to leave Titan was Sean Waltman. The onscreen '1-2-3 Kid' had missed most of the year recovering from a drug problem, after turning up to a television taping in Des Moines back in April so impaired that he was unable to perform. Waltman was disenchanted and wanted out, and McMahon decided that he was not worth the hassle. According to Waltman, "Vince told me, 'Look, if you wanna go work for that billionaire asshole and you can make more money there, then I will give you a week to think about it and you can go if you want.'" After some wrangling over the terms of the split, McMahon was true to his word and granted Waltman a contract release five months before it was due to expire.

Waltman showed up in WCW for the first time on September 16 alongside friends Nash and Hall as part of the nWo. The faction had been on a recruitment drive since the Hogan turn, and Waltman was the sixth member to be added following WCW original Paul 'The Giant' Wight and another recently released ex-WWF employee, Ted DiBiase. Unable to use the 1-2-3 Kid name that had made him famous, he was instead creatively named 'Syxx' in allusion to his induction as the sixth man in the group.

---

due to the WWF using the term "Always Believe" and his face paint logo.

[46] It would take eighteen years for Vince McMahon and Jim Hellwig to finally bury the hatchet and work together again. Thanks to conduit Paul Levesque - by that point McMahon's son-in-law and a key official in WWE - a deal was struck to induct The Ultimate Warrior into the 2014 Hall of Fame. McMahon and Hellwig put the past behind them and made peace over a weekend that also saw The Ultimate Warrior appear on WrestleMania and Raw, and visibly shed two decades worth of ill-feeling. Then, in an astonishingly poignant set of circumstances, Hellwig died the following day after collapsing in a hotel car park on his way home from the festivities.

The ever-growing list of WWF stars of the eighties' working for WCW further expanded with their surprise acquisition of Roddy Piper in late October. Piper had not been a full-time WWF regular since 1987, and was away filming a movie when the call came from WCW asking if he was interested in coming in to work a program with Hulk Hogan. "He was one of the main guys we needed," says Hogan, "He was one of the last pieces of the puzzle." Despite having worked for McMahon for over a decade, most recently at *WrestleMania*, Piper decided to cash in on his name value while he was still mobile enough to offer something in the ring. He had been away filming movies anyway so figured that McMahon would not miss him. Furthermore, $2.2 million over two years was a deal that Vince was never likely to match.

It did not take long for McMahon to get wind of Piper's defection, though he made sure not to let on when he called Piper in October prior to his WCW debut with a proposal. "Hey Roddy, what better guy to induct "Superfly" Jimmy Snuka into the WWF Hall of Fame than Rowdy Roddy Piper?" Piper felt a twinge of betrayal. He had specifically been told by Bischoff to keep the agreement to himself so that news did not leak out before his debut, and as such he had been unable to give Vince the courtesy of telling him about the WCW move. He simply sighed and told his friend and now ex-boss, "Look, Vince, I can't..." McMahon did not leave him hanging there for long, "Yeah, I heard," he bluntly replied.

Roddy leaving did not bother Vince as much as he had Piper believe, though he was disappointed that he had not received a token courtesy call on his way out. Others within the Titan system could understand why Piper defected to Atlanta, and why WCW wanted him, "He could do less and it would mean more, he still had great name identity from the first *WrestleMania*," says Jim Ross. Fellow office member Bruce Prichard felt it was more about personal enlightenment, "He went to prove a point to Hogan, Vince, and himself that he was still Roddy Piper," he theorises. Piper himself had no qualms about admitting his single, true motivation for pitching up with Bischoff in WCW, "Why did I leave the WWF? Money! More money!".

TEN

TWO MONTHS FOLLOWING WCW's REVOLUTIONARY nWo angle, Vince McMahon responded by having Jim Ross make a shocking announcement: Diesel and Razor Ramon were returning to the WWF. Behind the scenes at Titan, even those closest to Vince had no idea what he was up to. As it turned out, neither did Kevin Nash and Scott Hall. It was a classic case of pro wrestling bait and switch. To counter the increasingly frequent departures of his well-known stars, Vince had come up with the brainwave that he would recycle existing WWF trademarks and make beta versions of his already established characters. So what if Nash and Hall had gone to WCW, he pondered; he would simply make improved, alternative versions of them. He reasoned that he owned Diesel and Razor Ramon, and that the *characters* were the real stars, not the people portraying them.

Once they were let in on the plot, everybody else in the company privately thought the idea would be a categorical debacle. As was ordinarily the case, none had the moxie to express those sentiments to McMahon. It would not have made much difference anyway, because he did not particularly care if the characters failed. He was more concerned with fuelling speculation to get a positive result in the Monday Night Wars.

To fill the role of Diesel, Vince turned to Dean Malenko protégé Glenn Jacobs, a six-foot-nine son of a U.S. Air Force officer, who had last been seen in the WWF performing as an evil dentist called Isaac Yankem. To look more like Diesel, Jacobs dyed black and straightened his naturally curly red hair before donning the attire. He did a convincing job. Of a similar height and build to Kevin Nash, from a distance it was hard to tell the difference.

For Razor Ramon, McMahon brought in Calgary native Rick Bognar, who had plied his trade on the Canadian independent scene before finding work in Japanese blood and guts promotion Frontier Martial-Arts Wrestling, and Genichiro Tenryu's WAR group. It was while he was working in ECW as Big Titan that his hidden talent was discovered: he did a spot-on impression of Scott Hall. "I used to do imitations of wrestlers all the time in Japan. It was fun, I was just goofing off," explains Bognar. Backstage at an ECW event in Allentown, Pennsylvania on May 18, promoter and booker Paul Heyman approached Bognar to tell him the plans for his involvement that evening. Before he could speak, Bognar jokingly cut in and asked, "What the fuck do you want me to do, mang?" in a deadpan Scott Hall accent. Heyman was impressed. "Oh my God!" he exclaimed animatedly, "Can you do that out there in front of the audience?"

Heyman grabbed a walkie-talkie and asked Bognar to do the impression again to an unwitting Troy 'Shane Douglas' Martin, whom it was well-known throughout the industry had serious heat with Hall, enough to ultimately lead to his WWF departure in 1995. Bognar played along and watched as Douglas' face turned a shade of beetroot red. Upon letting him in on the joke, Douglas laughed and asked the same thing that Heyman had, "Can you do it out there?" Bognar duly obliged, performing a low-rent version of Razor Ramon for the ECW audience dubbed "Slice and Dice Ramirez", complete with toothpick and trademark phony Puerto Rican accent. Little did he realise that amongst the amused audience in the arena that night was a WWF official on scouting duty, who reported what he had seen back to McMahon.

Bognar was offered a WWF tryout match three months later. He turned up to open the show at a mammoth television taping in Wheeling, West Virginia on August 19 against veteran journeyman Frank Stiletto, wrestling under the handle Rick Titan. Backstage prior to the bout, Bognar asked the lifelong jobber what he wanted to do in the few minutes they had been allotted, but Stiletto advised him that it was not that sort of match. "This is all about getting you over, kid," he told him, "This is your chance to get hired by the big leagues." Bognar was normally generous in the ring, in the habit of giving his opponent plenty of offence, but he soon realised that he was in a different world than what he was familiar with. Rather than performing an even contest, Bognar in his words, "beat the shit out of him" in the match.

Bognar was scheduled to work his second tryout match that night against Tracy Smothers, an opponent he felt he could have a satisfactory match with because their styles meshed well. He was devastated when told that the bout had to be pulled due to time constraints, and left the building depressed that he had lost his shot. Two weeks later he returned home from the gym and was shocked to find a message blinking on his answering machine from Vince McMahon, who had left his home phone number and asked that Bognar call him back.

Bognar immediately perked up, but upon starting to dial the number he experienced a modicum of trepidation, wondering why Vince would be leaving his home number rather than having him call the office. He realised it must be something significant, though he never could have guessed the proposal that McMahon would offer. "Yeah, Rick," Vince started, "The people want Razor Ramon back and I heard you do a great Razor Ramon." Bognar's heart sank as McMahon continued, "I own the trademark to the name, the costume and the character. Rick, I want you to be my new Razor Ramon."

"Ah, shit," thought Bognar silently to himself, but he immediately realised that if he wanted to live out his career ambition of working for the WWF, then turning down the notoriously stubborn McMahon would not be in his best interests. "I felt it could be the only chance I would ever get to be in the WWF and live my dream," he says, "I thought that if I said no to Vince then he would probably be pissed at me and never hire me again." With that in mind Bognar accepted the offer to play Razor Ramon mark two, though he remained concerned that the role would signal the death knell for his career.

He turned to two of his friends from ECW, Sabu and Chris Benoit, asking them for their opinions on the matter. After mulling it over, both concluded that the role was an opportunity he should grasp. Even though it could potentially ruin his career, it was also a foot in the WWF door that might eventually propel him to stardom. Bognar himself remained under few illusions about his future prospects whilst performing the Razor Ramon character. "I knew what was going to happen there and then, and it did happen - only an idiot couldn't figure that one out," he admits. "I knew Vince was partly doing it to piss off Scott Hall and Kevin Nash, to tell them, 'I created you,' but I just wanted my chance to say I had been there and done that."

Jim Cornette was as surprised as anyone else upon hearing the announcement that Diesel and Razor Ramon would be returning to the WWF. He had spent the prior day at McMahon's house in Connecticut writing the following week's television, where no-one had breathed a word of it to him. As he remembers, "It all happened in literally a two-day period. I was away from Vince for a day-and-a-half, and in that time he announced it on *Livewire*. When I got to Oklahoma for a house show some of the guys were coming up to me and asking, 'Nash and Hall are coming back?' I had no idea what they were talking about. I told them, 'No! I know nothing about this, and I was just at Vince's house writing TV.' I called Bruce Prichard and he told me the idea. I guess Vince had woke up one morning and said, 'I own them, so we're just gonna have them.'"

Before the imposter duo were unleashed on television, Cornette was tasked with helping them learn the trademark moves and mannerisms associated with the Diesel and Razor Ramon characters. He was given a tape featuring five each of Hall and Nash's matches from their time playing the roles, and spent an evening meticulously jotting down each trait, manoeuvre, and idiosyncrasy in a yellow legal pad.

"I wrote down every move that Kevin Nash did and I got to six - and that was with the hair flip. Razor was a little more difficult," he remembers. Soon afterwards he met with Bognar and Jacobs at a secret warehouse in Connecticut (where the WWF had a ring permanently erected) so that the pair could practice the roles. Even though both were fairly adept at aping the gimmicks, neither Cornette nor the wrestlers, or anyone else for that matter, thought that the plan was going to work. "Still, nobody there thought it was a good idea," says Cornette, "It's just that nobody dared try to talk Vince out of it."

As soon as Jim Ross revealed on the September 6 "Championship Friday" special edition of *Raw* that Diesel and Razor were returning to the WWF, Kevin Nash's cell phone immediately began ringing. He was in Shreveport that evening working a WCW house show when he first learned of the WWF's stunt, and soon he was bombarded with questions from all directions. He professed his innocence, claiming he knew nothing about the announcement and was as surprised by it as everyone else. Despite his protestations, Turner company executives were panicked. Given what Brian Pillman had pulled a few months earlier, Eric Bischoff too suspected that somehow he had been "had" again.

WCW lawyer Nick Lambrose paged Nash and told him to call a now irate Bischoff, who was screaming down the phone when they finally spoke. He had cause to be concerned. While no loopholes were written into Nash or Hall's contracts that would allow either of them to leave, unbeknownst to most the pair were not yet actually working under the terms of their full contracts. The oversight was due to WCW's scramble to sign Nash and Hall before their ninety day notice period with Titan ended. While contractual terms were agreed with both, some details still needed to be ironed out. With the deadline looming, Turner lawyers wanted to tie the pair in before their WWF contracts automatically rolled over, so had them sign deal memos to secure their WCW jobs. Due to WCW's disorganisation, the performers had not subsequently inked formal contracts with the company. Eric Bischoff would deny this in the future, but according to Nash, he and Hall were hustled into a room at the following television taping, where they had hard copies of their full contracts placed in front of them. They were each offered an additional $400,000 per year on top of their already agreed deals to sign them there and then. As neither had any plans to leave anyway, they did so without hesitation. WCW's knee-jerk reaction to Titan's cheap stunt had cost them the best part of a million dollars.

AT THE WWF's *Mind Games* pay-per-view, a backstage camera caught a tantalising glimpse of Razor and Diesel doing a number on Savio Vega, a ploy to get people talking for the following night's episode of *Raw*. On the Monday night television show, Jim Ross was handed the unenviable task of introducing the proxy performers, though not before cutting an edgy promo that once again highlighted the scatterbrained WWF mentality. Ross was supposedly shooting, delivering an interview that touched on reality. He expressed some genuine pent up feelings about his dealings with Vince McMahon and the WWF in the prior three years, but the purpose was to then reveal two characters who insulted the audience's intelligence. In the diatribe, he began:

> Tonight ladies and gentlemen, before I was so rudely interrupted with a commercial break, we're gonna conduct this interview right now. And in just a couple of moments I'm gonna bring 'Big Daddy Cool' Diesel and Razor Ramon right out here.

> But before I do, I'd like to beg your indulgence for just a minute or so and tell you something that I've got on my mind. There's something I've been waiting to say for a long, long time. And when I'm through telling you many of you are going to question my loyalty to the World Wrestling Federation. So let's clear that up right now: I have no loyalty to the World Wrestling Federation! I've only got loyalty to good ol' J.R.

> Let me tell you why: In 1993 I left a great job in Atlanta, Georgia. I left the Atlanta Falcons of the National Football League to go to the recognized leader of sports-entertainment, the WWF. I came here to be the primary play-by-play man in the WWF. I don't think anybody here's going to disagree that I'm the best play-by-play man in the whole damn business. So when I show up for work the first day at WrestleMania IX in Las Vegas, Nevada they give me a sheet to wear. They said, 'Oh it's gonna be a toga. You'll look good in a toga, J.R.' I leave the National Football League for a toga. It's crap. And then ladies and gentlemen I go to the first King of The Ring in Dayton, Ohio. And I guarantee ya, you listen to that broadcast, I carried the broadcast from ringside.

> And then did you ever wonder where ol' J.R. went to? Why isn't J.R. doing play-by-play anymore? Let me tell you why: because the egotistical owner of the World Wrestling Federation - and you know who I'm

talking about, I'm talking about Vince McMahon, couldn't stand the competition. So J.R. disappears. And then on SuperBowl Sunday in 1994, I woke up with an affliction called Bells Palsy and my entire left side of my face looked like I'd had a stroke. You think I liked that? You think I like that my left eye doesn't open all the way because I got sick? Well let me tell you how warm-hearted Mr. McMahon is: Mr. McMahon called me in to his office on February 11, 1994 and he fired my ass! So I get back in my car and I'm driving to my home in that overpriced hell-hole Connecticut, and I'm trying to figure out how I'm going to tell my wife and my two little girls that their daddy had just got fired.

So then, remember when McMahon got indicted? They needed somebody to come back and do RAW? They called ol' J.R. And then they let me go again! So finally they called me back, hired me back for fifty cents on the dollar to come back and work in the front office. Do you think that all these guys leaving the WWF was an accident? Hell no it's not! You think that all these guys coming here was an accident? Absolutely not. I've been very busy. And right now, I wanna bring back one of your favourites. He's the Bad Guy, Razor Ramon

Eric Bischoff was backstage at *Nitro* in Cleveland when the segment aired, watching a monitor solely set up to keep tabs on *Raw*. Stood across the room from Nash when the WWF revealed their hand, his jaw dropped when he saw Rick Bognar wander through the curtain clad in Razor Ramon garb. His heart sank as it quickly dawned on him that he had wasted a fortune in a blind panic re-signing two of his performers to contracts they were already under.

Reaction from most corners to the faux Razor Ramon and Diesel was wildly negative. Dave Meltzer in his *Wrestling Observer Newsletter* noted that it, "reeked of desperation," and worried that the WWF was killing their adult audience - the same one the company needed to cater towards if they wanted to compete for top spot in the Monday Night Wars. Ever since *Nitro* had gone to two hours live each week, it had trounced *Raw* by an increasingly large margin. The September 23 show was intended as a momentum shift back in favour of the WWF, as Titan had done everything they could to load the one hour broadcast. As well as the Razor Ramon unveiling, they were putting the show out live, presenting a supposedly unplanned ECW invasion, and an Intercontinental Title tournament final match that would guarantee a title switch. It did not make a difference. WCW again hammered the WWF, with *Nitro* pulling a 3.4 rating to *Raw*'s embarrassing 2.0. It was another in a series of wake-up calls telling McMahon that something needed to change.

That however, did not extend to the pseudo Razor Ramon and Diesel characters, both of which lasted into 1997. Despite being unmitigated flops from the off, Vince had a greater purpose to their continued presence on television: he was goading WCW to respond so that he could use it as evidence in Titan's ongoing trademark infringement lawsuit against them. By fake shemping the Diesel and Ramon characters, McMahon felt it proved that Nash and Hall's WCW personas were a direct imitation of Titan's intellectual property. Dave Meltzer could see through this transparent entrapment attempt, writing:

> The other potential endings to this angle would be to simply put the heat on Jim Ross at the end by saying his source was wrong, or saying that - as often happens in high-level negotiations - that the negotiations fell through. WCW really can't react publicly to deny the story because of the lawsuit, because by reacting and saying that Razor Ramon and Diesel - or even not using those names and talking about the wrestlers Titan is referring to being under contract and not leaving - would play into WWF's hands in the lawsuit. It could be construed as an admission they were using Nash and Hall as Diesel and Ramon without using those names publicly.

WCW was wise to the ploy and did not respond directly, so Bognar and Jacobs were forced to continue in the roles to an increasingly tepid, and oftentimes outright enraged response. "I was working my ass off, but the New York crowd didn't want it. I couldn't do anything to please them," remembers Bognar. "There's a difference between heel heat and pissing the fans off, and getting real heat. Or them just telling you, 'You suck, go home! We want the old guy!' That's not heat, that's just bad."

CREATIVE IMPOTENCE was not Vince's only problem throughout the summer of 1996; he was also beginning to contemplate whether Shawn Michaels was the right person to serve as the company's flag bearer by wearing his WWF Title belt. Shawn had been wandering a rocky road for months following the 'Curtain Call' and his subsequent professional breakdown at *Beware of Dog*, but he had mitigated that with some stellar performances in the ring. House show business with him on top also remained strong despite the WWF's falling television numbers, which could be primarily attributed to WCW's expansion of *Nitro* to two hours rather than Michaels' drawing ability.

"If Shawn had not been as good as he was, I shudder to think where the business would have been without him," assesses Jim Ross, "He had evolved to the point where as an in-ring performer he was almost untouchable." Michaels knew it too. He would gleefully rile his fellow performers by screaming, "Follow that!" after every great display, challenging them to match his impossibly high standards. "It was a period of time where Shawn became very full of himself and arrogant," remembers Ted DiBiase.

While there was little doubt that Michaels was in a league of his own between the ropes, cracks were beginning to appear in the façade of the usually supremely confident performer. He was taking the WWF's weekly Monday night defeats harder than most, personally though wrongly shouldering the blame. "None of the guys would say it to my face, but through all the gossip they were letting me know that I wasn't getting the job done. I think a lot of them wanted to see me fail and relished seeing me getting blamed for the bad business. Wrestling was my life, and the idea of failing began to eat me up," he muses ruefully.

By late summer, Michaels was as short-fused and irritable as he had ever been. "I lashed out at everyone," he laments, "Wrestlers, agents, Vince. Everyone was fair game as far as I was concerned." McMahon was so worried about Shawn that he allowed himself to be talked into switching the WWF Title to Leon 'Vader' White. The aim was to rehabilitate Michaels as a slightly more aggressive version of his persona - one that could better connect with the WWF's predominately male audience - then have him regain the title in his hometown of San Antonio at the *Royal Rumble*. A match at *SummerSlam* in August was to be the first of their series.

White had struggled through a troubled year of his own. His shoulder was in constant pain due to his early return from surgery, there was the situation with Warrior that had flared up in June, and then he suffered the ignominy of Vince telling him to shed weight and get in better shape if he wanted to receive a main event level push. McMahon remained unconvinced about Vader in the top role, and as usual had to be persuaded of his merits by the voices of reason Jim Cornette and Jim Ross. They sold the idea by appealing to McMahon's partiality towards Michaels, arguing that the troubled champion would ultimately look better coming out of the program once the endgame had been reached.

Still unsure, McMahon had Michaels and White work a series of trial run house show matches in the build up to *SummerSlam*, but in a decision that baffled most, he had Michaels win cleanly in each city they visited. When not losing to Michaels, White was working against Sid Eudy with similar results, and prior to that he had been doing the chagrin-inducing thirty second jobs for Warrior. It was hardly the way to build up a future World Champion, and evidence to most that McMahon had no faith in the Vader project whatsoever.

The original plan called for a non-finish at *SummerSlam*, which would lead to a rematch at *Survivor Series* in Madison Square Garden. At the Garden, Vader would win the title and embark upon a two month reign before dropping it back to Michaels at the *Royal Rumble*. However, during one of their house show matches in the lead up to the initial *SummerSlam* bout, Michaels became vexed with White working too stiff in the ring. Halfway through the bout's allotted time, White was holding Michaels by the hair and peppering him with hard shots, when suddenly Shawn stopped selling and grabbed White in a hold. He then leaned in and growled, "Motherfucker, if you don't lighten up, your ass will be on a one way trip back to Colorado."

White had known Michaels for a decade - the two broke into the business together in the AWA in the eighties - and he was shocked to hear Shawn blow up at him in such a manner. Visibly distressed, White called for Shawn to take the match to its scheduled conclusion much earlier than planned, then he trudged backstage dejected. "Leon was in tears," remembers Vader's manager that evening Jim Cornette, "He was sobbing that Shawn had told him, 'If you yank my hair that way again, you're fired.' Leon was a stiff, hard-hitting guy, and Shawn was used to everyone catering to him and working with him a lot lighter. He didn't wanna work with Leon because he didn't wanna take the ass kicking that came with working Leon." White would later come to see Michaels' point, "He told me once he had worked back-to-back for three hundred days for the past ten years. Your body can't take that kind of punishment over too many days. I had to modify my style, not just a little bit, but drastically," he admitted.

Weeks before *SummerSlam* rolled around from Cleveland on August 18, Michaels spoke with McMahon and had future booking plans significantly changed. He told the chairman in no uncertain terms that he was not willing to work a long program with White because of his painful ring work, warning that he likely would not make it to *Survivor Series* if he had to wrestle against him every night. As he had done many times before, McMahon took on board what Michaels said and kowtowed to his whim. As a result, the house show program was canned[47], and Vader's planned title reign was

---

[47] Though the WWF did still run the match in cities where they had already advertised Michaels vs.

shelved. It was Michaels who suggested someone else in the role of monster heel to dethrone him: Sid Eudy. Whilst Shawn felt that Eudy was far less competent in the ring than White, his work was nowhere near as painful and did not take the same toll on his body. "Sid worked light as shit and Shawn could control him in the ring," notes Cornette.

After weighing up the options, McMahon decided that he was willing to go ahead with substituting Eudy in for White. "Vince didn't take much convincing because Sid looked like a million dollars," says Cornette. "His [less than wholesome] track record was brought up to Vince, but his justification for going with him anyway was simply, 'Well, *look at him!*'" Since returning to the WWF in July, Eudy's stock had risen dramatically. His intense persona, dripping charisma, and imposing physical presence had resonated with a fan base desperate for star power since the departures of Kevin Nash, Scott Hall, and The Ultimate Warrior, not to mention the hiatus of Bret Hart. Sid was just the tonic, and with each passing week McMahon could audibly hear the volume of the reactions to him swelling. Meanwhile, the response to Vader was tepid for the most part, a direct result of losing on a nightly basis up and down the country for months on end in front of thousands of fans.

Before the shift to Shawn and Sid, there was still the small matter of the heavily pushed Michaels and Vader *SummerSlam* match to deal with. McMahon wanted Shawn's hand raised, but also Vader to be kept strong enough to put over Sid in the following months to build him for the *Survivor Series* confrontation with Michaels. He decided that the best way to do that was to have Vader win on a count out, only for the match to be restarted and then end on a disqualification. WWF President Gorilla Monsoon would then authorise a third and final restart to produce a clear winner, where Vader would succumb to a pinfall defeat having first been allowed to kicked out of a Michaels superkick.

On the morning of the showdown in Cleveland, the two competitors laid out the basic blueprint for what they wanted to do in the ring that night. They were cordial and saw eye-to-eye backstage, but the geniality soon dissipated once the bout started. White was used to leading the rhythm and calling the spots in the majority of his matches, because that was traditionally the heel's responsibility. However, Shawn was so talented, not to mention headstrong, that he too was used to calling the shots. The deviation from the norm caused White to struggle, with his timing noticeably off on occasion and Shawn increasingly riled as the contest developed. "Shawn was very dominant in the ring," says White, "I always

Vader as the main event.

felt that it was the heel's role to call the match, but in the WWF, Shawn felt it was his role," he explains.

Towards the climax of what ended up a rewarding bout, Michaels had planned a clever spot that would see him soar from the top rope with an elbow drop, only for White to move out of the way. That in itself was nothing unusual. The innovative part would see Michaels shift his body in mid air upon seeing White evade him and land on his feet, before then hitting the move. Unfortunately, a bewildered White forgot the spot and did not move. Rather than simply hitting his usual elbow and covering White's mistake - about which no one watching would have been any the wiser - Michaels decided to publicly humiliate him instead.

Once Michaels realised that White was not going to evade the move, he shifted his body and landed on his feet, then stomped him repeatedly while yelling, "Move! Move you fat piece of shit!" Michaels exposed the error in such a way that it was obvious even to the casual fans in the audience what was going on. "It was one of the most unprofessional displays of bratty impudence that I have ever seen in a wrestling ring," noted one aghast wrestler who had watched from the locker room. White was more circumspect when looking back, "I made a few mistakes towards the end. I think it was a good match, but it could have been better had I not made so many mistakes," he confesses.

Years later Michaels was apologetic about the way he had acted, citing circumstances and his ongoing high stress level as the cause. "I shouldn't have yelled at Leon," he says wistfully. "What I did was unprofessional. I was snapping under the pressure," he admits. "Shawn was *always* that way," argues Jim Cornette, "He was a miserable prima donna before he even got the title, and he wasn't any more or any less miserable afterwards than he normally was. I made sure that I was never anywhere near him, because he was always a cantankerous shit."

CHANGING THE future direction of the WWF Championship meant the card for September's *In Your House: School of Hard Knocks*[48] had to be reshuffled, as Vader's unceremonious and comprehensive defeat at *SummerSlam* had effectively killed him off as a challenger. Original plans had called for Shawn Michaels and his mentor-cum-manager José Lothario to team up opposite Vader and his mouthpiece Jim Cornette - a piece of

---

[48] The show was named as such due to taking place in ECW stronghold Philadelphia. In keeping with that, the WWF decided to run an angle on their card with the promotion. Titan agreed to have a number of performers from ECW interject themselves in a match on the card after causing a disturbance in the front row, setting up a further future working relationship between the groups.

booking Cornette was relieved had to be changed. "That was Vince's idea and I wanted to do it like I wanted to go to the dentist and get my teeth grinded," he says, "I didn't want to be in the main event of a pay-per-view, because as I was on the creative team it would look like I had booked myself to be in that spot." With the plan nixed, the WWF decided to insert Mick 'Mankind' Foley into the headline mix for a one-off title match, necessitating the show to change its name to *Mind Games*.

Federation officials had been pleased with how rewarding Foley's series with Undertaker had been throughout the summer months. Many in management were also hoping that he could bring out the same level of intensity and motivation from Michaels as he had done with Mark Calaway, which would help significantly in rebuilding the ailing champion. The only concern was that the pay-per-view emanated from ECW territory: Philadelphia. Foley was still highly regarded by the hardcore faithful, and with Michaels already feeling a backlash from some sectors of the fan base Federation officials were worried that he would be given a heel reaction in the match. To quell that, they sent Foley out during the preview show and had him cut a promo on ECW and its fans, running them down, albeit without mentioning their name. It worked, and the resulting response to both competitors was exactly as McMahon desired.

The bout was the first time that Michaels and Foley had ever worked with each other, which ordinarily meant viewers could expect a fumbling contest between two unfamiliar performers. Not on this occasion. That night in Philadelphia the chemistry was instantaneous, with Michaels and Foley meshing as if they had wrestled each other nightly for years. As hoped, Foley brought out the violent, innovative best in Shawn Michaels. "Mick's character allowed my character to get a little aggressive, and I needed that as much as possible," Shawn recalls gratefully.

During the match, Shawn seized an opportunity to take a knowing shot at the critics who had condemned his behaviour at *SummerSlam*, inserting a spot into the bout that cheekily referenced his blowing up at Vader. After reversing an Irish whip from the corner, Michaels jumped onto the middle rope to set himself for a crossbody. Foley, as instructed by Shawn, did not follow as he "should" have, causing an apparently pissed off Michaels to run at him and scream, "Come on!" before landing a punch to his face. It was designed by Shawn and intended to look like a shoot, a subtle "fuck you" to the insiders who had been riding him since *SummerSlam*. The two followed it up by engaging in a real-looking but still entirely worked scuffle on the mat, while McMahon from his commentary position bellowed, "Michaels is dangerous. Michaels is hot!"

Much like he had opposite Undertaker at *King of the Ring*, Mankind brought to the table a level of brutality hitherto unseen in WWF rings. He and Michaels had been given free rein by McMahon to use all manner of assorted weaponry, be it chairs or a ringside table. Vince reasoned that the explanation as to why ECW was so popular in the city was down to a profuse employment of exotic plunder, so he had settled on the theory of "when in Rome". It was innovative chaos. Despite a cheap disqualification ending courtesy of interference from Vader that left some pay-per-view purchasers rolling their eyes and contemplating whether the oft-inconclusive *In Your House* shows were worth the monthly investment, the match was universally acclaimed by wrestling critics.[49]

Despite Shawn's impressive in-ring showing at *Mind Games*, outside of it he was beginning to visibly show the pressure that came with being the company's top dog. "By September, I was completely stressed out," remembers Shawn. Even his family, who he rarely saw due to his schedule, could sense that something was amiss with him during their brief get-togethers. "I know from being around him at that time that it was very hard on him," recalled his father Dick Hickenbottom.

Michaels' mindset was hardly helped by a call from McMahon telling him that he and Paul Levesque were no longer permitted to travel together due to their conflicting babyface and heel alignments. Levesque was Michaels' one solace on the road; the man he could confide in, who kept him positive. Equally important to Shawn, Levesque was also his designated driver. "Shawn was a lonely man on the island backstage at that point," observed Bob Holly, "He was drinking more, doing more drugs. He was in a whole other world."

Worried that Shawn was on the verge of a mental breakdown Vince turned to a trusted acquaintance, long-time employee referee Tim White, and asked him to take care of Michaels on the road. White had done something similar back in the eighties for his friend Andre the Giant - who was a notoriously heavy drinker. The difference was that Andre had needed a companion to help him get around due to his overgrown size, whereas

---

[49] Debate over the intended finish of the Shawn Michaels-Mankind match at *Mind Games* was a source of wrestling folklore for some time. Astute observers noticed that Vince McMahon appeared to relay instructions to Earl Hebner during the bout, which some took as him changing the planned finish "on the fly" from Mankind winning the title to the disqualification that transpired. As with many long-standing wrestling rumours, this was fantasy that morphed into reality through erroneous repetition. The finish was exactly what had been booked, the only difference was that Vader's interference which led to the disqualification was late. McMahon was simply relaying instructions to Hebner that instructed Michaels to formulate an alternative way of reaching the intended end point of the contest if for some reason Vader did not show up.

Michaels required a babysitter, someone to make sure he turned up for scheduled appearances and live events in a reasonable condition to perform. White was distraught with the responsibility of looking after the petulant World Champion and even considered quitting the company to avoid the task. It was a thankless job, and Michaels by his own admission made his life miserable. White would later tell friends that it was the worst period of his career.

Other members of the locker room were disgusted that the WWF Champion needed to be chaperoned like an infant. "I don't believe there's a place for people like that in the industry," rants Holly. "Why should somebody else have to take responsibility to get you to the show on time? If you're a grown man in the wrestling business and you can't get yourself to the arena or take responsibility for what you've got to do to get there, you have no place in the industry, no matter how talented or how much of a draw you are."

Shawn was so sour that he even took his anger out on his sixty-two-year-old mentor José Lothario, the man who first trained him to wrestle. Lothario had been brought in by the WWF to act as Shawn's on-screen manager, an idea first suggested by Bruce Prichard, who wanted to capture the father/son relationship of Rocky Balboa and Mickey Goldmill in *Rocky III*. Shawn was not comfortable with the idea, feeling he did not need a manager because it made him look "un-cool". He spent the months with Lothario by his side shunning his former teacher, turning his back on him and frequently yelling at him, unhappy about having to share his spotlight with anyone else. Witnesses to this behaviour in the locker room were appalled.

Former champion Bret Hart could see the pressure of being the main man getting to Michaels too. "Shawn was finding out that it was harder than he may have thought to go out there and blow them away every night, and do it without getting hurt," he comments. "The physical and emotional weight brought out the worst in him. He became increasingly bad tempered. No champion since Hogan had his own dressing room, but Shawn reverted back to the days when the champion felt the need to elevate himself above the rest of the boys."

SHAWN'S PROBLEMS worsened on September 29, when only months after main eventing the highest grossing Madison Square Garden card in company history, he headlined an event at the famous venue that drew the worst paid attendance at the building since Vince's father had promoted his first card there in 1956.[50] Less than 4,000 fans turned up for the Sunday afternoon show, which saw Michaels team with The Undertaker in the main event opposite Mankind and Goldust.

Despite what he felt, Shawn was not responsible for the poor turnout, which could instead be directly attributed to two other key factors. The first was a weak line-up featuring many of the intended-for-television performers brought in during the Cornette-led talent drive a few weeks earlier, none of whom the smart New York crowd considered worthy of working at the Garden. The second was a bigger issue; a month earlier the WWF had decided to stop paying for television syndication in most markets - including New York City - believing they could still draw strong houses in their established venues by only using local advertising and inserts on *Raw* that promoted the events.[51]

The decision had been a cost-cutting measure taken in August, which Titan accountants had analysed would save the company around $2 million per annum. Ever since Vince McMahon had bought out his father and took over the WWF, an aggressively assembled, custom-built television syndication network had been one of the primary backbones of his business. In the eighties, syndicated television shows aired in local markets and featured specific localised advertising for upcoming live events in the area. The programming was also where the majority of notable storyline developments would take place, so as to ensure that casual fans who only watched one wrestling show a week would choose the one containing advertising aimed directly at them.

Nevertheless, it came at a cost that was becoming increasingly difficult to maintain. To air its wrestling show on local television, the WWF was obliged to pay compensation, which in layman's terms meant they bought the television slot from the stations. It gave Titan control over their own area-specific advertising and was considered vital to increase their visibility when securing national advertising deals. By 1996, the revenue generated from those ads was deemed to be worth less than what the company were paying out. In a period of straitened finances for the WWF, it was an expense they could no longer afford to shoulder, especially as they felt that the onset of *Raw* as the WWF's flagship show on cable TV nullified the need for syndication.

---

[50] The card, which took place on November 26, 1956 under the Capitol Sports Wrestling banner, was headlined by Antonino Rocca against Dick the Bruiser. It was considered a disaster at the time, pulling just over 10,000 fans for a total gate of $30,000.

[51] There was also a third factor: the show came right in the middle of football season. Local team the New York Giants had a 1 p.m. home game that day against the Vikings, meaning anyone attending would not have made it to the MSG show.

Vince made the decision that effective from September 1996, the WWF would pull out of any syndicated television deals they had to pay compensation for,[52] and one of those was New York - his biggest market. Thus the promotion arrived in the city for the late September MSG card having had no local television presence in the area for the first time in modern memory. Even though McMahon felt that his major markets would not be affected and would still be able to pull in crowds for house shows, months earlier Dave Meltzer had suspected that might not be the case. "It is the bigger markets that they'll be most vulnerable in," he warned, "those are the markets they'll lose without compensation."

He turned out to be right. Following the MSG embarrassment, the WWF soon opened negotiations with New York based stations Channel 31 and the MSG Network in an attempt to garner a syndication deal, before finally securing a show called *Shotgun Saturday Night* at the end of the year. *Shotgun* was unlike anything else the WWF had ever tried: a dimly lit nightclub show that aired live and featured a far edgier product than the company had ever dared push before. It was an obvious attempt to capture the gritty feel of ECW and the attitude to match.

McMahon had wanted *Shotgun* to be the WWF's version of ECW so much that he even turned to Paul Heyman to help him out. Realising he was out of his element, Vince asked Heyman - a former publicity agent for New York's Studio 54 club - to find a venue for the shows. Heyman secured a number of hot New York nightclubs for McMahon, and in return Vince agreed to promote ECW pay-per-views during the *Shotgun* broadcasts. The first of those in January 1997 was certainly a stark departure from the WWF norm, featuring Terri Runnels flashing her breasts, cross-dressing wrestling nuns, and the suggestive ramblings of Tammy Sytch alongside a bewildered Vince McMahon on commentary.

THE BELT tightening had actually been going on since Vince's high court acquittal in 1994. The steroid trial - and some other notable lawsuits - had cost him tens of millions of dollars in the previous three years, and he realised cost-cutting needed to take place across the board in order to prevent the WWF from posting record losses. In September 1995, he called a meeting with all of his staff and took the decision to cut executive salaries across the board, reducing their income almost in half with 40% pay cuts. The wrestlers' pay was not a problem at the time because none of them

---

[52] Though some markets still syndicated WWF programming, no compensation deals involved in them. Rather, the stations would sell their own advertising and generate revenue that way, with the WWF getting local advertising on the wrestling show for live events as their part of the bargain.

were yet on guarantees, so trimming their payoffs and reducing the percentage he paid them in royalties would be a simple enough task. His decision caused outrage in Titan Towers, with many of Vince's long-time allies appalled that he was reducing their salaries so drastically. Alfred Hayes - one of McMahon's closest confidants for a decade - was so offended that he quit the promotion.

"He only singled out the wrestling people, the guys who used to be in the business," says J.J. Dillon, who had worked closely alongside McMahon since 1989. "When he called the meeting he said, 'All of you who used to be in the business can't think like wrestlers anymore. You have to think like businessmen.' I lost all respect for him after he did that."

The decision affected Dillon more than most. He had been struggling to get his finances in order for years due to decades of mismanagement, bad investments, and a monthly alimony he was obliged to pay. When the salary cut was announced, Dillon saw his annual income drop significantly, which left his already tightly balanced financial situation precarious.

The salary slash forced Dillon to begin seriously considering finding alternative employment, but the financial commitment to his house, and a need to support his family, meant he had few options other than to stay put. However, even before the pay situation, Dillon felt his relationship with McMahon was already stretched to breaking point.

Since he had started out, Dillon had committed himself to the wrestling business 24/7, which was a trait he shared with McMahon. It was well known throughout the industry that McMahon was a workaholic, devoting almost no time to anything else, not even sleep, which he felt was a hindrance and a waste of his time. He would regularly wake at 4 a.m. and fully expect everyone in his inner circle to do the same thing. For many, riding with McMahon was an exhausting life, but Dillon flourished in the role.

Everything changed when Dillon had children. Instantly they became his priority, and wrestling was forced to take a back seat. He began re-evaluating his life, and had a moment of clarity during a journey with McMahon. As he recalled, "Vince would drive at 100mph then get pulled over and given a ticket. Then he would drive right off at 100mph again. I was sat in the back of the car one day thinking, 'If he ever wrapped this car around a tree, what about my kids? Who would take care of them?' I started riding with Howard Finkel instead. Now Vince sometimes liked to refer to himself in the third person, and one day he came up to me and asked, 'What's the matter, you don't like Vince anymore?' I asked him if he wanted the truth, and told him that my priorities had changed. It didn't mean I had any less passion for the business, I was just balancing my priorities. Over a period of time, that probably strained my relationship with Vince."

Despite the issues that were starting to develop, Dillon became rooted in the company when Vince helped him purchase a house in Connecticut, straightening out some of his financial problems in the process. Dillon was in his debt. Around this time, McMahon implemented a new drug testing enforcement policy which he believed was so state of the art, that he sent it around the NBA, MLB and NFL, challenging each of them to come up with something comparable. Perhaps tellingly, it was Dillon's name that was listed as the director of the program, with McMahon's name nowhere to be found.

"Vince was arms length from it," remembered Dillon. "If anything came up as suspicious, it was my name that was listed on there and it would be me hung out to dry. If anything ever came up, all Vince would say was, 'He was the person in charge.' I was the fall guy."

The straw that broke the camel's back for Dillon was being leaned on to assist in covering up a failed test in order to protect a highly-positioned member of the roster. Dillon was already desperate to leave the WWF and had been for the previous year, but at this point he realised he could not handle working for McMahon anymore.

However, he was unable to leave until he had paid McMahon back the money fronted to him to buy his house, so he covertly sold the property without the WWF's knowledge, waiting until the day it closed on the market before acting. "I sold the house and took a $50,000 loss, but it gave me the freedom to up and go," says Dillon. "My wife rented a house in Atlanta so we had somewhere to send our furniture, then I walked up to Vince the day before his son Shane's wedding, and handed in my letter of resignation. I said, 'If you want to talk, let's talk.'"

Dillon, along with Vince and Shane, spent the next hour-and-a-half locked in Vince's office. The discourse was intense, with Dillon laying on the table his true feelings towards McMahon. "I told him I had lost all personal and professional respect for him because of what had happened, and that I couldn't work for him even one more day. He didn't see it coming. I packed up my office and handed in all of my company items to Human Resources. Vince was panicked, his wife Linda was in tears. They were afraid I was going to go public and create a scandal out of it."

In a constant state of high paranoia due to the tribulations of the Monday Night Wars, McMahon was deeply worried that Dillon was going to engage him in a public dirt-slinging contest. McMahon was so concerned that his ex-employee was going to call a press conference and create a wave of bad publicity for the company similar to the one that had nearly ruined him five years earlier, that he began desperately calling him to try and fix things.

When McMahon reached Dillon a few hours later, he challenged him on the potential exposé that he feared. The thought had not even entered Dillon's head. "Gee, talk about wrestlers being paranoid," J.J. told him, "That was the furthest thing from my mind." For Dillon, his departure was a matter of principle, but McMahon was still eager to mend the fence. "You have restored my faith in humanity," he stated, "Please, I want to make it up to you. Come by the office tomorrow and we will straighten this thing out."

Dillon was already halfway to Atlanta when the call came, and told Vince he was nowhere near the office and so unable to make it. McMahon implored him to call the HR department the next day, but Dillon pointed out that it was a Saturday and they were closed, thus no-one would answer. "They will answer," McMahon promised with absolute conviction.

Sure enough, when Dillon called the Titan's HR department the following day, he was answered immediately. Waiting for him was a new contract offer: $200,000 per year over the next two years, and a lump sum payment of $130,000 to pay off an outstanding credit note he had relating to issues with the IRS years earlier. Even in a time of budget cuts across the company, McMahon was so desperate to keep Dillon that he was willing to pay big bucks in order to do so.

Yet a few days later, a fax came through to Dillon's lawyer pulling the entire deal. The WWF claimed that Dillon had engaged in contact with WCW, and that he had used his company American Express credit card improperly in order to obtain plane tickets so he could meet with the rival promotion. "I had turned my card in six months prior," says Dillon, "I wasn't even using it anyway because I was trying to get my financial situation sorted. I think because I didn't do what Vince feared I would do - and with the wedding out of the way - he decided to pull the whole thing. I don't know for sure; I never called him or asked him." Dillon was quickly offered a job by Eric Bischoff in WCW based on recommendations from Tony Schiavone and Kevin Nash, and began working there on October 1.

Less than a month after Dillon had departed Titan, leaving his position as director of drug policy enforcement open, McMahon sent a memo to his talent roster detailing a relaxation of the company's drug testing policy that read:

This memo is to advise of certain changes in our drug collection and testing efforts, and to reiterate our position on the use of illegal and performance enhancing drugs. As each of you know, the company instituted systematic drug testing years ago on a group basis. Additionally, the standard talent contracts contain provisions strictly prohibiting the use of illegal and performance enhancing drugs which subject any offender to termination of their contract. As a result of our drug testing program, the incidence of use of illegal and performance enhancing drugs is so slight that group testing is no longer cost effective or necessary. Thus, we are, effective immediately, suspending drug collection and testing on a group basis. In doing so, we wish to reiterate that the strict prohibition against use of such drugs remains our policy and that any person caught violating our policy will be dealt with strictly. Additionally, we reserve the right to test any individual, at any time, for the use of illegal substances. If any individual tests positive for any prohibited substance, appropriate sanctions up to and including termination may be imposed.

The timing of the memo was telling. While on the surface it may have appeared to be simply another cost-cutting measure the company were taking in order to cover the glut of guaranteed contracts they were now paying, some sceptics felt otherwise. They saw the change as merely McMahon indirectly giving the go-ahead for his performers to start using steroids again; a reversion to type as a last resort to combat WCW. The change in company policy towards drugs protected the WWF should Dillon ever be inclined to reveal - potentially under orders from Bischoff - where the proverbial bodies were buried.

It was no secret to anyone in the locker room that McMahon had always believed that bigger bodies equalled bigger ratings. Many of the boys felt the memo now gave them *carte blanche* to take any shortcuts they desired to move ahead in the pecking order. That belief had already been partly-fuelled by the signing of bodybuilder Achim Albrecht, a former *Mr. Universe* winner whom all of the boys were sure was using steroids, and the return in August of Brian 'Crush' Adams. Adams had been publicly fired in early 1995 after his arrest on drug possession charges and resultant jail term. It reeked of hypocrisy when McMahon not only rehired him, but actually pushed him as an ex-con. He even went so far as to encourage his audience to chant "jailbird" at him.

It was the kind of reality-based storyline that Vince would have never signed off on in the past. Real life situations, be they positive or negative ones, were not allowed to creep into a WWF performer's television character. What happened off screen for all intents and purposes did not happen as far as WWF programming was concerned. To use Adams' conviction as a plot point for Crush was a groundbreaking decision, and yet another of many gradual shifts from McMahon towards an entirely different presentation of his product.

IT WAS around this time that McMahon began looking for a new babyface hero to carry the company into 1997. He still believed in Shawn Michaels the performer, but his faith in Michael Hickenbottom the man was wavering. Ironically given the *Wrasslin' Warroom* skits earlier in the year, it was two men from the past that McMahon attempted to turn to. The first, outlandishly, was Hulk Hogan, the man jointly responsible for WCW's recent ratings dominance and the same guy who McMahon had so viciously pilloried in the skits.

Hogan was in Denver with Eric Bischoff when he received a call telling him that McMahon was in the area and wanted to arrange a meeting with him. Bischoff immediately knew something was up, and Hogan was not shy about revealing the purpose of the call. "I can't believe it," he claimed, "Vince McMahon is here and he wants to talk to me about a deal." Despite how he sold it to Bischoff, the timing of the call and McMahon's presence in town were no coincidence; Hogan's contract was up for renewal and he wanted Bischoff to be well aware of what was going on - he knew it increased his asking price in WCW.

Hogan told the WCW Vice President that he was going to meet with Vince for talks, but assured him that he had no intention of going to work for the WWF due his distrust of McMahon. Regardless, Bischoff was worried. The nWo angle had made Hulk a hot commodity, and losing him to the WWF would have been a major blow to what WCW were doing. Hogan met with McMahon, later claiming he was offered an unprecedented $5 million per year deal with Titan to return at the *Royal Rumble* and win the annual thirty-man battle royal, then headline *WrestleMania* where he would win the WWF Title for a record-extending sixth time. For some it seemed a little fanciful; McMahon could not afford to throw that amount of money at anyone, even Hulk Hogan.

Bischoff knew it too, but was still relieved when four days prior to WCW's *Halloween Havoc* pay-per-view, Hogan put pen to paper on a three year deal with TBS that featured many of the same perks, creative control clauses and powers of veto that his original contract had contained. Hogan once again had proved that he was in a league of his own as wrestling's master manipulator. Only six months earlier, Bischoff had been wondering whether Hogan was worth the hassle anymore, due to his waning presence as well as a frustrating tendency to change booking on a whim. Yet suddenly he was guaranteed to be the top earner in wrestling for another three years.

Disappointed to have lost out on Hogan, McMahon looked to another eighties wrestling icon: 'Macho Man' Randy Savage. The colourful and eccentric Savage had been one of the few talent departures to WCW that had affected McMahon on a personal level, when he upped and left without so much as a goodbye in late 1994. McMahon had allowed himself to become close to the wrestler, travelling the road with him and even permitting Savage to regularly stay at his Connecticut home.

However, Savage had been privately unhappy for some time, stemming back to a perceived snub of his father Angelo back in 1987, who was overlooked for a spot in a throwaway legends battle royal on a house show and thus missed out on a final professional shindig with his peers. Savage let the rebuke eat at him for years, but due to the success he was enjoying as the second biggest star in the company behind only Hogan, he repressed his anger and worked through it.

By 1994 he was no longer used as a top level performer. In fact, he was barely used as a wrestler at all. McMahon was looking to youth, rebuilding his ailing promotion with a troupe of talent that he dubbed the 'New Generation', and he felt the forty-two-year-old Savage was no longer best utilised in an in-ring capacity. Infuriated by McMahon's implication that he was elderly, Savage decided to seek employment elsewhere and left for WCW without so much as a thank you or a goodbye.

By 1996 it was clear that the so-called New Generation were not moving numbers to anywhere near the levels that Titan had achieved during the company's peak years. Rather, the biggest business generators were to be found in WCW, where the WWF's reinvented prior generation were shifting tickets and increasing television viewership on a weekly basis. Savage was one of those, and McMahon recognised that he had been wrong to shun him. Much like Eric Bischoff had theorised when he brought in Nash and Hall, McMahon felt rehiring Savage would not only help WWF business but also leave a significant hole in WCW's.

Negotiations rumbled on for weeks, with Savage going between McMahon and Bischoff looking for the best deal. Bischoff was unsure as to Savage's worth, because in 1996 he was nowhere near the level of the blistering, frenetic, guaranteed match of the night level performer that he had been in the eighties. In some respects, Bischoff felt compelled to keep him around purely so that McMahon could not get him, rather than because he wanted him.

Savage's key bargaining chip was the threat that he would walk out of WCW alongside Hogan, allowing the two to transplant their WCW headline program onto WWF television. Losing both stars would hurt WCW badly, but losing one was not irrecoverable. Thus when Hogan signed his deal with WCW, Savage lost significant leverage and was unable to push Bischoff as far as he wanted. Initially he had been hoping to secure a deal for one hundred dates per year and with it a raise due to how annoyed he was with the figures that Nash and Hall were earning apiece. The problem was that Bischoff could not have paid him more than them even if he had wanted to due to their favoured nations clauses. He had no intention of doing so anyway, because he felt Savage was no longer as valuable to the company.

Belief throughout the industry was that Savage would return to work for McMahon, but there was a snag. Savage wanted a long-term wrestling deal and to be compensated as a main event talent, whereas McMahon was not willing to pay him to wrestle for more than one year, perhaps two at a push. He could not afford to do so, and the last thing he wanted to do was give Randy a one year contract for considerable money, only to have him head back to WCW after a year hotter than he was when he left them.

McMahon instead wanted Savage to sign a transitional contract that promised a substantial first year then far less over the other four, which would have him working in a different, non-wrestling role behind the scenes as an agent. Savage felt that it was a similar indictment of his age as the one that had offended him a few years ago, and the two parties remained far apart on what they wanted from the respective deal.

It is believed that during these talks, McMahon was then made aware for the first time of a taboo relationship that Savage had apparently engaged in with his daughter Stephanie. At that point he cut off any further negotiations stone dead and made a vow to never work with Randy again. It was a promise he never broke. It was not until after Savage's untimely death in 2011 that he even considered allowing references to him on company merchandise and marketing, and it took until 2015 before he finally backed down to fan pressure and allowed Randy Savage a place in the WWE Hall of Fame.

ELEVEN

ANOTHER MAJOR STAR WHOM VINCE McMahon was trying to secure to a long-term, big money contract was already a member of his roster - Bret Hart. Since his WWF Title loss to Shawn Michaels at *WrestleMania*, Hart had been on hiatus from Federation television, working only occasional international house shows. He had been spending his newfound free time resting a battered and worn down body for the first time in over a decade, while also trying to break into acting with a recurring part on Western-themed miniseries *Lonesome Dove*.

Hart had technically become a free agent in July thanks to the unique terms of his Titan agreement. Where most other WWF contracts only gave the performer a ninety day window to hand in their resignation or else the deal would automatically roll over, Hart's was different. His allowed him to give ninety days notice at *any* time thanks to a clause in the favourable contract he had signed in 1992. It had been inserted by McMahon to keep Hart sweet, a way to counter a strong play that WCW was making for him. Hart rejected their offer after assurances from Vince that he would be allowed to leave if he was ever unhappy, and McMahon then confirmed it in writing with the break clause. That contract was signed years before WCW was any real threat to the WWF, but it remained valid in 1996. Hart believed that his stepping away from the ring immediately after *WrestleMania* constituted giving his ninety days notice, and any dates he did overseas following that were merely him working out his contract. Therefore he theorised that if he were to receive an offer from WCW, he would be able to sign for them without having to put over everyone in the territory on his way out.

McMahon realised this was the case whilst in the midst of securing everyone else on his roster to guaranteed contracts: his only way of preventing further talent jumps to WCW. Worried about Hart's intentions, McMahon flew to Calgary in late July to discuss terms of a new deal with Bret and his wife Julie. The meeting came two weeks after Hulk Hogan had sent shockwaves through the industry with his *Bash at the Beach* heel turn, which had since helped *Nitro* reach unexpected heights in audience viewership figures. McMahon wanted to make sure that Hart - perhaps the biggest box office star he had left - was with him for the long-run. McMahon told him to name his price, but Hart was in no rush to commit to anything until he had allowed WCW the chance to counter offer. He still remembered what Nash had told him in India about the terms of his and Hall's enormous deals in Atlanta, and as a far bigger star than both he suspected he could make much more.

Hart returned to wrestle on the WWF's untelevised tour of South Africa in early September, but gave no further indication as to where his future might lie. Privately, he told friends that he did not want to leave the WWF, but he also realised that at thirty-nine years old it could well be his last chance to make big money in the industry. Going to Atlanta could allow him to retire comfortably, free of any financial worries for the rest of his life. Despite Hart's refusal to give anything other than vague assurances that he was staying put, the WWF jumped the gun and began promoting his appearance in an interview segment with Brian Pillman at *Mind Games* on September 22. Hart did not make the show due to filming commitments elsewhere, and he had no intention of McMahon strong-arming him into anything until he had heard from WCW first.

He did not have to wait long. Three days later when he arrived in Los Angeles to record a voice track for his high-profile guest spot on *The Simpsons*, he was surprised when Eric Bischoff showed up unannounced at his hotel room moments after he had checked in. The opportunist WCW Vice President had been tipped off about Hart's presence in the city by agent Barry Bloom, who felt that a private confab away from the wrestling business was a suitable way for the two to meet.

Bret was pleasantly surprised when he and Bischoff hit it off right away. They spent an hour casually talking about everything except wrestling, until Bischoff finally played his hand and addressed the elephant in the room. "So, what's it gonna take to bring you to WCW?" he asked matter-of-factly. Hart had been expecting the question to come at some point so he was prepared for it; he was going to start with a figure ridiculously high and see what the response was. He threw out a proposal that he knew would be rejected, but would also serve to give him an indication of whether WCW was worthy of his consideration. "I would want the same contract as Hogan, plus one penny," he stated coolly.

Hart watched as the colour drained from Bischoff's face. "I can't do a deal anything like that!" he stammered, "Not right now." Hart smiled and told the flustered WCW executive not to worry, because he was happy with the WWF and not looking to go anywhere. He was telling the truth, but he was also playing an outlandish game of hardball. If Bischoff thought he was not interested, then the higher WCW's inevitable return offer was likely to be. At the very least it would give him something to use in his negotiations with Vince to bump up his tabled WWF deal a few notches. Bischoff took the bait. "C'mon, at least give me something I can take back with me to my people," he pleaded. Bret seized the chance to throw out an equally astronomical though potentially realistic figure. "I would think about coming to work for you for $3 million per year and a lighter schedule than the one I have now," he replied.

The two left the wrestling side of the discussion there and returned to their earlier conversation. After the meeting concluded, Hart decided that even though Eric Bischoff was WWF public enemy number one, he actually rather liked him. He liked him even more two days later when he called to make an offer: $2.8 million per annum over three years, on a deal that incorporated movie work as well as wrestling, and promised a much lighter schedule as he had requested. Such was WCW's desire to bring Hart into the fold, that Bischoff was even able to convince Nash and Hall to waive their favoured nations clauses. Hart was gobsmacked at the amount on the table and told Bischoff that he would contemplate it and get back to him.

The sheer magnitude of the offer from Turner left Hart with a moral dilemma that he wrestled with for the next few weeks. He had a life-changing decision to make in regards to what was more important to him: money or his loyalty to Vince - the man who had given him the opportunity to become a star in the first place. "I had always figured I would end my career with the WWF," recounts Hart, "But WCW's offer was for an enormous amount of money - beyond anything I had ever imagined when I got into wrestling. It was tough. I didn't know what to do, even though the decision should have been simple - take the money. But money is not always everything. How much money do you really need sometimes? I found myself torn between doing the right thing for my family and my loyalties. Loyalty is important. Vince had always been like a father, and I felt that leaving him would be like leaving my dad. Especially when the chips were down. It was probably the biggest decision of my entire life."

"I can't match it," were the first words uttered from McMahon's mouth when Hart told him about the WCW offer. Bret assured him that he did not expect him to, he simply wanted him to make the best offer he could. "We both knew that I didn't want to end up in WCW," says Hart, "I hated the thought of being used as an assassin against Vince and the company that I had devoted my life to." Irrespective of that, Hart made sure to point out that he was in a position to make $9 million in three years, and that he had to be smart about his next move. "It would be like ripping up a lottery ticket," he told McMahon, who countered with the warning, "WCW would never know what to do with a Bret Hart."

The call ended with McMahon asking for time to ruminate. He promised to get back to Hart with an offer, so Bret assured him that he would not do anything until he had heard back from him. On October 9, the WWF were in Medicine Hat, Alberta for a house show. McMahon came along for the trip and made the brief flight to Calgary in order that he could present his counter offer to Hart face-to-face. True to his word, McMahon was offering the highest guaranteed contract that he had ever given to anyone. In total, it was for more money than what Turner were promising, though would be spread over twenty years rather than three and contained far more contractual dates than the WCW offer.

The deal was for $1.5 million per year as an in ring performer over three years (which was more than double what both Shawn Michaels and The Undertaker were making), $500,000 annually for seven years in a position as a senior advisor (a fee that was still around double what the majority of the better paid midcard wrestlers such as Mick Foley, Steve Austin, and Marc Mero were earning), and then $250,000 per year over ten years for a position as McMahon's long-desired "Babe Ruth of wrestling" role. It was the same role that he had tried and failed with Bruno Sammartino in the mid-eighties and Hulk Hogan in 1993. The position would call for Hart to be on standby for the occasional match or segment, and perhaps appear in as on-screen authority figure akin to the ones played by Gorilla Monsoon and Roddy Piper earlier in the year.

"I'll never give you a reason to ever want to leave," implored Vince as he laid out the prospective terms. Satisfied that McMahon had given him the best offer he possibly could, Hart shook hands with him on the deal. Vince smiled a relieved smile, thankful that the ordeal of negotiations was over and done with. Together they collectively agreed that Hart would make his long-awaited return to television on the October 21 edition of *Raw* from Fort Wayne, Indiana. Three days later, Hart published his regular column in the *Calgary Sun* newspaper, letting fans in on some of the details of the decision he had been tossing and turning over for the past few weeks.

I'd gone higher in wrestling than I'd ever allowed myself to dream of. It didn't seem that I had anything left to prove. When you're that high up it's a long fall down. I don't want to be one of those guys that hangs around long after he's past his prime and embarrasses himself and his fans every time he steps into the ring. I realize that wrestling is sports entertainment but, for my taste, lately there's been too much emphasis on the entertainment and not enough weight put on athletics and sportsmanship. There's an upstart group in the states whose extreme style is all about brawling. There's another group that, at around the time of *WrestleMania XII*, seemed to be where worn out wrestlers worked, although that has since changed and they've brought in a lot of exciting, technically knowledgeable guys. The WWF, had, in my opinion, lost some of its balance and become too youth oriented - Clowns instead of Pipers and Perfects. The WWF's catering to kids came to its ultimate end when Shawn Michaels became champion. I'm not saying that Shawn isn't talented because he is. In fact, I knew Shawn would be the one coming up behind me sooner or later. The only thing is that it happened "sooner." Shawn has always had a tremendous ego and maybe, based on his ability, it's justified. The problem is that they allowed his character to get out of control. They call him "flamboyant" and I call him obnoxious. I was annoyed and concerned about a lot of things in the business at around the time of *WrestleMania XII*. I didn't leave because Shawn Michaels became champion. In fact, the business could use more guys with Shawn's dedication. I'd reached a fork in the road and I needed to stop long enough to be able to read the signs. I've found that a lot of wrestlers develop a sort of tunnel vision--they eat, sleep and breathe wrestling. It's fair to say it's a symptom of the lifestyle. As much as I made a conscious effort not to neglect outside interests, the schedule was so brutal that all you could do in the end was submit and look forward to a time when there will be time.

In the six-and-a-half months since *WrestleMania XII*, I've given myself time to do some of the things I've had on hold for over a decade. I realized that I wasn't enjoying them nearly as much as I'd anticipated and it took me a while to understand why. I figured out that part of it is because I have something much more serious than tunnel vision. I was born with wrestling in my blood and there's no medicine that's going to cure me. As much as I didn't want to admit it to myself, to me, wrestling can never be just a job. I couldn't really relax knowing that the sport was speeding off in what I consider to be the wrong direction. I realized that I was wrong when I thought I had nothing left to prove in wrestling. In fact, it just may be that my toughest fight is ahead of me. I'm going to try to prove that one man can make a difference when it comes to restoring the credibility and dignity that professional wrestling has lost. I have no delusions about single-handedly changing things over night, but maybe if I can get the tide flowing in the right direction, wrestlers and fans will see my point and help to row the boat upstream. My memories are not yet greater than my dreams. I decided to return to the ring but where and when remains a big question.

A wrestling organization who is a competitor to the WWF has offered me an amazing amount of money to work for them. I'd be working less days than with the WWF and making a lot more money. I realized that in a few years I could be sitting on a beach somewhere and never have to work another day in my life. Being that the WWF is a family owned business I didn't think they could ever come up with enough money to match this offer. I've said before that I'm not greedy for money but that I'm greedy for respect. I guess for most people it would be a simple decision. If they pay you more and work you less, that's where you go. But for me it wasn't that cut and dry and that's when I realized that wrestling isn't just a job. My family has generations caught up in it. I started asking myself hard questions about loyalty, integrity and weighing that against the fact I have four kids that could benefit from the money long after I'm history. I owe the lifestyle I enjoy today to the WWF. I do feel a sense of loyalty to Vince McMahon, but his company, its directions and its priorities, have changed.

In the words of the Million Dollar Man, "Everybody has a price." I've lost sleep over it but I've made my decision. It was like choosing between two lovers--they both want you and they'd both treat you good and they both have their own little benefits. No matter how good the one you end up with is, you're always going to wonder what you've missed.

Despite seeming to hint that he was heading for WCW, Hart was simply throwing out a red herring to keep his WWF return a surprise. McMahon was set to announce Hart's much anticipated television return on the October 14 edition of *Raw*, but there was a snag. Hart had been faxed a contract markedly different to what had been discussed, and he refused to confirm his appearance on the following week's broadcast until the deal was signed and sealed. Vince was immediately fearful that Hart had changed his mind and taken a counter offer from WCW, so decided against hyping his scheduled appearance. Those inside the company not privy to the negotiations took the omission of Hart's name from the program as a sign that he was WCW-bound. With the WWF losing the ratings war it would be big news to have Hart's first appearance in half a year on the broadcast, so it made no sense not to hype it. The failure to mention Hart seemed like a silent admission from McMahon that he was resigned to losing him.

It was not the case. Even though Hart had received another counter offer from WCW, he had given McMahon his word. Despite working in a business filled with perfidious charlatans and mendacious glad handers, Hart was loyal to the core and considered his integrity to be paramount, more so than money. His decision was made and his intention was to stay with McMahon, but he was starting to become increasingly annoyed with the hold up in getting his contract finalised. He began to suspect that Vince was stalling because he was suffering from buyer's remorse on the deal.

Three days before the Fort Wayne broadcast, Hart received another copy of his contract that was so far removed from what he and Vince had talked about in Calgary - not to mention heavily weighted in favour of the WWF - that his lawyer sternly advised him, "Do not sign that contract. Only an idiot would sign that." Hart once again refused to appear on *Raw* unless the situation was resolved, so he turned to his former business manager and the WWF's current Head of Operations in Canada, Carl De Marco for help.

De Marco implored McMahon to move hastily in securing Hart, warning that losing him would destroy the WWF's business in Canada, not to mention give WCW an unassailable lead in the ratings war. With others around him expressing similar sentiments, McMahon finally ceded and had his office call Hart with an apology, claiming his legal department had sent out the wrong contract. Hart had heard it all before, having been fed a tale not dissimilar the last time he was under negotiations. He was partly amused, though equally frustrated that the same old excuses were still being wheeled out.

However, such was the passion with which De Marco pleaded Hart's case that he was able to not only speed up proceedings, but also managed to wrangle some perks and concessions designed to protect Hart. The veteran wrestler had been around long enough to see what happened to performers when they lost favour with Vince, and he had no intention of allowing something similar to happen to him should he and McMahon end up at odds for any reason. Hart was given a unique boon that aped Hogan's WCW contract in some respects: creative control. However, unlike the omnipotent Hogan, Hart only had what was deemed "reasonable" creative control for the final thirty days of his contract. It was a failsafe to protect him from losing to everyone in the territory or creative forcing him into scenarios damaging to his persona if he was to leave.

McMahon eventually caught up with Hart an hour before the *Raw* broadcast featuring his return went live, and both finally inked their names on the deal. McMahon looked anxious and pensive throughout the signing, clearly worried about the sizeable financial commitment he was making. He had only recently started giving his performers guaranteed money and this was by far the biggest contract yet. Having refused Hall and Nash similar deals earlier in the year and consequently losing them to WCW, he realised that he was now paying Hart double what it would have cost to keep them both.

As agreed, Hart headed to the ring that night and cut an unscripted monologue that lifted the curtain a little on what he had been deliberating in recent months. Many described it as the best of his career. In the speech, Hart outlined his intention to stay with the WWF for the rest of his life, addressed the passing of his nephew Matthew Annis from rare disease necrotizing fasciitis in July, and fired some shots at Shawn Michaels for his recent decision to pose semi-nude for gay magazine *Playgirl*.[53] It was a pre-agreed snipe, intended to start a slow burn build for the pair's mooted rematch at *WrestleMania*.

Hart wandered to the ring for his first live appearance on Federation programming in half a year, dressed casually in jeans and a t-shirt rather than his trademark pink and black garb. The intention was that fans would believe they were hearing the words of Bret Hart the man, rather than of the character 'The Hitman'. Jim Ross stood in the ring to conduct the interview and cut right to the chase, asking Hart about his future. It was the only thing he would ask:

> Well, I missed everybody. I just want to say that for the past couple of weeks or maybe a little more, I've had to deal with a lot of things. For one there was a certain rival wrestling organisation that... all I can say is that they made me a great offer and they dealt with me with integrity, in nothing but an honourable fashion, and I can't say anything bad about how they represented themselves or me. I was faced with this incredibly tough dilemma that if I decide to come back to wrestling if I should in fact come back to the WWF or find new adventures somewhere else. It was not that long ago that I said, "I'm not greedy for money, I'm greedy for respect," but until you have to actually step into my shoes and make that kind of a decision, when you get a great offer and you have to

---

[53] Shawn would later deny knowing that *Playgirl* was a gay magazine, though the boys quipped that the only male wrestling fans who liked him were gay. All it did was further fuel the widespread belief in the locker room that Michaels was a closet homosexual.

decide which one you're gonna take... And I've done a lot of soul searching, nobody has any idea about how much soul searching I have done over this. But when it comes down to it, everything I've ever done and everything that I plan on ever doing - I owe it all to my WWF fans, and I won't be going anywhere. The WWF? Well I'll be with the WWF forever.

I want to address why I left in the first place. People wonder if I left because maybe I'm a sore loser, and maybe I am. Shawn Michaels, the World Wrestling Federation champion, I want to make something very clear because it might not have seemed like it at the time, but Shawn Michaels beat me fair and square right in the middle of the ring and there's no excuses for it. I might not be real thrilled about it, but I knew when I climbed right through the ropes for that sixty minute match, and I lost and I have no excuses for it. You know, I consider Shawn Michaels my opponent, not my enemy. But you know, Shawn Michaels there is just something about you that really bugs me. Shawn Michaels, you might be a little bit younger than I am and you might even be a little more popular, and there's people out that might think that Shawn Michaels is even a little bit cuter than I am. Shawn Michaels is a great wrestler and he's done a great job as champion, but there's two things that Shawn Michaels will never, ever be. He will never, ever be as tough as me, and he will never, ever be as smart as me. I think Richard Nixon said it best, "You learn from defeat, and you come back and beat 'em the next time." Which is why I have decided to accept the challenge of the best wrestler in the WWF today, and in the *Survivor Series* I will face... 'Stone Cold' Steve Austin. I might be a little rusty and maybe I won't be, but Steve Austin, I want you to know one thing: Madison Square Garden is not a church but it's holy ground. And Steve Austin, 'Stone Cold', we'll see who kicks whose ass in Madison Square Garden.

Since I've been off I've had a chance to really think about a lot of things, and I owe everything I've got to my fans all around the world. I've got the most incredible fans all over the world. It's an incredible privilege to have fans like that. And it's something I take quite seriously being a role model, and I think that the one thing that has been missing from the World Wrestling Federation for the last six months... has been me. I just wanna say that people ask me why am I coming back, why do I wanna come back. It's not that much fun sometimes - especially if you can afford not to, to get kicked around and get beat up. It's a tough job and a hard way of life. I got chance to go home and spend time with my family, and there's one little boy in Canada who basically worshipped me. I was his hero. And it's something I take an incredible amount of pride in. And one day this little boy got real sick, it didn't take very long it took just a matter of a few hours, and this little boy became the sickest little boy in all of Canada. And I went to his bedside and I promised this little boy on his last legs when they didn't think he would make it through the night, I promised this little boy that if he would just pull out of that, if he would just come though, if he could just kick out, that I would come out of retirement for him. And as soon as I said that in his ear he started to come out of it. Well, I wish I could tell you I have a happy ending here, but I don't. Just when we thought this little boy was going to turn the corner, he didn't, and that little boy passed away. And that little boy was my nephew. But the reason that I have decided to come back - and people can think all they want to and they can guess that I have come back, and I planned this out a long time ago, but the fact of the matter is, from that very day, I promised myself that that I would come back and I would give wrestling fans and little kids all around the world somebody that they can look up to. Somebody that doesn't necessarily... Hey, I can't dance and I don't pose too well for girly books, but I am the best there is, the best there was, and the best there ever will be, and I'm back. Thank you very much.

Hart's return was welcomed by many of the boys, who had long since tired of Shawn Michaels' prima donna attitude and increasingly frequent tantrums. Hart's *Survivor Series* opponent Steve Austin had even privately contacted Bret, practically begging him to return to the WWF. Austin, like many others, believed that Hart was the only person who could keep Michaels in check and put an end to his unruly behaviour. Michaels himself was far from thrilled with the news. Not only did he see Hart as direct competition, but he was also furious that Bret was getting paid double what he was earning. Michaels firmly believed that he was superior in every way to Hart, who he felt was becoming an industry dinosaur hanging on to his spotlight for too long. Shawn was of the opinion that it was his time to shine, but with Hart back he knew it would make his life much more difficult. The difference in their pay scales simply added insult to injury.

Vince McMahon too was anxious about the amount of money he had been forced into guaranteeing Hart to secure his services, which became a source of constant ranklement for him. Sixteen months after making the deal, McMahon appeared on television show *Off The Record* and admitted how he felt about Hart's bloated contract, "After I had done the deal, I was sorry that I had. I was sorry when I signed the deal financially. Bret, even prior to the leveraging factor of WCW versus the WWF, told me he wasn't about the money. It was about being comfortable and being treated the way he had been - with respect - in the WWF for years and years. That meant more to him than money. Yet he leveraged himself against Turner's operation and bid himself up so much. Everyone around me at that time was saying, 'Oh my God, you can't let Bret go, you just can't! This is the straw that breaks the camel's back, Vince, you can't let Bret go!' I listened to them and I think I was sorry that I did from a financial standpoint."

A year following Hart re-signing, McMahon reneged on the deal when he told Hart he could no longer afford him, adding that he was free to reopen negotiations with WCW. McMahon had mined one final good year out of Hart, who he felt was increasingly at odds with what the WWF were trying to present. Hart was devastated, but not surprised. McMahon had been constantly breaking promises to him throughout the year, not to mention running him down from behind the commentary desk as old and washed-up whenever the opportunity presented itself.

The result was an occurrence that would go down in wrestling folklore as the infamous 'Montreal Screwjob' at the 1997 Survivor Series. The incident saw a desperate McMahon - terrified that Hart would show up in Atlanta with the WWF Title - legitimately ring the bell on an unwitting Hart during a match with Shawn Michaels for the WWF Title. In doing so, he unceremoniously and humiliatingly ended a storied WWF career, making himself public enemy number one with Hart's supporters in the process. Ironically enough, Montreal inadvertently ended up being the final piece of the puzzle the WWF needed to combat WCW in the Monday Night Wars.[54]

LONG BEFORE Vince McMahon broke Raw viewership records in segments with Steve Austin after reinventing himself as the most despised heel in the business, he was searching for an opponent for the fast-rising star from within the ranks of his wrestling roster. To many, the choice of Brian Pillman was an obvious one. The two best friends were ex-tag partners in a former WCW life and had infectious chemistry together. They were also the two most extreme personalities on the roster, with Pillman's

---

[54] While WCW consumed itself, Montreal gave the WWF an accidental top heel in McMahon, who turned out to be the perfect foe for blue collar anti-hero Steve Austin. Their program together did record business, ultimately sparking the revival of the WWF as it entered the full throngs of the "Attitude Era".

unpredictable character a perfect counterpart for the no-nonsense, smack-talking Austin.

After subtly teasing a confrontation between the two, McMahon finally let them go at it on an episode of *Superstars* taped on October 22 in Pillman's hometown of Cincinnati. Pillman was still suffering from the fallout of his Humvee accident, with the daily grind of life on the road hampering the healing of his ankle, and thus he remained unable to wrestle. Instead, he was in town to conduct an interview with Austin, hyping the *King of the Ring* winner's forthcoming match at *Survivor Series* with the returning Bret Hart.

Pillman played the part of a proud friend pleased that his former partner was getting the chance to wrestle Hart on the big stage. Austin was not comfortable with Pillman's overly-familiar demeanour and lambasted him, calling him a "little crippled freak." Given that the program aired in most markets at 11 a.m. on a Saturday, it was pushing the boundaries of decency and acceptability for the timeslot. When Pillman started excitedly spouting Bret Hart's famous, "best there is, best there was, best there ever will be," catchphrase, it suddenly became brutally violent. Austin jumped Pillman, smashing him in his injured leg with a cane that he had been using for support. He soon went even further, placing Pillman's ankle between the unforgiving metal of a steel folding chair and stomping it repeatedly until lower card wrestlers and company officials intervened.

It was a notorious angle, with the act of placing an opponent's extremity into a steel chair and jumping on it becoming known throughout the industry as "Pillmanizing". Like with so many other scenarios that transpired on WWF television during the era, the idea was actually born in the dimly lit Philadelphia bingo halls of ECW. Back on March 9 at *Big Ass Extreme Bash '96*, Shane Douglas had performed the exact same move to Raven following their ECW Title match, though to considerably less fanfare. It was blatant plagiarism, but most WWF fans were none the wiser; they simply thought they had seen an exciting, original angle.

The idea behind having Austin assault Pillman was to write him off television so he could get yet another operation on his ankle, and he underwent surgery the following day. He was starting the healing process from scratch, and the prognosis was that he would be out for at least six months.[55] However, the story between the pair did not end there. Two weeks later, Vince's ongoing creative schizophrenia was brought into sharp

---

[55] Pillman returned to in-ring competition on May 5, his first match in over a year, in a post-*Raw* dark match. His television debut came almost three weeks later in a squash match victory over jobber Tony Williams.

focus when he presented an angle far more shocking than anything he had ever dared try before.

WHEN MCMAHON was able to negotiate a shift to an 8 p.m. starting slot for *Raw,* an hour earlier than the usual 9 p.m. start which had seen the show follow housewife favourite *Murder She Wrote*, he was delighted. Not only was *Raw* given a much more demographic-friendly lead in with *Walker, Texas Ranger*, but now WCW no longer had the jump on him with *Nitro*'s one hour head start. Vince believed that casual viewers were tuning into Turner's show with the intention of later switching over to the WWF, but had forgot about *Raw* by the time it started. With the two broadcasts starting on an even keel, he hoped that would change.

To generate interest in the time slot, Vince wanted to do something controversial. Brian Pillman and Steve Austin had performed with an edge that veered close to the line of moral acceptability for months, but they had always been reined in enough so they did not offend any more than a handful of people. What was scripted for them on the November 4 episode of *Raw* did not merely cross a line, it left it as a faint dot in the distance. It also nearly caused the WWF to get thrown off the *USA Network*.

It was Bruce Prichard who had first pitched an idea to McMahon calling for Austin to storm Pillman's home and finish what he had started two weeks earlier on *Superstars*, only for Pillman to respond by invoking the castle doctrine and attempting to defend himself with a pistol. It was a scene lifted directly from *Cape Fear*, though Vince would never have known it because he refused to watch movies - he felt them a profligate use of time. McMahon was hesitant initially. The use of a gun on his programming was something he had always vehemently opposed, as he knew it was a veritable Pandora's box of controversy, one that once opened could not be closed.

However, because shock television was the latest fad in craze-hungry America, Vince was eventually persuaded to go ahead with the gun angle, finally conceding to some heavy leaning from Prichard and *WWF Magazine* editor Vince Russo. They convinced the chairman that the storyline was in keeping with the likes of *The Jerry Springer Show* and other controversy-laden programming of that ilk which were so in vogue. Some of McMahon's more conservative staff were concerned with the use of a handgun in a pro wrestling angle. "I would have never brought a gun out," argues Cornette, "It's the one thing in wrestling you never did, because if someone brings out a gun then they've gotta use it."

Undeterred by the naysayers despite his own concerns, McMahon pressed ahead with his storyline, sending a camera crew to Pillman's family home in Walton, Kentucky to shoot the controversial scene. He had personally visited the house three days earlier with Prichard to ensure everything was set-up as he wanted. His intention was to film the footage the following day, but at the last minute he changed his mind. Instead, he decided to let the performers adlib the entire ordeal, filming it live during the airing of the pre-taped *Raw*. He felt the one-take environment better encapsulated the spirit of what they were shooting, giving it an added edge that pre-taped footage rarely possessed.

Following a pre-show warning on *Raw* that advised the episode would be "graphic and violent," McMahon launched into the scene with announcer Kevin Kelly stationed outside of the Pillman household. Kelly set the stage for the events about to unfold, serving as both a narrator for the television audience and a proxy conduit for McMahon to speak through. After teasing the viewers with speculation about what might happen, the feed returned to Pillman's "suburban Cincinnati" home, with the drama reinforced by a lingering close-up of the crocked wrestler's plaster-encased ankle. It was legitimate, the result of the surgery he had recently endured, but intimated as having been caused by the Austin chair assault two weeks earlier.

Pillman slouched casually on his couch while real life wife Melanie gave her best shot at acting, wearing an expression of grave concern in the background. When Kelly prodded the Austin issue, Pillman declared that hostilities were now personal between them, and thus there was now a different set of rules. Via remote link-up, McMahon interrupted and shared the news that Austin was circling the neighbourhood, then played on Pillman's supposed vulnerability by probingly asking if he felt like a hostage in his own home.

"Ha, Steve is a dead man walking. Because when Austin 3:16 meets Pillman nine millimetre gun," - at which point Pillman revealed that he was in possession of a pistol - "I'm gonna blow his sorry ass straight to hell." Hovering somewhere on the scale between low-budget horror movie and live police chase, the scene took a turn for the dramatic when an off-camera voice shrieked, "Steve Austin is out there now!" The feed ended and returned to the matches filmed two weeks earlier in Fort Wayne, Indiana, with the promise that the broadcast would return there later.

The latest development saw Steve Austin arrive, appearing on camera for the first time having found the house and crossed the property line into the yard. He spent the following few minutes amusing himself by throwing around two heavy-set extras purported to be Pillman's friends, inserting an element of slapstick as he bashed both across the head with children's toys and the door of a spacious family car parked on the driveway, then hurtled them into Pillman's garage door. "It was a hot and heavy night and it was like a full-blown shoot," recalls Austin, "We had to do it all in one take. Brian never did get that garage door fixed because it broke the hinges real bad." Following the assault, Austin circled the property looking for a way into the house, with Vince seeming a little disturbed by it all. "There's a very uncomfortable feeling in that live shot we just saw," he cogitated, ostensibly worried that matters were about to go further than he had originally intended. It was too late to call an audible and change the script now; McMahon had made the call to go ahead with the storyline, and he had to accept the consequences.

Back at the Pillman household Brian stared blankly into the distance clutching his Glock pistol. He had a deadness to his eyes that conveyed to viewers the real possibility that he was about to shoot and kill Austin live on air. McMahon chimed in that what people were seeing was a publicity stunt that was going wrong, and that Austin was trying to make a name for himself. The statement only heightened the drama, adding a further element of reality to the segment. It was a jarring experience for the television audience. They were presented with a gripping melodrama unfolding live before their eyes that was supposedly not part of the script, nestled uncomfortably and in stark contrast to unimaginative caricatures such as The Stalker, The Sultan, and Rick Bognar's Razor Ramon.

Meanwhile in Kentucky, Austin smashed through a window in Pillman's back door and entered the house *a' la* Jack Nicholson in his famous "Here's Johnny" scene from *The Shining*. In response, Pillman bolted out of his seat and aimed his pistol, ready to blow Austin away as soon as he entered the living area he and Melanie were situated in. Before anything happened, the screen went black once again. While McMahon speculated as to what might have occurred, director Kerwin Silfes dialled in from the production truck stationed at the Pillman residence, noting that the electricity had gone out in the house and they had lost their feed. Desperate for an update, McMahon was told that the rest of the production team had holed themselves in the truck out of fear, with no idea what had happened or where Austin was. It was all part of the storyline, but the presentation felt very real.

McMahon spent the remainder of the show reminding viewers to stay tuned for the grand finale of the WWF's take on *Cops*, promising to get the feed restored for the gritty and possibly gruesome conclusion. Naturally the video link was back up and working before *Raw* went off the air, and

Vince's audience were greeted with a scene of panic. Pillman was screaming, his eyes now wild and darting as his friends and WWF officials struggled to keep him calm. Meanwhile, Kelly updated everyone that no shots had been fired because Austin had scarpered when he saw the weapon.

"Oh my god he's back," whimpered Kelly, as another scuffle broke out upon Austin's return. The usually slick camera work became intentionally shaky and blurred in the melee, adding a further layer of authenticity to the presentation. Unnamed extras tried to drag Austin away, Melanie screamed and begged for the police, and colour commentator Jerry Lawler on the live link pleaded with Kelly to grab the gun from Pillman before someone was killed.

But Kelly did not dare approach the frenzied Pillman, who was maniacally yelling, "Let him go, that son of a bitch got this coming. Let him go! I'm gonna kill that son of a bitch! Let him go, get out of the way! *Get out of the fucking way*! Let him go!". There was a final fade to black accompanied by the sound of gunfire - then immediately the show ended, leaving impressionable viewers wondering if someone had been shot, and parents questioning what the hell had happened to pro wrestling since they had last watched Hulk Hogan and Andre the Giant a decade ago. Dave Meltzer remained unimpressed, believing the stunt to be desperate clamour to hotshot a strong rating.

> It was compelling because (like the fake Razor, the fake Double J and the weekly fake bombshell news stories that are teased and never materialize) of the fascination with just how desperate-appearing the WWF television appears to be. WCW is in the same war, and they do the same teases, but manage to do so within the framework of putting on a continuing wrestling show.

The television ratings told the story. While *Raw* had again been soundly beaten by *Nitro* that night, there was a point during the broadcast that *Raw* caught up to its competitor and was neck-and-neck during one of the quarterly breakdowns. It was the first time the WWF had managed that in months. Conversely, there was also a price to pay for the intensity of the storyline; demographic reports showed that around 125,000 pre-teen viewers were so disturbed by what was occurring at *casa* Pillman that they had switched channels to *Nitro* when tensions became too much for them to bear.

Austin and Pillman were frustrated that the angle had not beaten *Nitro*, as both were convinced that it was going to snap their rival's winning streak.

Despite that, Vince still felt it was a watershed moment. All of the talk within the industry and in the dirt sheets the following day was centred on what the WWF had pulled. "It was a turning point for wrestling in what was acceptable as entertainment, and Brian was proud to be a part of that," reflects Melanie. Steve Austin recalls that despite Titan having recently banned its performers from talking with anyone associated with WCW (due to fear of information leaks and further defections - though few adhered to the directive), he bumped into a number of ex-colleagues and friends from the group on a flight the day after the gun angle aired. He cordially shot the breeze with old acquaintances, many of whom were quick to praise the intensity of the angle and the boldness of the WWF's daring new direction.

IT WAS also the talk of the *USA Network* offices, with many at the station furious with the content that Titan had aired. Few realised that McMahon had been given the green light to orchestrate the whole scenario by other more liberal *USA* executives in an attempt to try and boost *Raw*'s flagging ratings. However, in an ironic twist that harked back to the 'Curtain Call' in May, McMahon found himself on the receiving end of a berating for something that had been pre-approved.

Prior to the shoot, McMahon had made concessions and agreed to tone down some of the angle's content. Initial drafts had called for a bump from Melanie, which would have led to Pillman firing two shots at Austin before the feed was lost. *USA* was not keen on the violence towards a woman and the actual firing of the gun on-screen, so McMahon rewrote the parameters of the script to suit. Those at the network who agreed to the stunt had no idea how realistic the scene would be portrayed; they thought it would be another hokey wrestling angle. "Nobody really expected it to come off that good. It was something that made you go, 'Is that real?'" mulls Michael Hayes.

When the *USA* switchboards began to light up with floods of complaints from furious parents with affected children who had believed the footage *was* real, the mood at the network began to sour. There was a tidal wave of negativity from the corporate world against Vince's organisation, with key Titan advertisers such as *Milton Bradley* - whose Karate Fighters toys had been plugged several times during the broadcast - infuriated at what had taken place on a supposedly quaint wrestling show aimed at little kids.

"That angle was executed to perfection, it was one of the best angles I ever did," reminisces Austin, "But it came across as too real for pro wrestling, and the WWF got a lot of heat for that." It was more than heat;

highly positioned members of management at *USA* were concerned with how far the WWF had taken their latest exploit, and even though similar if not more intense programming could be found on the network within shows such as *Silk Stalkings*, there was also little doubt that those broadcasts were scripted entertainment. What the WWF had delivered was presented as if it was not fiction. Others at *USA,* notably Vice President of Sports Programming Wayne Becker, were furious that the word "fuck" had been uttered over the airwaves. Becker was so appalled with what he saw, that he demanded the WWF and their sinister theatre be removed from the airwaves with immediate effect.

USA Network Chairwoman and Chief Executive Officer Kay Koplovitz had an inkling that McMahon was going to try something edgy to draw attention to the WWF, because he had already been giving her headaches throughout the year doing exactly that. She had been exasperated with him more than once for pushing the envelope, be it with the slanderous Ted Turner skits, Goldust's homoerotic gyrations, the increase in the use of bad language or copious middle finger gestures creeping into his programming. This was the latest in a series of McMahon's stunts that caused her to pore over *USA's* contract with Titan in fine detail, seeking a potential standards and practices violation loophole to get out of it should such drastic action be required. Koplovitz was growing weary of Vince's increasingly desperate tactics in trying to stave off WCW. In fact, she was fed up with the whole New WWF circus.

Even though she knew that McMahon had been given permission to run with the divisive shoot, Koplovitz could sense the frustration towards the WWF within her ranks. Feeling that she was left with little choice, Koplovitz hauled Vince in for a meeting with her and a team of aides to discuss the future of *Raw*. Somewhat curiously, the summit took place in the same Manhattan borough that *Raw* had emanated from each week during its early years, back when it was still a show aimed at and geared towards pre-teens and their families. Rather than protest about the injustice of his being there, Vince played it coy as Koplovitz forced him to sit through a video that featured everything he had done on his television show over the past twelve months that the network found offensive, objectionable, or felt violated the terms of his *USA* contract. When it finished, Koplovitz warned Vince that what he had been doing lately was no longer for kids, and as *Raw* was marketed as a children's show it would not be tolerated on her network. "Vince, we are not doing this anymore," she warned, "It has to be lighter. It needs to go back to the original formula."

McMahon had little choice but to kowtow, and issued an insincere public apology on the following weekend's edition of *Livewire*, expressing regret for the language used but tellingly, not the misdemeanour or use of the gun. Then later on the same show, he had loyal henchmen Michael Hayes and Jim Ross point out that many fans had actually enjoyed the tone of the program and wanted more of the same. Under orders from Vince, Ross read out letters apparently sent in by fans, promising they would reject WCW in favour of the WWF permanently if *Raw* did shows like that more frequently.

Another caller, a perturbed mother from Florida, instead advised Vince that the WWF needed to clean up its act, complaining that the use of a gun was unnecessary. Uncomfortable with the lecture, Vince visibly squirmed ever so slightly under his collar as he listened. Others would defend him, "You can say that McMahon went too far and that he went over the line, but quite simply it worked," says Mean Gene Okerlund, who was with WCW at the time of the broadcast. Kevin Kelly, who played a key role in the stunt, similarly defended it years after the fact, "What would you do if you were in that situation, and your family is being threatened and you're helpless to stop this attacker? You're gonna reach for a gun," he argues. "It's something I think a lot of people in this country, with second amendment gun rights, could relate to."

As polarising as the exploit had been, the immediate swell of reaction it generated did not go unnoticed by McMahon and the rest of his writing team. It was by some considerable margin the most attention that the WWF had been afforded since the start of the Monday Night Wars. Vince had always believed that as long as people were talking about the WWF then they were doing the right thing, and here that was undoubtedly the case. He was starting to realise more and more that a shift towards further edgy programming was the answer in combating WCW, who could not dream of responding by following them down that route due to the limits imposed on them by TBS.

In the past, WCW had been hamstrung by censorship from above, with Turner brass even going so far as to demand the cessation of the long-established wrestling term "foreign object" for any illegal weapon. Wrongly interpreting the word "foreign" to be a slight against non-Americans, the ultra-PC parent company had demanded a change and that the nonsensical term "international object" be implemented instead. It was decrees like that which had made WCW a laughing stock for so long prior to the Eric Bischoff-led revolution, but even he knew that trying to do anything too far outside of the group's comfort zone would land him in trouble.

Despite Koplovitz's warnings, Vince decided to finally let go of his long-held predispositions towards cartoon wrestling and fully take the plunge into the untested waters of shock-value television. He had observed the edgier storylines that he had been cautiously integrating into his product getting the best reactions of anything he was doing, and he felt the time was right to drop any remaining pretence about what the World Wrestling Federation was going to be. The Pillman and Austin angle had been the catalyst, but it was still only the beginning. "We had created a great deal of controversy with the home invasion thing, it was totally new and it got a lot of people talking," recalls Jim Ross. "I didn't think we would go back to it, but it opened the door."

Of all people, wrestling traditionalist Jim Cornette had actually been the one who first tried pushing McMahon towards a more adult direction. He realised that the fans of the WWF from the boom period were now teenagers and young adults, and that to appeal to them the company needed to change the way they presented wrestling. "I wanted to make it real edgy and violent, more like *Cops*. I didn't want three cameras on backstage angles, I wanted security cameras to make it seem more real, but I was never allowed to do it," he imparts. "The thing with Vince is that you can say the same thing fifteen times until you are blue in the face and he looks at you like you've got turds hanging out of your mouth. Then one day he wakes up and has an idea - which is everything I had been saying to him for months - and in his head it's the first time he had ever heard of it.

"In 1996 I was advocating realism in the ring and with the gimmicks of the guys, but Bruce [Prichard] and Pat [Patterson] always wanted the funny-ha-ha, and then Vince Russo would chime in pushing *Jerry Springer* style programming. As a result 1996 ended up being an even bigger transitional year for the WWF than 1995 had been. On one part of the show you would have The Goon with his cute little wrestling boots that looked like skates, then elsewhere you would get Brian Pillman pulling a gun!"

UNFORTUNATELY, THE real Brian Pillman story would have a typically shocking and tragically imminent end. On October 5, 1997, the day of WWF pay-per-view *Badd* Blood, Brian was found dead in his Budget-tel Motel room in Bloomington, Minnesota at the age of thirty-five. The coroner's report listed the cause of death as down to arteriosclerotic heart disease, though a combination of pain medication, cocaine and other substances played a significant part. Those who had been around Brian in the preceding months were hardly surprised.

It was not long before even his close friends stopped talking to him out of fear he had a death wish, as unfortunately, Pillman had taken the role of the 'Loose Cannon' too far, even playing it at home when only Melanie and his children were around. Life imitated art, and was one of the grounds for Melanie filing for divorce. Less than a year after she had stood in her home and played the role of frightened wife, Melanie found herself back on *Raw*, only this time in the very real position of grieving widow contemplating raising five children (and one more on the way) as a single parent. The move to put the stricken Melanie on the box just twenty-four hours removed from her young husband's tragic passing was a particularly heartless and tacky one from McMahon, who was taking shock-based reality television to whole new levels of classlessness with the stunt.

TWELVE

OW THAT THE FLOODGATES WERE open, there was no
stopping the bullish McMahon as he charged away from kid-
oriented programming towards a volatile brand of risqué,
aggressive television.[56] For some on the roster such as former All-American
defensive tackle Ron Simmons, that meant a complete change in character
direction.

Simmons had been catapulted to stardom when he was drawn from a
ballot by then-WCW chief Bill Watts, picked to represent the company as
its first ever recognised African-American World Champion. He beat Vader
on August 2, 1992 in Baltimore, Maryland, but the trajectory of his career
dropped off considerably after losing the belt back to Vader at the end of
December. He found himself cast aside, and by 1994 he was mired in the
midcard. Eventually WCW decided not to renew his contract, a situation
that Simmons later suggested was down to bigotry. He wound up spending
the next two years wrestling for ECW and then touring Japan.

In the middle of 1996, Titan finally came calling. Bruce Prichard was the
conduit in arranging a meeting between Simmons and McMahon, though
the job offer came thanks to a recommendation from Jim Ross. Like many
of the men championed by Ross in those days, Simmons had made a name
for himself in WCW during the announcer's own time in Atlanta, with his
decorated football background a trait that Ross deeply admired. Even
though the former NFL star had not wrestled in the mainstream for two
years, he was an easy sell to the talent-bereft McMahon. A former WCW
Champion, albeit one from four years prior, was a commodity he was keen
to have at his disposal.

When Vince laid out his plans for Simmons during their first meeting,
the wrestler initially thought he was being ribbed. "I sat down with my
team, and this is what we envision you as," began McMahon, "We see you
as this gladiator. This Spartan." Simmons was intrigued and initially behind
the idea, but then McMahon started showing off the drawings Creative
Services had provided him with to use as a visual aid. "This will be
something like what you'll be wearing, this helmet right here, it's made of

---

[56] Kay Koplovitz and the USA Network remained squeamish at the content of the WWF's show, but
McMahon continued to defy their wishes. In early 1998 when the WWF began beating WCW
regularly each week, suddenly the lewd, violent content was not a problem anymore.

leather," added McMahon. Simmons scoured the drawing, which depicted him wearing a helmet resembling something a frequent seizure sufferer might adorn, and a gladiator's outfit that looked like a fancy dress costume gone wrong. At a loss for words, Simmons began to laugh. He was amused at McMahon's sense of humour - ribbing him during his job interview - until he realised that he was the only one in the room laughing; McMahon was serious.

Simmons' heart sank when it dawned on him that if he wanted a job in the WWF, he would be reduced to competing in skimpy attire that rivalled Dustin Runnels' *WrestleMania* bare-all lingerie for bad taste and indecency. Realising McMahon's mind was made up, he had little choice but to stammer, "You know, I think that's great. It's absolutely fantastic! I think it will be the best thing that I've ever done." Thus Faarooq Asad was born - a name confusingly taken from the penultimate King of Egypt, Farouk I - and to compound the nonsensical mentality of the gimmick, Simmons was given promiscuous flirt Sunny as his ill-fitting manager.

He later suggested that the challenging disposition of his character was not simply down to creative incompetence, but was rather done by design. "The idea [behind it] was to give you something not as approachable or appealing to people and make it work, so you could get out there and learn what they wanted. That really trained me in what the people wanted and how to work the crowd. It was a learning experience. At the time I had no idea what Vince was doing, but that's what he did with a lot of guys, and he did it with me."

Those in the office who had known Simmons for years were appalled with Vince's vision for him. "He was an All-American athlete at Florida State and a former World Champion, but he came out dressed as a goddamn gladiator," grumbles Jim Cornette. "It was things like that which made me hate my life when I was there. It was so frustrating." Cornette, in keeping with some of the edgier characters that the WWF had been promoting at the time, initially proposed that Simmons' Titan persona would resemble something more akin to notorious Nation of Islam leader Louis Farrakhan. He also suggested having Simmons renounce his "slave name" *a' la* Muhammad Ali, but at the time McMahon was uncomfortable going in that direction. Just a few months later, he would perform a dramatic U-turn.

IN NOVEMBER, the WWF presented *Survivor Series*, the first Titan pay-per-view to grace Madison Square Garden in two-and-a-half years. Even though the show came a month prior to the culmination of the calendar year, in many ways it served as a climax to everything that Vince had been working towards in 1996. It also set the stage for the future of his company; performers on the card would make up at least part of the main events on thirteen of the next fourteen *WrestleMania* shows[57]. It was an evening of glorious returns, grand arrivals and - for some - validation.

Curiously, a throwaway eight-man tag team match on the undercard encapsulated the state of the WWF as a whole, featuring as it did a veritable hotchpotch mix of wildly contrasting ideals. On the babyface side was the debuting Charles 'Flash Funk' Skaggs, the returning Rodney 'Yokozuna' Anoa'i, directionless ethnic stereotype Juan 'Savio Vega' Rivera, and blast from the past James 'Superfly Jimmy Snuka' Reiher. On the heel end of the ring were Glenn Jacobs and Rick Bognar in their farcical Diesel and Razor Ramon roles, the politically harangued Leon 'Vader' White, and Ron Simmons - who had recently been given a freshly injected dose of attitude.

With Faarooq Asad not connecting on any level with his audience, Vince realised that he needed to change tact with Ron Simmons to get the most from his investment in him. He decided to go in an entirely different direction to the would-be gladiator gimmick, recycling Jim Cornette's idea of Simmons as a chagrined black man fighting against prejudice. He repackaged the idea and presented it as his own, adding a unique personal twist on Cornette's original premise. He wanted Simmons as the despotic leader of a quasi-militant group, complete with racially-driven overtones and a band of like-minded followers. With McMahon having decided to go full-steam ahead with a provocative brand of programming, he pulled the trigger on the idea and the Nation of Domination faction was born.

"It wasn't racist... at first," offers Simmons, "It was more me being a dictator and the vicious leader of the gang. I was to be the most obnoxious and overbearing person on television, slightly edgy and bigoted. It's not something you have to rehearse when you come from the background I have, and you have seen the things I have seen." The group's name was taken from a similar unit formed in Jerry Lawler's USWA, with its ethos loosely based on the black nationalist organisation the Black Panther Party, as well as the Nation of Islam. The Nation of Domination's members

---

[57] A run interrupted only by amateur wrestling greats Brock Lesnar and Kurt Angle, both of whom had turned professional and were given the chance to headline *WrestleMania XIX* in 2003. It was not until *WrestleMania XXVII* in 2011 that the main event again featured performers who had not been at *Survivor Series*, though Dwayne 'The Rock' Johnson was heavily involved. Johnson's return to the WWE resulted in him headlining the next two *WrestleMania* shows opposite John Cena, before the main events of *WrestleMania XXX* and *WrestleMania 31* became only the third and fourth incarnations of the annual extravaganza since the 1996 *Survivor Series* show to not feature any performer who had appeared on it.

adopted Pan-African colours, a unifying group salute, and engaged in unprovoked attacks on members of the roster, all the while with Simmons spouting injustice-inspired tirades against those who he felt had wronged him.

Simmons debuted the original incarnation of the Nation for the first time on pay-per-view at *Survivor Series*, and when his former WCW tag partner Charles 'Too Cold Scorpio' Skaggs was hired towards the end of the year many suspected he would be the latest inductee into the heel faction. Instead he was cast as a babyface, with McMahon once again reverting to type and rebranding him as the derivative Flash Funk, a zoot suit and furry boots wearing stereotypical seventies hoodlum.

Jim Cornette guiltily admits culpability for inadvertently giving Skaggs the name, blaming a conversation that had occurred during one of the many endless creative meetings by Vince's pool. McMahon had already decided that Skaggs would dance and jive, but he was not satisfied with any of the names suggested for him. "Why can't he just be Scorpio?" pleaded Cornette, only to be told by McMahon, "Oh no, we've gotta change that." Cornette - who was a big fan of eccentric Motown artist Rick James - suggested that Skaggs be renamed "Funk" due to James' nickname "the king of punk funk". Bruce Prichard chimed in with "Flash" as a forename because of the character's supposed stylishness, and thus Skaggs became Flash Funk. Cornette holds himself accountable, "I thought, 'What the fuck? It doesn't even matter anymore.' It was Stockholm Syndrome. You stay there [in the WWF] long enough and you start thinking like they do."

The hiring of Skaggs came about due to a secret working agreement that McMahon shared with ECW promoter Paul Heyman. "Vince and Paul had a great relationship," says Jim Ross. "We [the WWF] were helping them [ECW], because we looked at it as, 'Well, maybe at some point in time we'll be able to get access to some of these stars.'" While McMahon viewed ECW with a degree of caution, he also realised that since the death at his hand of wrestling's territorial system, it was a convenient place to shop for and nurture fresh talent. He had already enjoyed a degree of success with other ECW alumni such as Steve Austin, Mick Foley, and Brian Pillman, and he wanted first refusal on any other members of the roster that took his fancy.

McMahon met with Heyman in September and the pair reached a deal which allowed Vince to send rarely used members of his talent pool to ECW for seasoning. In return, he wanted to flesh out his own roster with former Fabulous Freebird Terry Gordy, smooth tag team outfit Doug Furnas and Dan Kroffat, and Too Cold Scorpio. Heyman had no qualms with the first three, but Scorpio posed a problem. While he privately admitted that he had creatively done everything he could with the character, the snag was financial. ECW had a long-standing deal with record publisher Tommy Boy Records that saw the label promote one of its tracks as Scorpio's entrance theme. Each time he appeared, they were credited onscreen, in return paying ECW $1000 per week in sponsorship for the exposure. Upon Heyman informing McMahon of the lost revenue he would be facing, without batting an eyelid the WWF head promised to cover it. Immediately he had his finance department issue weekly cheques to ECW's holding company HHG Corp, a deal he honoured until the group folded in 2001.[58]

With the issue resolved, Skaggs was cleared to make his Federation debut at *Survivor Series*, though his introduction as Flash Funk was some way removed from his ECW send-off at *November To Remember* the previous night. At the ECW event, he turned heel on the crowd with the declaration that, "I'm not gonna miss none of you motherfuckers," then defeated three jobbers in quick succession. In keeping with the traditions of the business, Skaggs eventually did the job on his way out, succumbing to former WWF star Louie Spicolli to the delight of the ECW Arena.

In Madison Square Garden as the jiving Flash Funk, Skaggs was immediately reduced to a comedic parody. "What the heck? What *is* this?" pleaded Jim Cornette from the announce desk, echoing the thoughts of every outraged Scorpio fan watching. Contrarily, Vince felt that Flash Funk represented the vanguard of modern culture. He awkwardly attempted to show his own chic side by dancing along to Funk's entrance music, subsequently adopting a forced ebonical dialect and purring, "Ah ha! I know that's right," like a *haut monde* Barry White. With Titan's recent failure to land Hulk Hogan fresh in the memory, McMahon could not resist taking a sly shot, and instructed Jim Ross to get in a petty dig in at 'the Hulkster'. Ross duly obliged, commenting on the brightly bedecked Funk, "I've never seen the yellow and red look so good here in the Garden."

Elsewhere on the babyface team, the return of Rodney 'Yokozuna' Anoa'i was supposed to be the start of another long-term run for the respected Samoan. The mammoth grappler had recently returned from a stint at a slimming clinic at the behest of the WWF, as the promotion were concerned over his well-being. The thirty-year-old Anoa'i had piled on mass to such a degree that he tipped the scales at around 800lbs. It was a

---

[58] The agreement to pay ECW $1000 per week eventually led to rumours that Paul Heyman was on the WWF payroll. These rumours were unsubstantiated, but spread enough to cause many fans and people in the industry to believe them as gospel.

dangerously unhealthy weight and Titan had due cause to be worried, though they were equally concerned that Anoa'i would not even be able to wrestle in certain states due to strict guidelines lain down by regional athletic commissions.

Unfortunately, Anoa'i did not take the weight loss seriously and flunked out of the program immediately. That he came back to the ring larger than ever was not lost on anyone, especially irked members of management. The *Survivor Series* encounter would ultimately prove to be his final match with the WWF. Little under four years later Anoa'i's weight problems had taken such a toll on his body that his organs were unable to take the strain. Despite having dropped to around 600lbs, he died alone in his Moat House Hotel room in Liverpool, England on October 23, 2000, with the cause of death listed as a pulmonary edema.

While Yokozuna was unknowingly performing his WWF swansong, the return of Superfly Jimmy Snuka was always intended to be a one off, feel-good spectacle for the fans in the Garden, a venue where he had performed some of his most memorable moments. In WWF lore he was forever linked with the building thanks to a famous leap from the top of a steel cage onto Don Muraco back in October 1983. That in itself was typical WWF revisionist history; Snuka had performed the exact same move little over a year prior during a match with then-WWF Champion Bob Backlund, but because he was a heel at the time the memory of that initial stunt was stricken from history.

Snuka was already in town for the WWF's annual Hall of Fame ceremony held the night before at the New York Marriott Marquis hotel. He was one of nine inductees sworn into the intangible Hall, alongside the likes of lifelong jobber Johnny Rodz, 'rock 'n' wrestling' forefather Captain Lou Albano, and Vince's father Vincent James McMahon. Those entered were carefully chosen, with the WWF specifically avoiding anyone who worked for WCW, or those who might defect there and potentially cheapen the honour under instruction from Bischoff.

As honourable a gesture as it was for McMahon to recognise those from the past who had helped him build his empire, few took the annual extravaganza seriously due to the absence of several notable names from the WWF's rich history. Without the likes of Hulk Hogan, Randy Savage, Bruno Sammartino, and Bob Backlund, they argued it would never be legitimate.[59] Increasingly struggling to furnish the Hall with performers whom he felt would not screw him over by pitching up in Atlanta,

---

[59] Hogan was eventually inducted in 2005, Bruno Sammartino and Bob Backlund in 2013, and Randy Savage in 2015.

McMahon decided to discontinue the ceremony until 2003, two years after he had bought WCW and was no longer in genuine competition with any other wrestling company.

Snuka's role at *Survivor Series* was an unannounced surprise, though his involvement was limited to a handful of trademark moves and his famous Superfly Splash from the top rope. Rick Bognar was the recipient on this occasion, suffering the ignominy of the fifty-three-year-old Snuka pinning him, and being one of only two men eliminated from the bout (the other being the soon-to-turn-heel Savio Vega). Everyone else was disqualified, with the match thrown out as a cheap draw after less than ten minutes of combat. It was the victim of time shaving, with everything else on the card having gone longer than expected.

AT LEAST the participants could be thankful they were on the pay-per-view portion of the card at all, which was more than could be said for the performers involved in the opening match on the preview show. Unlike the diverse array of characters competing in the latter elimination bout, the free-to-air contest was entirely made up of conspicuous throwbacks and talent struggling with stale gimmicks. Pitting babyfaces Jesse Jammes, Aldo Montoya, Bob Holly, and Bart Gunn against The Sultan, Justin 'Hawk' Bradshaw, Salvatore Sincere, and Billy Gunn, in many ways the contest embodied the antithesis of what the New WWF represented. The irony would be that the majority of those involved became key personalities in the Attitude Era once they shed their cartoon personas.

Brian 'Jesse Jammes' James, son of veteran wrestler and then WCW agent Joseph 'Bullet Bob Armstrong' James, had worked for the WWF on and off since 1994. He initially appeared as The Roadie, a heel manager gimmick that saw him serve primarily as 'Double J' Jeff Jarrett's towel boy. Plans eighteen months earlier had called for The Roadie to break away from Jarrett and the two to work a program together, but Jarrett's departure from Titan seemed to spell the end of that.

Not so in Vince McMahon's eyes. Even though Jarrett was now plying his trade in WCW and there was no possible payoff, he forged ahead with the feud anyway. Vince was undeterred, recasting James as the "real" Double J, a glorified tribute act who was promoted as the man responsible for Jarrett's success. Fans did not buy it, seeing Jesse Jammes as a cheap rip-off version of a character they had enjoyed watching. It was Diesel and Razor Ramon mark two all over again, and it generated the same apathetic response.

It was a reaction one of his opponents, Monty 'Billy Gunn' Sopp, was becoming increasingly accustomed to. Having been part of the babyface Smoking Gunns tag team for the past three years and having exhausted all possible scenarios in a weak division, Sopp had recently turned heel to a tepid response. Due to his six-foot-four-inch frame, impressive athletic prowess, and a shock of platinum blond hair, some had Sopp pegged as a future singles star. However, in the ring he was struggling to show any of this potential. After *Survivor Series*, Sopp and James became embroiled in a critically panned feud for much of 1997, and were on the cusp of WWF releasing them altogether. They were given one last-ditch shot at getting over in a thrown together oddball tag team, albeit one that appeared doomed to fail.

Similar to how management's apathy had basically left Steve Austin to his own devices prior to him smashing the perennial glass ceiling, the newly dubbed New Age Outlaws were given a degree of creative license. Their directive was simply, "Go out and get over," and that freedom allowed the personalities of their bawdy characters to emanate. To the surprise of everyone, the pair made it work thanks to their instant chemistry as a unit and a fresh shtick. They eventually became multiple time tag team champions and one of the hottest acts in the industry. The Outlaws became so over so quickly, that in 1998 they were granted a berth in the WWF's top Attitude Era faction, D-Generation X, alongside Paul Levesque and a returning Sean Waltman.

Another heel, The Sultan, portrayed by hefty Samoan former tag team champion Solofa Fatu, was a character that harked back to the seventies. The premise of the gimmick was that The Sultan was a genuine shah, the ruler of an ancient Middle Eastern empire[60] who had renounced his dynasty and traded his sultanate for a career bending bones. Covering his face to avoid recognition as Fatu by eagle-eyed fans, the story spun by the announcers was that The Sultan's tongue had been cut out and his face disfigured. It made little contextual sense, but it was the best a jaded creative team could come up with to explain it.

In addition, Titan cast two former WWF Champions from the pre-Hulkamania years to serve as The Sultan's elite guard. The first was former Iranian Olympian and one-time real-life shah bodyguard Hossein Khosrow Ali Vaziri, better known as the Iron Sheik. It was his first Federation role for nearly five years, having last been seen serving alongside Sgt. Slaughter as a controversial Iraqi-sympathiser. Alongside him was his former in-ring rival Bob Backlund, the second longest reigning WWF Champion in history. He was performing the heel role of morality policeman, taking a stand against Federation performers he judged to be decadent. With the Sultan purportedly coming from a similarly conservative background, he was the ideal candidate for doling out flagellation to those deemed by Backlund as having sinned.

Despite McMahon giving him a fairly strong early push that should have got him over as a dangerous heel, fans had little patience for such an archaic persona. In an era of increasingly realistic angles and characters, The Sultan stretched the boundaries of believability more than any other act on the roster. Despite that, McMahon persisted and pushed Fatu into an Intercontinental Title match at *WrestleMania* with another ailing performer, his real-life cousin Dwayne 'Rocky Maivia' Johnson.

The Sultan rapidly fell out of favour when it became clear even to McMahon that he was not getting over, and Fatu left the promotion for two years to recharge and freshen his act. He returned in late 1999 as Rikishi, unmasked, much heavier and with bleached-blond hair. Now a portly dancer clad in a mawashi - somewhat akin to his cousin Yokozuna - Fatu finally achieved main event stardom.[61] The next time he and Johnson met in a singles match on pay-per-view, it was as one third of a triple main event at *Survivor Series* in 2000.

Robert Howard shared Fatu's frustration at being burdened with a no-hope gimmick. In his role of colourful racing car driver Bob Holly, he typified an era that the New WWF was struggling to break away from. Like Fatu, he would have to undergo a significant personality transformation before he achieved success in wrestling's modernised landscape. But first he was forced to endure one of Vince McMahon's infamous brainwaves, when he was paired with Monty Sopp's former tag team partner Mike 'Bart Gunn' Polchlopek in the New Midnight Express.

The original incarnations of the Midnight Express managed by Jim Cornette and featuring various pairings of Dennis Condrey, Bobby Eaton, Stan Lane, and Randy Rose were regarded as one of the finest tag teams of the eighties, enjoying successful spells in the NWA and various regional territories. McMahon had tried to sign the duo of Eaton and Lane, along with Cornette during the Hulkamania era, but he was turned down after offering merely an opportunity rather than a comparative financial deal to what the team were already earning. By 1998, the team were long gone from

---

[61] Rikishi ended up being by far the most successful character that Solofa Fatu ever performed. Under the Rikishi guise, Fatu was even inducted into the WWE Hall of Fame class of 2015.

the mainstream, so McMahon decided to re-invent them, and make them, "bigger than ever".

The idea came to him while travelling with Jim Cornette and constantly hearing fans refer to the tandem whenever they ran into the former manager at rest stops or conventions. McMahon, whose knowledge of wrestling outside of the WWF was severely limited at best, was intrigued and decided to put Cornette back on television with a modern version of the tag team. He turned to Howard and Polchlopek, who were both mired in the undercard nadir, giving them corny alliterative names to go with their striking blue and yellow tights. As with virtually all examples in wrestling with the prefix "new", the tandem bombed and was split within a few months of forming. Cornette later stated that he felt the whole charade was likely a rib, designed to show him up or at the least stop fans asking about the Midnight Express.

After the failure of the New Midnight Express, Howard would get lost in the shuffle for another year before reinventing himself as Hardcore Holly. The role allowed him to trade in his gimmick of farcical goofball with a propensity for losing, and become a legitimate badass wielding weaponry. The character overhaul stuck, and he lasted a further thirteen years with the company, enjoying a tenure that ran unbroken until 2009.

Howard's Midnight Express cohort Polchlopek was in a similar situation to ex-Smoking Gunns partner Monty Sopp when *Survivor Series* came around, struggling to adapt to singles competition after the tandem's split. He meandered for a while with little success, then after losing to Sopp in June he disappeared for six months prior to the Midnight Express run with Howard. Polchlopek seemed to be on course to getting his career back on track when he demonstrated his real-life toughness in winning the WWF's ill-fated MMA-inspired and almost entirely legitimate *Brawl For All* tournament in 1998. Unfortunately, in doing so he also managed to irk WWF Head of Talent relations Jim Ross.

The intention of the fight series was to serve as a vehicle for promoting the introduction of one of Ross' long-time favourites 'Dr. Death' Steve Williams, a former college football star for the University of Oklahoma, of whom Ross was an avid follower. Williams was a renowned hard man in a wrestling industry exclusively populated by tough guys, possessing a phenomenally fearsome reputation. With Ross keen to give Williams an immediate push to the top of the card for a program with Steve Austin, the *Brawl For All* was devised with the belief that the newcomer would steamroll through the competition with ease. What nobody had accounted for was that Williams was far from in fighting shape. He was coming into the competition with a catalogue of injuries, the result of years of hard-hitting matches in Japan. The non-worked nature of the tournament meant that the WWF could not control its outcome, and when Williams came up against Polchlopek - a former Tough Man contest winner - he tore his hamstring mid-fight before getting knocked out with a vicious left hook.

Titan were furious. They had been so sure Williams was going to emerge victorious that they had already paid him the winner's fee as part of his contract. Not only that, but the humiliating defeat left Williams out of action for the rest of the year. With his reputation in tatters, he was no longer a viable opponent for Steve Austin even when he did return. Rather than give Polchlopek the spot intended for Williams, he was instead punished for daring to win the *Brawl For All*. He was used again only so that Titan could make an example out of him, pitting him in a mismatch with tubby charity boxer Eric 'Butterbean' Esch at *WrestleMania* in 1999. Polchlopek was knocked out quickly and left the WWF later in the year, heading to Japan to resume his wrestling career.

Like Polchlopek, Kliq ally Peter 'Aldo Montoya' Polaco also had to leave Titan to enjoy the most rewarding spell of his career. Polaco was fighting a losing battle in the WWF, forced to compete adorned in a bright yellow mask that strongly resembled a jockstrap, and colourful tights representing the Portuguese flag. Polaco's friendship with the Kliq was the only thing that kept him employed, though when his dates dried up significantly in 1997 he asked for his release so he could go and work for Paul Heyman in ECW. The promotion was the perfect place for Polaco to flourish. He swiftly underwent an attitude overhaul and transformed himself into Justin Credible, bulking up and adding a contemptuous cockiness to his personality. Polaco was over enough in the role that he eventually became ECW's version of World Champion, before getting another WWF run in 2001 following ECW's bankruptcy.

Of the eight competitors in the *Free For All* match, only Tom 'Salvatore Sincere' Brandi faded from mainstream view. He had actually performed beyond the Federation's expectations of him in his stereotypical Mafioso role, outlasting each of the other TV-only stars hired alongside him in the summer. Brandi became a fully-fledged member of the roster, though the limitations of his character ended up his downfall. The following year he was "outed" as "just a gimmick" by Marc Mero, who referred to Brandi by his real name. It was an angle that achieved little, serving only to strip Brandi of the proxy personality he was given. He soon left the company, though still enjoyed a twenty year career on the independent scene.

The most successful of the eight was John 'Justin Hawk Bradshaw' Layfield, who eventually dropped his played-out mountain-man gimmick in favour of another McMahon tag team retread: The New Blackjacks (alongside an equally rudderless Barry Windham). When that inevitably did not work out, Layfield eventually formed a successful tag team known as the Acolytes (and later the Acolyte Protection Agency, or APA) with Ron Simmons in 1998, finally achieving success as a no-nonsense brawler. When he flew solo again in 2004 he was repackaged as the J.R. Ewing-inspired JBL, becoming one of the most unlikely World Champions in history. While Layfield quickly grew into his newfound lofty role at the summit of the company, and eventually evolved into a worthy heel champion, his career path could have so easily been very different. That cold November night in the Garden, a mistake nearly cost him his job.

With time short, the eight men in the pre-show bout were determined to make a case for themselves in the brief window they were allotted. They realised their lowly position on the card was a reflection of their collective current statuses in the company. Looking to determine their own fates, the octet executed their planned sequences at pace so as to cram in as much action as possible, hoping to catch the eye of a watching agent or official. Unfortunately for Layfield, not everyone was watching closely. Match referee Tim White was only paying the contest cursory attention, which as a result nearly accidentally derailed his career.

Layfield was booked to win the match as the sole survivor, which he hoped would be the start of a push up the card. Federation brass was high on him, because like Sopp he ticked all the right boxes that Vince looked for in a star. It was clear from the commentary that Layfield was destined for a bigger role than toiling on the undercard. "He's got unlimited potential," offered Jim Ross, "He's gonna be something special here before too long."

After eliminating Bob Holly from the match with his patented stiff lariat, Layfield was quickly rolled up from behind by Jesse Jammes for what was supposed to be a two count. Unfortunately, White was distracted by a new earpiece that he and the other referees were wearing for the first time that night, so was not paying full attention. He instinctively counted the three despite Bradshaw's shoulder clearly coming off the mat, wrongly eliminating him from the match. "Did he get him? I think he got him. I'm not so sure that was a three count," asked a puzzled McMahon from the announce desk. In an instant, White realised what he had done. "Oh my God, kid, I am so sorry!" he pleaded to Layfield, who could do little else except trudge angrily to the back.

Immediately he was met at the curtain by an incandescent Gerald Brisco, who was running the Gorilla position that night. Brisco lambasted Layfield, letting him know in no uncertain terms that his push was dead and he would be lucky to even keep his job. Brisco did not realise that White was to blame. He thought Layfield had forgot to kick out of the pinfall attempt, or for whatever reason was purposely sabotaging the match. In those times of war, mistrust and accusations of treachery were rife throughout both the WWF and WCW. For all Brisco knew, Layfield could have been a covert saboteur working for Eric Bischoff. To his credit, Layfield refused to pass the blame to where it belonged. "I couldn't stooge Tim out, so I just took it," he later recounted.

In the ring, a sheepish White relayed instructions from the back to the remaining performers, with booking changed around so that Bart Gunn could get a measure of revenge on storyline brother Billy. The last few moments following Layfield's exit were hurried, with time running out on the *Free For All* broadcast. Eliminations came thick and fast before Billy tied Bart up in the ropes so he could secretly tell him the new plan for the bout's finale, which they proceeded to awkwardly execute. As he would in the future, Mike Polchlopek benefited from a spot designed to help get someone else over, and like in 1998, it ultimately did nothing to enhance his on-screen persona.

BACK IN August on the same Wheeling, West Virginia taping where Rick Bognar had been desperately trying to impress WWF officials and land his dream job with the company, a rookie called Flex Kavana was doing much the same thing. Kavana was third generation performer Dwayne Johnson - the son of former WWF Tag Team Champion Rocky Johnson, and grandson of 'High Chief' Peter Maivia - who had made both his wrestling and WWF debuts on the same night in a tryout match back in March.

Johnson had first come to the WWF's attention at the start of the year when the confident youngster blindly called Pat Patterson to introduce himself, asking the respected official to come and see him work out with his dad. When he eventually realised he was talking to Rocky Johnson's son, Patterson agreed to meet with Dwayne at a local restaurant. Patterson was immediately struck by his imposing footballer's build and natural charisma. "I couldn't believe the look on him. He looked great. He looked like a star," remembers the veteran.

Patterson called Vince the following day and was full of glowing praise for Johnson, advising he was a can't-miss prospect who needed to be looked at immediately. Desperate for fresh talent, McMahon agreed to give

Johnson a shot and brought him to a *Superstars* taping in Corpus Christi, Texas for a series of tryout matches. Johnson impressed enough in his subsequent auditions with Steve Lombardi and Chris Candido that he was immediately given a contract - partly to prevent WCW from getting their hands on him. Titan then sent him to Jerry Lawler's USWA promotion in Memphis for seasoning.

Six months later he was back, having traded in his bland birth name for his USWA handle Flex Kavana, and bringing with it a swagger and an air of confidence that would go on to define his career. At the Wheeling taping in August he defeated relative unknown David Haskins in a dark match, then the following night in Columbus was put against veteran ring general Owen Hart. At the time, Hart was running a tried and test wrestling trope; a phony injury angle that saw him wear a cast on his left arm long after any injury would have healed, then use it as a weapon in matches for guaranteed easy heat. Johnson had been too busy honing his craft and hitting the gym in Memphis to keep up with Federation programming, so he had no idea that Hart's injury was a work.

Johnson only noticed the cast for the first time when the pair were in the ring. He simply assumed that Hart was doing the same thing that wrestlers always did and working through an injury that would keep any normal person out of commission. "Oh shit, I don't want to hurt the guy any more than he is already hurt," thought Johnson to himself, deciding that the best thing would be to avoid the apparently hurt appendage entirely and work holds exclusively on Owen's right arm. That was a major no-no in the intricately weaved tapestry of long-established wrestling lore. The rule in the industry (apart from in Mexico which adopted a reverse policy) was to work all holds on the left side of the body. Having everyone reading from the same hymn sheet made it easy to work with unfamiliar opponents from anywhere in the world. That way everyone knew what everyone else was going to do and how to do it, keeping the dance smooth and fluid.

Johnson started fumbling around awkwardly with Hart's right arm, struggling to adapt against a deeply ingrained practice. "It felt terribly awkward," he remembers, "It was like trying to write with your left hand when you're naturally right-handed." To those in the back watching on the monitors it seemed like an arrant blunder, with some wondering how Johnson was even at the stage where he was granted tryout matches when his fundamentals were so glaringly lacking. For a brief moment, Hart wondered the same thing. The experienced pro scalded the rookie. "Hey, what are you doing? That's the wrong arm, take the left kid," he whispered. "I thought you were injured!" stammered Johnson, who felt a knot twist in his stomach and his cheeks turn bright red with embarrassment. He felt like an idiot. Johnson was hardly soothed by Hart uncontrollably laughing out loud right there in the middle of the ring, but the greenhorn was able to pull himself together enough that the remainder of the bout passed without any problems.

"So, how was he to work with?" McMahon asked Hart afterwards. "He was good," assessed Owen, "He is probably better than half of the guys on the roster." Rather than a damning appraisal of the troupe of talent McMahon currently possessed, Hart's assessment was intended as a glowing commendation of Johnson. Vince was pleased. He knew that as well as daring programming, youth was the other key component in battling WCW. If Johnson was truly as talented as Patterson and Hart were telling him then he wanted him on the main roster immediately. Two weeks later Johnson received a call from McMahon's trusted front office executive J.J. Dillon, telling him his stint in Memphis was over and that he was to report to the WWF's warehouse training facility in Stamford, Connecticut for some final preparation under the tutelage of Tom Prichard.

Three months later, Johnson was summoned to Titan Tower for a face-to-face meeting with Vince McMahon and Jim Ross. They broke the news that he was going to be thrown into the WWF mix at the deep end by making his official television debut at *Survivor Series* in Madison Square Garden. The rookie was thrilled. He knew that if he was trusted on a pay-per-view emanating from the Garden then the office had faith in him. He was somewhat less enthused when they informed him of the handle he would compete under: Rocky Maivia. The name was intended as homage to his father and grandfather, but Johnson hated the idea. He wanted to carve his own niche in the business. He did not want to follow the barefooted Samoan footprints of his grandfather, or the racially profiled funky black man route of his father. McMahon and Ross assured him that would not be the case, rather that the moniker would serve as a respectful deference to his lineage and a nod to the fact that he was unique in being the WWF's first ever third generation performer.[62] After some coaxing, Johnson made peace with Rocky Maivia and agreed to try his hardest to make it work.

So big were McMahon's plans for Johnson, that he was not only competing in a match that night at the Garden, he was booked to win the whole thing. He would be the sole survivor from a team of four, single-handedly responsible for defeating two well-established members of the

---

[62] Though like many things in the WWF, this was merely promotional fluff. Vince himself was a third generation performer. Jeff Jarrett's father (Jerry) and grandfather (Eddie Marlin) were both wrestlers too.

regular crew. McMahon, Ross, and Patterson were so confident that Johnson was a future World Champion that they were determined to give him a mega-push to guarantee he got over. On the night of the show, Gerald Brisco broke the news to Johnson, who calmly took what he knew to be a huge opportunity in his stride. "That's great, what do you guys have in mind?" he replied with an assuredness and poise that belied his twenty-four years.

The notoriously ruthless New York crowd were considerably less enamoured with Rocky Maivia's unveiling than WWF brass, greeting him with a collective shrug of contempt as he bounded to the ring sporting a cheesy perma-grin that he had been instructed to wear at all times. It was hardly a surprise: making his entrance clad in duck egg blue tribal tassels and a haircut ostensibly inspired by a Bichon Frisé, Rocky Maivia felt like a generic blue-eyed babyface who had been transplanted there from the eighties.

SOME OF his team mates that night were precisely that. One was Barry Windham, a former WWF Tag Team Champion who had wrestled on the first *WrestleMania*. He had recently returned to the Federation to be re-imagined by McMahon as The Stalker. It was a confused persona that saw Windham wear camouflage face paint and army slacks, performing a scarred battle solider version of serial killer "Night Stalker" Richard Ramirez. He had logically started life as a heel in pre-taped hype vignettes, but puzzlingly morphed into a babyface prior to his in-ring debut. The result was the act dying an instant death. Coming at a time when Vince was changing tact with his characters, the arcane role did not resonate with viewers and was shelved before the end of the year.

In the WWF, that was par for the course for Windham - widely revered as one of the most talented workers of his generation - but a puzzle that McMahon was frequently unable to solve. Some championed him in 1985 as having the potential to be the next Hulk Hogan level star, but Windham was unable to cope with the hectic WWF schedule and quit. In 1987 he was among the best wrestlers on the planet, routinely composing hour-long classics with Ric Flair in the NWA. When he rejoined Titan in 1989 he expected to be competing under his established name and used as a main event star, but instead he was forced to adopt a gimmick. He became The Widowmaker, though stubbornly refused to change anything about his persona. Disillusioned with his casting, he disappeared after only four months in the role.

By 1996, Windham, much like Ron Simmons and Vader, had seen his years of hard work in WCW evaporate upon the arrival of Hulk Hogan and his harem of antiquated ex-WWF wrestlers. He too meandered for two years before Jim Ross was able to land him a job with Titan. Ross was hoping to capitalise on some of the untapped ability that he believed Windham still possessed, though by now he was a sad shell of his former self. After twelve minutes of the *Survivor Series* contest, Windham was cleanly pinned by Goldust,[63] a scenario that would never have happened if the WWF had any serious long-term plans for him. Out of shape and wrestling at the tempo of someone twice his age, it was clear that Windham was no longer cut out for the increasingly fast-paced style of the WWF.

He was in much the same boat as the third member of the team, Jake Roberts, who was drafted into the match as a replacement for the injured ex-Olympian Mark Henry. Following the modest part he played in helping catapult Steve Austin into the stratosphere, the aging Roberts had transitioned into a program with announcer and fellow in-ring part-timer Jerry 'The King' Lawler over the summer. Their program was another that was laced with more than a little reality, based around Roberts' past problems with addiction. Once one of the most chillingly sinister heels in the business, Roberts was reduced to portraying a recovering alcoholic, fighting to overcome his demons and stay sober while temptation lingered. Unlike Windham, who had no affinity with the alien role thrust upon him, Roberts had few problems slipping into character.

While the famously tee-total Lawler mocking Jake each week was in poor taste but innocent enough at first, friends of Roberts felt the angle went too far when they saw him suffer alcohol poured down his throat by an unrelenting Lawler. He was even forced to stumble to the ring and act like a drunkard before revealing the whole thing to be an exotic brand of possum, designed to lure Lawler in so he could quickly beat him. It was a tacky route for Titan to traverse. Roberts was still genuinely struggling to stay clean, finding that even giving himself to Jesus Christ could not stop the unquenchable thirst he had for alcohol and various other vices. For the WWF to deride him for his troubles and scoff at his failure to adhere to a new moral code was the promotion at its most crass. Even though it was only a storyline, the angle played a part in sending Roberts into a spiral back to the murky world of substance abuse. It was a paralysing burden that would eat away at him, consuming him for nearly two more decades until he finally cleaned up his act for good in 2012.

---

[63] In a previous WCW life, Barry Windham and Dustin Runnels were tag team partners and promoted as best friends.

THE FINAL member of the babyface team was Marc Mero, the man Vince McMahon had been so keen on signing back in March, who was now firmly rooted in the midcard with little room for movement beyond that. Trying to justify his salary, McMahon had given him a brief reign with the Intercontinental Title at the end of September, but it only lasted a single month before he was beaten by one of his opponents on the heel team, Hunter Hearst Helmsley. While Mero had wowed audiences with his flashy, high-octane offence, he had not connected on an emotional level to make them care about him beyond his exciting aerial moves. He floundered for the following three months before damaging his knee and missing half a year of action. He returned a fraction of his former self, no longer motivated and completely overshadowed by his far more popular wife Sable.

For Paul Levesque, the Intercontinental Title win marked an end to five months of continuous losses and his spell in the political doghouse. His immediate return to a plum spot within the company did not sit well with some members of the locker room. "After a couple of months, they figured he'd paid his dues and they gave him the Intercontinental Title. That sure showed him," moaned Bob Holly. Despite his career turnaround, Helmsley was still the second man eliminated from the heel team, ousted by Marc Mero in a final attempt to give him some credibility.

It might have worked had he not then immediately been pinned by the limited Brian 'Crush' Adams, who following his Federation return had slipped right back into his role as lumbering heel with a push not befitting his mediocre skill-set. A close friendship with Mark Calaway helped his cause considerably, and in many ways his grungy look and storied past fit the WWF's new direction better than anyone else in the match. More so even than the floundering Goldust, who had been phased down significantly following his defeat to Ahmed Johnson in June. He was about to undergo a babyface turn to deflect the heat that still surrounded the contentious character. It was a strange situation for Dustin Runnels, who watched perplexed as others on the roster were going through transformations to make them more controversial, while he was seeing his own effectiveness rapidly reduced.

The turn came in December, a month on from *Survivor Series*, and involved two of his teammates at the Garden, Helmsley and Lawler. Hunter making a move on Goldust's valet Marlena served as the catalyst for his shift in allegiance, and when he helped Marc Mero fight off Helmsley's advances towards Sable he became a fan favourite. The turn was cemented later in the night when Lawler matter-of-factly asked him, "So, are you?" "Am I what?" answered Goldust incredulously. Lawler hesitated, then blurted out, "A, you know, a queer?" To the biggest babyface pop of his career, Goldust simply stated, "No!" and the audience hollered with a damning mixture of relief and joy. The most un-PC character that Vince had ever promoted had fittingly become a good guy in the least politically correct manner possible by "inning" himself.

It was Crush and Goldust who were given the job of putting over newcomer Rocky Maivia at the conclusion of the contest, losing despite having a seemingly insurmountable two-on-one advantage. Maivia first pinned Crush, catching him by surprise with generic go-to babyface move the flying body press, before finishing off Goldust with his shoulder breaker finisher. The Garden cheered out of courtesy, but Maivia had not been made into the overnight sensation officials had hoped he would be. To many, he came off as overly-enthusiastic and disingenuous, with fans sensing that he was simply reaping the benefits of his family's groundwork. Some in the office worried that McMahon had given Johnson too much too soon, making the same mistakes as he had when over-pushing Lex Luger and Diesel in the past. He was trying to force Rocky Maivia to get over because he had chosen him to get over - there was nothing organic or natural about it.

Unhappy about the WWF trying to force them to support a character they did not care for, fans nationwide quickly began to turn on Rocky Maivia with fervent vitriol. He became a hate figure amongst hardcore fans, reviled for not having earned his spot and for his deeply unoriginal persona. They viewed him as bland, generic, and a chore to watch, the outmoded vanilla babyface they as a collective had grown to loathe. Soon they began bringing handmade placards to live events declaring their hatred. Then the chants started: "Die Rocky, Die".

Johnson was unnerved by it, lacking the experience in both years and between the ropes to properly deal with the abuse. As usual, Pat Patterson was there to offer an arm around his shoulder and words of encouragement and advice. Realising that the youngster was panicked by the fan's rejection of him, Patterson told him not to worry because at least they cared enough to chant his name. Johnson tried to ride out the negative reception he was generating, though it was to no avail. The more he was on television the more fans hated him. It would take a full-blown heel turn to move him beyond that and into a spot that the WWF audience could relate to, with a heel turn and a place in Ron Simmons' Nation of Domination eventually proving to be the answer.[64]

Two years following his *Survivor Series* debut, Johnson, now simply called 'The Rock', lifted his first of ten World Titles, and went on to become one of the biggest names in the history of the sport. He also managed to do the one thing McMahon never truly could: infiltrate the mainstream. Having left wrestling early and transitioned into the world of Hollywood, in 2013 Johnson was the top grossing actor on the planet, with his movies pulling in a combined $1.3 billion in revenue. It was a figure that more than tripled Hulk Hogan's revenue from his entire acting career.

THE ANTICIPATION for the return of Bret Hart amongst fans did not appear to be shared by Vince McMahon. He was still smarting from the size of the deal he had signed off on, due in part to the figurative gun held to his head by Carl De Marco during negotiations. For his first televised match back, McMahon decided to recast the aging former champion in an unfamiliar role; that of a complaining, bitter veteran, unhappy with the direction the WWF was heading in.

It was barely an angle. Hart genuinely was uneasy with the heightened levels of lewdness and brutality that made up the WWF's new meta-fictional approach to wrestling programming. Over the course of 1997, as Vince's unprincipled television shows began to render the WWF a lawless, amoral dystopia, Hart found himself more at odds with the company's mindset than ever. "It's become smut TV," he huffed, "It's a lot more sexual and raunchy. I don't think you watch wrestling for sex."

Even before Hart began to vocally (and publicly) shun the WWF product, McMahon still felt he had an axe to grind with him. Along with broadcast colleague Jim Ross, he spent the duration of Hart's *Survivor Series* match with Steve Austin running him down with subtle digs. "I felt like they were going out of their way to portray me as old and beat up, while I was only doing my best to make Steve look strong," complained Hart. In spite of what Vince might have been trying to convey from behind the announce desk, he could not mask the reality of the situation to the viewers at home: The 'Hitman' and 'Stone Cold' assembled a masterpiece, a contest far better than Hart's clash with Vince's golden boy Shawn Michaels at *WrestleMania* in his last major outing. Hart had not missed a beat, and in Austin he had found someone whom he respected not only as a worker, but also - unlike Michaels - as a man. Hart had kept a close eye on Federation programming while he was absent from WWF rings, watching with interest

---

[64] Johnson's position in the Nation served as a conduit for him to vent his genuine frustrations at the negative reactions he was receiving. He managed to be so entertaining at being pissed off, that he ironically became one of the biggest babyfaces in the industry.

as Steve Austin quickly climbed up the card. He sensed immediately that 'Stone Cold' was the future of the WWF, and he unselfishly wanted to play a part in helping build him into a star. When discussing terms of his return to action, Hart had even hand-picked Austin as his first opponent, a gesture that the Texan was deeply appreciative of.

Austin's ascent since *King of the Ring* had been so rapid that fans now fervently clamoured to see him perform. He was different, fresh, and modern, and such a departure from the ubiquitous ennui that his blue-collar cynicism was generating more cheers than boos. He was a whole different gamble for McMahon, whose wrestling canvas had always been strictly painted with well-defined strokes of lavish black and white. Steve Austin was an entirely unseen concept - a shade of grey - bridging the divide between babyface and heel, forming his own inimitable path as a 'tweener'.[65] The overwhelmingly positive response to Austin when he stepped through the curtain at *Survivor Series* attested to that, with many of the New York fans reacting to him like a messianic vanquisher. It was not only jaded Gen X'ers tired of an infantile product, but women, children, and their families too. Such was the magnetism of Austin's viscerally intense personality that everyone wanted to jump on the Austin 3:16 bandwagon.

Even though Hart was given an equally rousing reception, especially from a hardcore sector of the fan base grateful that he had opted to stay with the WWF, there was an inescapable split in the audience's loyalties. Sat at ringside, McMahon watched as Austin flashed two disrespectful middle fingers at Hart prior to locking up - in many ways a physical manifestation of the New WWF - and seemed relatively surprised that the gesture was met with cheers from the crowd. "He can be a little crude," offered Jim Ross apologetically.

Hart dominated the early sequences of the bout, crafting a tale of the wisened master systematically schooling the new naiveté. He aptly demonstrated why his nickname for so many years had been "the excellence of execution", as he bended Austin's limbs with an array of holds first taught to him decades prior by his father in the Hart family dungeon. For his part, Austin did his best to make each one look as painful as possible, twisting and contorting his face into a furled grimace. When he began to fight back, McMahon decided to launch his first verbal assault on Hart. He fired a disparaging volley against the former champion, pouncing on an opportunity to question his stamina. "Bret seems to be a little slow in getting up," he jabbed.

---

[65] Tweener is the industry term for a wrestler who is neither a babyface nor a heel in the traditional good guy/bad guy sense, but rather someone who floated between both.

Some of Vince's other calls at *Survivor Series* strongly hinted to insiders that he was regretful of having given Hart such a loaded deal. "I don't see a lot of offense here," he grumbled as Hart again worked a wrestling hold, entirely cheapening the intentionally slow-burning structure of the match. Jim Ross leapt into sycophant mode and rushed to the proverbial side of McMahon, setting him up for another glancing shot across the bow. "Bret can't execute the cover," he barked. Appreciative of the setup, McMahon took over the reins and asserted, "He just didn't have it, JR!"

The pace of the contest remained deliberate early on. Hart was concerned about tiring early in such a long match following his seven months absence. It was too slow for the instant-gratification seeking McMahon, who as a general rule had always favoured the sizzle of a performance over the actual steak of the wrestling. He decided to break off from calling the action and take time out to champion the new blood that had performed so ably already that night. It served a double duty, as in promoting the younger performers he once again called attention to Hart's own advancing age.[66]

Looking to capture the spirit of the increased aggression levels prevalent throughout the WWF, Austin and Hart deliberately ignored the rulebook and took their fight outside the confines of the squared circle. They pushed the boundaries, fighting over the security barricade into the crowd and causing the railing to collapse. When the battle reached the opposite side of the ring where the announce teams were situated, Austin took Bret down to his back and grabbed his legs, placing his knees under Hart's backside before falling down and pivoting him up in the air with a move called a slingshot. Hart crashed into the Spanish language desk, however unlike at *Survivor Series* a year earlier where he and Kevin Nash had first pioneered table use in the WWF, the table did not break. Austin took the wood's resistance personally and decided to give breaking it another shot. He placed a prone Hart over the table and leapt from the ring apron, driving an elbow into the Canadian's sternum. It was to no avail - the table stayed standing.

Impressed with Austin's determined mode of attack, Vince posed a question to his viewers, "What's left of Bret Hart? Does he have enough left to pull it off?" The message he wanted to convey was clear: Austin was

---

[66] Exploits like this would later lead to Hart believing McMahon had played him in a protracted long-con when their twenty year deal fell apart nineteen years early in the fall of 1997. He felt McMahon had slowly broke his once chastened character's reputation apart bit by bit, with the intention being that when Vince let him out of his contract he would be of far less value to WCW than he would have been had he signed for them in mid-1996. McMahon had got one last good year out of Hart, then cut him adrift when he felt he was no longer worth the investment.

the better man, dominant and focused. If Hart were to snare a victory then it would be down to a fluke, not because Austin was in any way inferior to him. Ross again hopped on board with the narrative, sniping, "Bret's gotta realise this is not 1991. It's not even 1994," clearly planting the suggestion that Hart's better years were behind him. Though Hart had no awareness of the announcers' character assassination of him over the course of the match, his immediate upping of the tempo almost seemed like he was trying to prove them wrong. After getting the better of a furious fist fight, Hart delivered a nod to those paying closest attention by using Austin's own stun-gun move against him. Not to be outdone, 'Stone Cold' returned the favour with a superplex, a high impact move always guaranteed a response.

Hart upped the ante even further, impressing even McMahon by throwing his legs back over his head and capturing Austin's leg, twisting into a flashy cradle pinning predicament. Austin kicked out, but in the context of the story he had been reminded that the wily Hart had hitherto unseen tricks in his arsenal, so he went to the well and dropped him with a Stone Cold Stunner. Hart was permitted to kick out of Austin's popular finishing move, which came as a surprise to many in the audience who assumed it was over. Austin began to show cracks in the 'Stone Cold' façade by losing his cool, conveying his frustration with a series of further covers, each of which Hart managed to escape at the last second. Austin then returned to his hometown roots as he tried to beat Hart at his own submission game, locking on a hold that bore stark similarities to Bret's own Sharpshooter - the Texas Cloverleaf. Hart had never submitted in a match before, and he ensured that would not be the case here either when he broke the hold by reaching the bottom rope.

Seemingly running out of ideas, Austin resorted to scrapping and clawing, assaulting Hart with a flurry of kicks to the head and punches to the gut. Regaining focus, he sent Hart hard, kidneys-first into the ring post, then further demonstrated his own technical wrestling acumen with the execution of a rarely seen bow and arrow hold. Nevertheless, Hart was not about to be beaten at his own game, perspicaciously flipping out of the move and into his Sharpshooter to an impressed response from the crowd. Austin showed that he had done his homework on Hart and evaded the hold, then locked in a submission of his own: his old Million Dollar Dream finisher. This was the setup to the end of the match, with Hart taking a page out of his own playbook and his match with Roddy Piper at *WrestleMania VIII*, kicking off the top rope and pushing backwards so that he landed on top of a felled Austin for the win. McMahon immediately jumped to

Austin's defence, noting that he only lost because he did not release the sleeper hold, such had been his apparent desire to make Hart pass out.

Hart was satisfied with the match. He had achieved his goal of Austin walking away a bigger star in defeat than he had been coming in, while simultaneously justifying his own worth to McMahon. Although he shook Hart's hand as he left ringside while cooing, "Unbelievable," McMahon was unable to resist a further dig at him when prompted by Jim Ross. JR could not help but praise the effort of Hart after the match, because at heart he was firstly a fan of great wrestling. He extolled the virtues of Hart, expressing a belief that so adept was Bret's performance that he did not believe the evening's main event stars Sycho Sid and Shawn Michaels would have been able to beat him if they had been in the ring with him that night. McMahon raised his eyebrows and rolled his eyes, resolutely declaring, "Well, I don't agree with that *at all*," apparently outraged at the mere suggestion that Hart could beat the champion or the champion elect. It was an especially counterproductive thing for him to say given he was already advertising Hart going up against the winner of the evening's main event at December's *In Your House: It's Time* pay-per-view.

When Hart eventually learned of the way McMahon had buried him during the contest, he angrily approached him about it. He demanded that if Vince was not happy with the deal they had negotiated then he was giving him the chance to break it, because he would just go back to Eric Bischoff and take his offer of making a fortune in WCW. Instead, McMahon backtracked immediately. He apologised profusely, professing that any offence caused was entirely unintentional, before reiterating that he was happy with the contract.

IT WAS with a degree of irony that the same night which played host to the return of 'the Hitman' also signalled the fall from grace of champion Shawn Michaels. Opponent Sid Eudy, initially chosen out of necessity merely so that Michaels would have a monster to eventually slay, had managed to generate so much momentum in the preceding months that he was now the only logical choice to beat Shawn. His mesmeric charisma and unstable demeanour were far more appealing to male fans under twenty-five than pretty-boy Michaels, and the Garden let both he and McMahon know it.

Unlike with Steve Austin, who was viewed as something of an anti-hero, the hearty response generated by Sid was more down to the crowd's inherent dislike of Michaels. As he himself admits, "The fans turned on me. I was a white-meat babyface, and the MSG crowd hated that kind of character." They did not waste any time in expressing those sentiments, loudly cheering at the onset of Eudy's *Psycho* inspired entrance music, clamouring to reach over the railings and touch him as he travelled down the famously narrow Garden aisle way. The sheer sight of Michaels on the big screen making his way to the curtain backstage inspired a chorus of angry boos. Shawn immediately knew it was going to be a rough night.

The lust-ridden young women in the crowd screeched and hollered as his music hit, but they were soon drowned out by the overwhelmingly negative majority. Shawn partly attributed it to the American public's desire to see someone fall after building them up, pointing out that the same audience had loved him when he was stealing the show with Scott Hall at *WrestleMania X*, and were fully behind the 'Curtain Call' earlier in the year. "Once I made it to the top and my character became a babyface, those same fans turned on me. I couldn't do anything right," he complains.

Sid's opening flurry of brutish punches were met with a chorus of approval, with Michaels receiving only girlish screams when he launched haymakers of his own. The pair opted to take the opposite approach than Hart and Austin by working at a breakneck pace from the off, but it was immediately apparent to Michaels that he was going to have his work cut out if he wanted to steal the show. As well as the hostile crowd, he also had to figure out a way to make the mechanical Eudy work to his high standards. Michaels struggled to lug Sid around, so instead opted to throw himself into every move that his opponent delivered. His intention was to make the match memorable with exaggerated selling and big bumping rather than through his own offensive assaults.

After leaping high into the air to make it appear as if Sid was effortlessly pressing him above his head, Michaels took a breather on the outside of the ring where he was immediately met with a salvo of foul-mouthed abuse from the front row. He could only listen with contempt prior to flashing a brief forlorn stare into the camera, before quickly snapping back into action. He returned to the ring and focused his assault on Sid's enormous legs, chopping him down to the ground like a mighty redwood. The crowd booed relentlessly, causing Michaels to survey the audience with shock. When they broke into a "Sycho Sid" chant to taunt him, Michaels snapped and a mouthed, "Fuck you," before locking on a figure four leglock.

Determined not to have a repeat of the incident he had experienced at *Beware of Dog* earlier in the year, Michaels remained steadfast in his desire to pull a competent match out of Eudy, so he decided to give the crowd what they wanted and play the villain. He shouted over at Sid, telling him to reverse the hold. It was a traditional babyface spot, but Michaels knew that no matter what he did now, the Garden was not going to root for him. He later expressed regret for having been so easily swayed by the fans into working heel, musing, "That wasn't my role and I shouldn't have done it. As a professional, I shouldn't have reacted to the live crowd. I should have been playing to the television audience."

Michaels continued to direct his focus on Sid's legs like a rabid wolf. Once again his opponent's woodenness caused him problems. "He couldn't work a lick," grumbles Shawn, "He was one of the most difficult guys that I have ever been in the ring with. He was so big and hard to move, just so tense." Michaels eventually heaved Eudy into position with a great degree of difficulty, his frustration compounded by the Garden's continuous barracking of him. He shot the fans a wicked sneer as he drove Sid's knee hard into the canvas, before letting him fight back and beat him up on the outside of the ring.

Eudy was not adept to change like Michaels. He struggled to keep a pre-planned match together at the best of times, no less change everything on a whim, so continued to portray the heel role that he had been instructed to play prior to the match. He drilled Michaels with hard kicks and knees to the face, each of which were met with cheers. When Shawn mounted his own comeback in response then ascended to the top rope, he was once again showered with a rain of boos. When Sid caught him and delivered a backbreaker, it was met with a deafening reaction, prompting even McMahon to finally acknowledge through gritted teeth that as many people were rooting for Sid as they were Shawn.

Shawn acted dead on his feet, playing a game of rope-a-dope with Sid and letting his opponent punch himself out before returning fire. After employing stick-and-move tactics coupled with a leg assault, Michaels was now fighting Sid at his own game, showing his own strength with an impressive bodyslam. Michaels climbed the ropes again, looking for his patented elbow drop, but was caught square in the chin with a huge boot. Not acclimatised to lengthy matches of such intensity, Eudy was gasping for air by that point. He slowed the tempo to a crawl with a sleeper hold, allowing himself to catch a breather and talk over the final phases of the contest with Michaels.

The next spot saw Sid tease a chokeslam, one of his go-to manoeuvres, which Michaels broke free of with an iniquitous eye poke. McMahon felt he had to cover for his champion's villainous actions, explaining that he had escaped Sid's bear-like clutches, "as best he could". When Michaels followed up by attempting to hit his superkick finisher the crowd feared the worst for Sid. They were ecstatic when he caught Shawn's foot to prevent it, then countered with a mighty one-armed chokeslam, with Shawn leaping eight feet into the air to espouse its impact.

Sid seemed to have the bout in hand, but to the frustration of announcer Jim Ross he wasted time with a hand gesture disseminating last rites. Shawn was thus able to counter his powerbomb attempt into a cradle for a believable near fall, as the audiences both in the building and at home became gripped by the drama of the match. Sid, seemingly frustrated to boiling point at his inability to finish the job, turned and grabbed a camera from one of the technicians at ringside and motioned that he was going to lay out his opponent with it.

With Michaels prone in the corner of the ring, his mentor José Lothario climbed onto the apron to plead with Sid not to go through with the dastardly deed. Sid listened, briefly, then in a moment of inspiration he decided to drill Lothario instead. With his on-screen father figure rolling around in agony on the floor, Michaels hit a desperate superkick on Sid then immediately rushed to Lothario's aid instead of going for the cover. It was an "out" for Michaels, a way of making it look like he would have won the match if not for his compassion towards José.

The storyline soon veered into the realms of tastelessness, with Michaels cradling Lothario in his arms while Jim Ross solemnly expressed his concern that the sixty-two-year-old was suffering from a heart attack. As with many of the other trashy, quasi-realistic angles that Vince was increasingly employing, it teetered on the precipice of good taste. Once again - as with the 'Pillmanizing' angle in October - it was stolen from ECW. The night before at *November to Remember*, Tommy Dreamer had used the exact same spot on Brian Lee to help his friend Terry Funk to victory. It seemed that those at Titan responsible for coming up with angles and match finishes were liberally lifting them from ECW, safe in the knowledge that Vince - who did not watch wrestling outside of the WWF - would never know any differently.

In the ensuing chaos the referee took a tumble after a collision with Michaels, while outside the ring Lothario still rolled around unattended, clutching his chest with no sign of any assistance from paramedics or anyone in the locker room. Unintentionally, it made the WWF's health and safety policy look like a shambles, and McMahon appear heartless for not leaving his announce desk and helping the ailing veteran. Meanwhile, the wrestling match continued. Sid drilled Michaels with the same camera he had employed to assault Lothario, before finally hitting his patented powerbomb for a less than clean win and the WWF Title. The eight month reign of Shawn Michaels was over, and his unseating was greeted with the sound of rapturous applause. Sid Eudy, who had quit the company at the start of the year - and only six months earlier was working on a farm in Arkansas - was now the king of the WWF.

THE REACTION to Shawn Michaels at *Survivor Series* had been difficult for Vince McMahon to swallow. It also left him in a quandary. The locker room and many of Vince's management staff had long expressed their opinion that Shawn was not the right man to build the company around, but the response he generated and the performances he put forth had always countered their objections. However, the Garden was the Garden, Vince's way of hearing directly from the pulse of his most die-hard fan base. If they were turning on Shawn, then other audiences were sure to follow. As 1996 drew to a close, McMahon realised he faced a decision about whether to go ahead with his plan to put the title back on Michaels at the *Royal Rumble*, or if it was time to go in a different direction and take a chance on someone else.

There was no hiding from the fact the Michaels had not drawn as champion like Vince had hoped. The momentum that he had going into the *Royal Rumble* leading to its strong pay-per-view number had long since waned, with only one show following his title win having generated in excess of 200,000 buys.[67] The WWF's traditional second biggest show of the year *SummerSlam* had struggled with Shawn headlining against Vader, pulling a meagre 0.58 buy rate for a total 194,000 buys. *Survivor Series* was the best number the WWF had managed in over six months, though that could be attributed to the return of Bret Hart as much as Shawn's spot in the main event.

Although change was already afoot in the WWF, McMahon knew that he needed to push the boundaries even more to properly fight WCW's insurgence. An unpopular babyface champion who nobody in the dressing room liked and who did not move metrics in the desired fashion was not the long-term future of his company. Nor, felt McMahon, was the curmudgeonly Bret Hart. He was a remnant of the old noir, so far removed from the ethos championed by the New WWF that he had become a relic practically overnight. The woeful 0.35 buy rate that his subsequent December pay-per-view outing with Sid drew was testament to that.

The reality of what he was doing finally clicked for Vince. He realised that more than ever he needed to be bold in moving forward with his vision. There was no turning back. He was willing to consider anything,

---

[67] *In Your House: Good Friends... Better Enemies* with a 0.65 buy rate equating to 210,000 purchases.

regardless of moral principles, to modernise his anachronistic company and bring the WWF kicking and screaming into the modern era. For the first time he fully recognised and accepted that his audience had completely changed. The children who had grown up in an era of, "Say your prayers and take your vitamins," were now the disaffected young adults who wanted something fresh and different. Something exciting and engrossing.

It would take time to completely rebrand and change course, because sponsors and the network would surely oppose him. Nevertheless, if the numbers held up then he could attract alternative advertisers looking to sell to a different demographic than his current ones. He had been on the ropes throughout most of 1996, but with his characteristic assuredness and conviction, McMahon stepped into 1997 more determined than ever to fight. It would turn out to be the most tumultuous, stressful and perhaps critical year in the history of the World Wrestling Federation, one that served as the catalyst for the company's rebirth as the undisputed and unrivalled brand leader in sports entertainment.

REFERENCES

Books

Steve Austin, Dennis Bryant, Jim Ross. *The Stone Cold Truth*. WWF, 2003

Eric Bischoff, Jeremy Roberts, *Eric Bischoff: Controversy Creates Cash,* WWE, 2007

Basil V. DeVito, Jr., Joe Layden. *WWF WrestleMania: The Official Insiders Story*. HarperEntertainment, 2001

Bret Hart, *Hitman: My Real Life in the Cartoon World of Wrestling*, Grand Central Publishing, 2008

Bob Holly, Ross Williams, *The Hardcore Truth: The Bob Holly Story*, ECW Press, 2013

Jerry Lawler, *It's Good to be the King...Sometimes*. WWE, 2002

Dustin Runnels, Mark Vancil, *Cross Rhodes: Goldust, Out of the Darkness*. WWE, 2010

Mick Foley, *Have a Nice Day - A Tale of Blood and Sweatsocks*. HarperCollins, 1999

Diana Hart, Kirstie McLellan, *Under the Mat - Inside Wrestling's Greatest Family*. Fenn Pub, 2001

Tom Billington, Alison Coleman, *Pure Dynamite - The Price You Pay for Wrestling Stardom*. Winding Stair Press, 2001

Shaun Assael, Mike Mooneyham, *Sex, Lies and Headlocks - The Real Story of Vince McMahon and World Wrestling Entertainment*. Broadway Books, 2004

Ted DiBiase, Tom Caiazzo. *Ted DiBiase - The Million Dollar Man*. Gallery Books, 2008

Bobby Heenan, Steve Anderson. *Bobby the Brain - Wrestling's Bad Boy Tells All*. Triumph Books, 2002

James Dixon, Arnold Furious, Lee Maughan, Bob Dahlstom, Ben Richardson. *The Complete WWF Video Guide Volume III - The New Generaton 1993-1996*. History of Wrestling, 2013

The Rock, Joe Layden. *The Rock Says...* Harper Entertainment, 2000

Shawn Michaels, Aaron Feigenbaum. *Heartbreak & Triumph: The Shawn Michaels Story*. WWE, 2006

Dave Meltzer. *Tributes - Remembering Some of the World's Greatest Wrestlers*. Winding Stair Press, 2001

J.J. Dillon, Scott Teal. *Wrestlers Are Like Seagulls: From McMahon to McMahon*. Crowbar Press, 2005

DVDs

Stone Cold Steve Austin: The Bottom Line on the Most Popular Superstar of All Time. WWE, 2011

The Shawn Michaels Story: Heartbreak & Triumph. WWF, 2007

Jake The Snake Roberts: Pick Your Poison. WWE, 2005

The True Story of WrestleMania. WWE, 2011

Triple H: Thy Kingdom Come. WWE, 2013

nWo Back in Black, WWF, 2002

The Monday Night War. WWE, 2004

For All Mankind - The Life and Career of Mick Foley. WWE, 2013

Born to Controversy - The Roddy Piper Story. WWE, 2006

The Self-Destruction of the Ultimate Warrior. WWE, 2005

Hitman Hart: Wrestling With Shadows. Paul Jay. 1998

WWE Greatest Rivalries - Shawn Michaels vs. Bret Hart. WWE, 2011

Brian Pillman - Loose Cannon. WWE. 2006

nWo - The Revolution. WWF, 2012

The Rise & Fall of WCW. WWE, 2009

Ladies and Gentlemen, My Name is Paul Heyman. WWE, 2014

The Rise + Fall of ECW. WWF, 2004

The Rock - The Epic Journey of Dwayne Johnson. WWE, 2012

Lawsuits

Titan Sports, Inc., vs. Turner Broadcasting Systems, Inc., World Championship Wrestling, Inc., and Eric Bischoff (1997)

World Championship Wrestling vs. Titan Sports, Inc., d/b/a The World Wrestling Federation, and USA Network (1999)

Magazines

"Let's Talk with Brian Pillman". *Powerslam.* 24

"Vader Interview". *Powerslam.* 231

Online Articles

Cult of Whatever. "*Scott Hall Interview.*" 2013,
            https://www.cultofwhatever.com/2013/07/scott-hall-interview/

Wrestling Inc. "*Rick Bognar Interview.*" 2013,

http://www.wrestlinginc.com/wi/news/2013/1208/568093/rick-bognar-looks-back-at-his-time-as-fake-razor-ramon/

Wrestling Inc. "*Vader Interview.*" 2014,
http://wrestlinginc.com/wi/news/2014/0930/582514/vader-talks-signing-with-wwe-and-his-push/index.shtml

Broken Skull Ranch. "*Blog - Stone Cold Stunner.*" 2012,
http://brokenskullranch.com/archives/875

Pro Wrestling Torch. *"Below the Bottom Line: Philosophies Change for Good Reason"*. Wade Keller.
http://pwtorch.com/artman2/publish/Torch_Flashbacks_19/article_1798.shtml#.VWXF00ajFQ4

Camel Clutch Blog. *"Interview With Paul Orndorff"*. Eric Gargiulo.
http://camelclutchblog.com/paul-orndorff-interview/

411Mania. *"Flashback Goodness: WWF In Your House - Mind Games [1996]"*. The Goodness
http://411mania.com/wrestling/flashback-goodness-wwe-in-your-house-mind-games-1996/

WWE. *"The Kliq Curtain Call"*. Ryan Murphy.
http://www.wwe.com/classics/the-kliq-curtain-call-roundtable-26223071

Prodigy. *"Interview With Marc Mero"* Bob Ryder. 1996,
Transcript: http://www.hack-man.com/Wrestling/Interviews/wres-news-marc-mero-9603-interview.html

Orlando Sentinel. *"Wrestlers Win 1st Round in Battle to Regulate Them"* Michael Griffin. 1992,
http://articles.orlandosentinel.com/1992-02-08/news/9202081166_1_professional-wrestling-wrestling-matches-wrestling-fans

John Layfield Facebook. "*Survivor Series Backstage Story and Smackdown Pics*" John Layfield. 2012,
https://www.facebook.com/media/set/?set=a.10151277091078534.489328.194176253533&type=1

"New Jack Interview". Dave Scherer, Jess McGrath, The Rat
http://www.angelfire.com/nj2/newjack/interveiw2.html

411Mania. *"The Top 20 WWF Matches of the 90s"* Scott Keith. 2002,
http://411mania.com/wrestling/klassic-keith-the-top-20-wwf-matches-of-the-90s-part-two/

Podcasts & Radio Shows

Steve Austin Show. "Episode #10/11- Kevin Nash" 2013,
http://podcastone.com/Steve-Austin-Show

Steve Austin Show. "Episode #32/#36- Scott Hall" 2013,
http://podcastone.com/Steve-Austin-Show

Steve Austin Show. "Episode #51 / #56 - X-Pac" 2013,
http://podcastone.com/Steve-Austin-Show

Steve Austin Show. "Episode #114- Eric Bischoff" 2014,
http://podcastone.com/Steve-Austin-Show

Steve Austin Show. "Episode #122- Big Van Vader" 2014,
http://podcastone.com/Steve-Austin-Show

Steve Austin Show. "Episode #174- It's Pro Wrestling Goddamnit!" 2014,
http://podcastone.com/Steve-Austin-Show

Live Audio Wrestling. "Interview - Vader" 2012,
http://fightnetwork.com/news/30838:interview-vader-march-2012/

Under The Mat Radio. "Episode #11 - Ahmed Johnson" 2013,
http://www.blogtalkradio.com/pwkgw/2013/12/17/under-the-mat-episode-11-ahmed-johnson

Gary Mehaffy. "Rick Bognar Interview" 2014,
https://www.youtube.com/watch?v=R_D4VnYdytE

WGD Weekly With Steve & The Scum. *"Ron Simmons Interview"* 2014, http://recordings.talkshoe.com/TC-129237/TS-840573.mp3

The Sports Courier. *"Kevin Kelly Interview"* 2010, https://www.youtube.com/watch?v=LL6ApgUbhWM&list=PLF EE01526BB3C535C

Shoot Interviews

Timeline the History of WWE 1995: As told by Kevin Nash. Sean Oliver, Kayfabe Commentaries

Shawn Michaels Shoot Interview. Rob Feinstein, RF Video

Eric Bischoff Shoot Interview. Rob Feinstein, RF Video

Ringside With Vader. Sean Oliver, Kayfabe Commentaries

Ringside With Vader. Sean Oliver, Kayfabe Commentaries

YouShoot - Kevin Nash. Sean Oliver, Kayfabe Commentaries

YouShoot - Jim Cornette. Sean Oliver, Kayfabe Commentaries

Timeline the History of WCW 1996: As told by Kevin Sullivan. Sean Oliver, Kayfabe Commentaries

Timeline the History of WWE 1997: As told by Jim Cornette. Sean Oliver, Kayfabe Commentaries

Shoot Interview with the Ultimate Warrior. Ringside Collectibles

Kevin Nash No Holds Barred Shoot Interview. Scott Hudson, WrestleReunion

Kevin Nash Shoot Interview. Joe Dombrowski, Prime Wrestling

Vader Shoot Interview. Rob Feinstein, RF Video

Vader Studio Shoot Interview. Bostonwrestling.com, 2014

"The Bullet" Bob Armstrong Shoot Interview. Highspots.com,

Sid Vicious Shoot Interview. Doug Gentry, RF Video

Guest Booker... With Bruce Prichard - Screwing Bret. Sean Oliver, Kayfabe Commentaries

YouShoot - Kevin Sullivan. Sean Oliver, Kayfabe Commentaries

TV Shows

Off The Record. Michael Landsberg, 1998

WWE Network Specials

The Ultimate Legend. WWE, 2014

WWE Countdown- Biggest Blunders. WWE, 2014

WWE Countdown- Memorable Debuts. WWE, 2014

Monday Night War - The War Begins. WWE, 2014

Monday Night War - The Rise of nWo. WWE, 2014

Monday Night War - Embracing Attitude. WWE, 2014

Monday Night War - The Hart of War. WWE, 2014

Monday Night War - The Austin Era has Begun. WWE, 2014

Monday Night War - The Kliq. WWE, 2014

Legends of Wrestling - nWo. WWE, 2011

Legends of Wrestling - Monday Night Raw. WWE, 2012

Legends of Wrestling - Renegades & Outlaws. WWE, 2012

Legends of Wrestling - Achievers. WWE, 2010

Legends of Wrestling - WrestleMania. WWE, 2008

Legends of Wrestling - The Monday Night War. WWE, 2007

DX: Confidential. WWE, 2014

Author Conducted Interviews

Jim Cornette
J.J. Dillon
Lanny Poffo
Tracy Smothers

All television rating data provided by Nielsen Media Research

All pay-per-view buyrate data provided by the Wrestling Observer Newsletter.

The following issues of the Wrestling Observer Newsletter (http://www.f4wonline.com/) were used for research purposes to help compile this tome.

January 2 1996, January 6 1996, January 15 1996, January 22 1996, January 23 1996, January 29 1996, February 5 1996, February 12 1996, February 19 1996, February 26 1996, March 4 1996, March 11 1996, March 18 1996, March 25 1996, April 2 1996, April 8 1996, April 15 1996, April 22 1996, April 29 1996, May 6 1996, May 13 1996, May 20 1996, May 27 1996, June 3 1996, June 10 1996, June 17 1996, June 24 1996, July 1 1996, July 8 1996, July 15 1996, July 22 1996, July 29 1996, August 5 1996, August 14 1996, August 19 1996, August 26 1996, September 2 1996, September 9 1996, September 16 1996, September 23 1996, September 30 1996, October 7 1996, October 14 1996, October 21 1996, October 28 1996, November 4 1996, November 11 1996, November 18 1996, November 25 1996, December 2 1996, December 9 1996, December 16 1996, December 30 1996

ACKNOWLEDGEMENTS

Thanks to the following, without whom this book would not have been possible: Benjamin Richardson for his fastidious proofing, fact-checking, reworking, and reimagining of many of the words in these pages. Not to mention the wonderful cover art. Jim Cornette, for agreeing to go over the stories from the year in fine detail, and with an enormous amount of patience. His character references and insight into the inner workings of the WWF were, as with *Titan Sinking*, invaluable. Justin Henry for his enthusiastic support of the project, assistance with fact checking and for writing the foreword. Lee Maughan for researching and writing the section in the book covering the Japanese wrestling scene, the Randy Savage-Jerry Lawler feud and the UWF. A big thank you to J.J. Dillon, Lanny Poffo and Tracy Smothers for opening up to me in interviews about their own experiences of 1996, and their insight into the behaviour of others. Dave Meltzer, for his incredible weekly Wrestling Observer Newsletter, a vital source of information, facts and stats, not to mention being on hand to confirm facts and stories. Scott Keith for his hard work over the years documenting wrestling in his own distinctive way, and for his support and championing of *Titan Sinking*. My wife and children for their constant support. My parents for encouraging me to pursue my various endeavours. And finally, all of the people who read and enjoyed *Titan Sinking* enough that I was convinced to write the sequel.

INDEX

INDEX

INDEX

INDEX

INDEX

INDEX